Embezzlement and High Treason in Louis XIV's France

Embezzlement and High Treason in Louis XIV's France

The Trial of Nicolas Fouquet

VINCENT J. PITTS

Johns Hopkins University Press
Baltimore

Printed in the United States of America on acid-free paper
2 4 6 8 9 7 5 3 1

Johns Hopkins University Press
2715 North Charles Street
Baltimore, Maryland 21218-4363
www.press.jhu.edu

Library of Congress Cataloging-in-Publication Data
Pitts, Vincent J. (Vincent Joseph), 1947– author.
Embezzlement and high treason in Louis XIV's France :
the trial of Nicolas Fouquet / by Vincent J. Pitts.
pages cm
Includes bibliographical references and index.
ISBN 978-1-4214-1824-7 (hardcover : alk. paper) — ISBN 978-1-4214-1825-4 (electronic) — ISBN 1-4214-1824-x (hardcover : alk. paper) — ISBN 1-4214-1825-8 (electronic) 1. Fouquet, Nicolas, 1615–1680—Trials, litigation, etc. 2. Trials (Embezzlement)—France. 3. Trials (Treason)—France. 4. Louis XIV, King of France, 1638–1715. I. Title.
KJV135.F68P58 2015
345.44′0231—dc23 2015006253

A catalog record for this book is available from the British Library.

Special discounts are available for bulk purchases of this book. For more information, please contact Special Sales at 410-516-6936 or specialsales@press.jhu.edu.

Johns Hopkins University Press uses environmentally friendly book materials, including recycled text paper that is composed of at least 30 percent post-consumer waste, whenever possible.

Contents

Illustrations

Acknowledgments

For many courtesies and much patience, I would like to thank the staffs of the Bibliothèque nationale de France, the Bibliothèque de l'Arsenal, the Bibliothèque Mazarine, the Bibliothèque de l'Institut de France, and the Archives nationales (France). I am truly grateful to Mme Lynda Frenois, director and curator of the château of Vaux-le-Vicomte, and to M. Alexandre de Vogüé, its co-proprietor, for their exceptional efforts on my behalf. On this side of the Atlantic, the extraordinary resources of the Yale University library system, including the Beinecke Rare Book Library and the Yale Law School Library, greatly facilitated my research.

It is hard to express adequately my gratitude to academic readers who have given generously of their time and expertise to comment on the manuscript at various stages. Orest Ranum's encouragement and support for this project from its beginning to its conclusion, and his profound insights into the nature of seventeenth-century French society, are more than appreciated. John Carey, Marvin Cox, Kathryn Edwards, Charles Heckman, Martin Margulies, Wayne Strasbaugh, Jason Warren, and James and Camille Weiss all brought their special perspectives to the task at hand and provided me with much useful advice and commentary. I have also benefited greatly from comments and suggestions by nonacademic friends, whose help has also been invaluable: Michael Carbone, Raymond Kosinski, and John Metz. A special word of thanks is owed to my nephew, Nicholas Clark, whose prowess with the computer has helped me navigate from "now" to "then," and back again, on many occasions.

Let me also acknowledge the efforts of Robert J. Brugger and his team at Johns Hopkins University Press, whose efforts have helped transform the manuscript into a book that I hope will be worthy of its subject.

For much hospitality over the years and for a deep interest in this project as well as earlier ones, I am much indebted to French friends: M. and Mme Daniel Allix; M. and Mme Jean-Yves Perrotte; and the late Mme Anne Develay, whose enthusiasm for the history of her beautiful country never flagged, and with whom I first visited Vaux-le-Vicomte more years ago than I would like to admit.

Embezzlement and High Treason in Louis XIV's France

Introduction

From 1661 to 1664, France was mesmerized by the arrest and trial of Nicolas Fouquet, the superintendant (*surintendant*) of finance and one of the most powerful men in the kingdom, on capital charges of embezzlement and high treason. It was certainly not the first such fall from grace followed by a spectacular trial that the French had witnessed. Since the late Middle Ages, theatrical events of this type had been used by kings of France to demonstrate the quality and swiftness of their justice, particularly when the culprit was one of the great of the realm who had betrayed the royal confidence. Sometimes these trials involved members of the high nobility: the constable de Saint-Pol under Louis XI, maréchal de Biron under Henri IV, or the duc de Montmorency under Louis XIII and Richelieu. At other times they involved prominent servants of state from lesser backgrounds: the financier Jacques de Semblençay under François I or maréchal de Marillac, another victim of Richelieu's. In most cases, the drama unfolded in a ritualistic fashion: an arrest, a hastily arranged trial before a specially appointed court to ensure the desired verdict, and swift and condign punishment, usually a public execution at the hands of the headsman or, in the case of a commoner, by the hangman.

Those were the expectations at the time of Fouquet's arrest. A special court was appointed to try the accused, with the judges carefully selected by the authorities, and thousands of seized documents to serve as proof of the superintendant's criminal activities. But Louis XIV and Fouquet's enemies, headed by the redoubtable Jean-Baptiste Colbert, did not get the result they anticipated. Instead of a quick judgment and condemnation, the process consumed three full years. Despite the pressure to return a guilty verdict with a capital sentence, in the end the court threw out all but two of the many charges brought against the disgraced superintendant, including the most terrible of all, a charge of high treason for plotting armed rebellion against the crown.

For the relatively minor charges for which Fouquet was convicted, the court voted a punishment of exile. To the astonishment of the prosecutors and the royal government, public opinion, or at least the opinion of those elite segments of society which can be sampled, originally highly censorious of Fouquet, had moved almost entirely in his favor and applauded the decision of the court. The young Louis XIV, at the beginning of his "personal reign," had suffered a terrible humiliation, one he never forgave those judges for inflicting on him. To rectify matters from the royal perspective, Louis XIV broke all precedent. Making use of his right to assume personal jurisdiction over any judicial matter, Louis intervened, not to mitigate the sentence but to increase it, changing the punishment from banishment to perpetual imprisonment on grounds of *raison d'état*. There was no precedent for such a step in the annals of French justice, nor was there another such intervention for the duration of the ancien régime.

Notwithstanding this extraordinary measure, there was little doubt in the minds of contemporaries that the crown had suffered an enormous political defeat. Fouquet the man stood convicted and was to spend the rest of his life in harsh and spitefully managed captivity in a remote fortress in the Alps. But there was no denying that despite a hand-picked court, perjured witnesses, and fabricated evidence, the crown had failed to prove its case on any of the significant charges brought against the superintendant. Instead of a piece of royal theater masquerading as justice, the crown had become party to a runaway show trial. The defense challenged the justice and fairness of the proceeding and made its case by impeaching the motives and veracity of the prosecution. It demonstrated that the offenses allegedly committed by the defendant were commonplace practices of the state and its high officials, largely concealed from the public. Most tellingly of all, Fouquet's defense attempted to prove that the chief beneficiary of these corrupt practices was none other than the late prime minister, Cardinal Mazarin.

Fouquet and his supporters laid bare the financial and administrative mechanisms of the state in a way that only seemed to confirm the accusations of corruption and mismanagement against the royal administration made scarcely a decade earlier by the high judiciary itself during the Fronde, the civil wars that plagued France between 1648 and 1652. Many of Fouquet's assertions implicated Mazarin, and the credibility of such assertions in the eyes of Fouquet's judges—as indicated by their verdict—seemed almost to vindicate that insurrection. Coming at the end of the 1650s, a decade marked by continuing friction between the crown and its judiciary, the trial unfolded as a belated aftershock to that earlier upheaval. As Daniel Dessert has pointed out, what made the trial of Fouquet so ambiguous and contradictory was that it exposed the activities of an entire social group—and a very powerful one at that—when its sole purpose was to find a single member of that group guilty of wrongdoing.[1] This was the key weakness in the prosecution's case, and one that Fouquet exploited brilliantly, forcing his judges to confront the question of justice when faced with truth.

If Louis XIV never forgave the judges who inflicted that humiliation on him, neither did he ever forgive Fouquet, never according him a pardon and release, or even a significant amelioration of the harsh conditions of his captivity. In Louis XIV's eyes, perhaps the most unforgiveable of the crimes Fouquet committed was to betray the "king's secret," revealing at trial the inner workings of a system that enriched the few and powerful at the expense of the majority of the king's subjects, especially those who were least able to bear it. Part of the king's justification for changing the sentence was the possibility that once safely on foreign soil, Fouquet might air more secrets of state: hardly a reassuring argument and an implicit confirmation of Fouquet's assertions.

By putting up a magnificent and unexpectedly effective defense, Fouquet treated the French public to a real show trial, one which, by impeaching the state's exercise of power, set up a dichotomy between power and justice and thus called into question the legitimacy of the proceedings.

As in the case of other such trials, opinion often remained divided about the underlying guilt or innocence of the defendant long afterward. In the late nineteenth century, two distinguished French historians, Jules Auguste Lair and Adolphe Chéruel, examining the same evidence, came to opposite conclusions about Fouquet's culpability. In more recent decades, a number of scholars, notably Daniel Dessert, Françoise Bayard, Claude Dulong, Jean-Christian Petitfils, Richard Bonney, and Julian Dent, have painstakingly reconstructed the financial apparatus of the early modern French state and in the process have shown the complex links that bound French financiers, other elements of elite strata, and the crown in a poisonous but somehow symbiotic relationship, at the expense of nonparticipants and the tax-paying lower orders of society. In the process, and almost incidentally, these scholars have verified many of Fouquet's revelations.

Relying on this research into the workings of the French financial system of the seventeenth century, most contemporary historians have concluded, sometimes with reservations, that Fouquet was undoubtedly a participant in the types of financing of the French state commonly, though illegally, practiced in that time. But since the entire apparatus of state was geared up to operate that system, the fairness of his prosecution remains in doubt. In short, as Fouquet argued, he had become a convenient scapegoat for the sins of a much larger group and a surrogate for a far more important figure: Mazarin.

Fouquet's trial and the passions it aroused inevitably bring to mind that other great show trial in French history, that of Alfred Dreyfus. Some of the parallels are indeed startling: the determination of high officials to obtain a conviction at any price; the tampering with evidence and suborning of perjury among witnesses; the insistence that reasons of state or national security overrode the normal rules of procedure and evidence. Like Dreyfus, Fouquet began his ordeal as an isolated and despised figure, with public sentiment (insofar as one can speak of such in seventeenth-century France) very much against him. But over time, a handful of determined supporters turned public opinion against the government's case. By the end of Fouquet's trial, the crown and its ministers were on the defensive, as Fouquet's advocates convinced many of his innocence, or perhaps, of the guilt of too many others not charged to make his prosecution just.

Unlike Dreyfus, Fouquet never benefited from an eventual happy ending. He was to spend the rest of his life in a remote prison in the Alps in virtually solitary confinement for much of that time. But his defense exposed matters that Louis XIV and Colbert would have preferred to leave secret and demonstrated how risky a show trial can be for the government that brings it, even when the odds are heavily stacked in the prosecution's favor.

For modern historians, Fouquet's trial opens a window onto the early years of Louis XIV's reign. It allows us to see the practical limits of "absolutism" when confronted with institutional obstruction. Inadvertently, and despite the best efforts of the prosecution, the trial provided a forum for renewing criticisms of the fiscal policies and financial mechanisms prevalent under Mazarin. Those disputes, which were central to the Parlementary Fronde (1648–1649), remained unresolved and contentious throughout the 1650s. In this context, the trial can be seen as a continuation of those quarrels. The trial itself was to have implications for the evolution of the French judicial system. The debates over legal issues during the trial, especially those relating to the rights of defendants, prosecutorial misconduct, and the autonomy of judges in the administration of justice, foreshadowed those same arguments raised during the reformation of the civil and criminal codes of procedure at the end of the 1660s (the "Code Louis"). Some of Fouquet's judges were members of the committees that fashioned those codes, and their debates reflect many of the same divisions that had emerged during the trial.

The Fouquet trial also illustrates the "show trial" mechanism and the risks this can entail when the convening authority loses control of the narrative and the proceedings, thereby allowing the defense to establish a convincing, often devastating, counternarrative of events.

In human terms, of course, Fouquet's trial offered a profound and inherent drama, pitting a solitary and disgraced man against the power of the state. The unscrupulous use of that state power to secure a conviction, a theme with too many repetitions down the centuries, is well represented in Fouquet's ordeal.

It is not the intention here to retry the case or reexamine the evidence to determine the "guilt" or "innocence" of Fouquet. That is a moot question. The modern historian is unlikely to get much beyond the findings of his judges: despite troubling circumstances and "grave suspicions," the prosecution did not prove its case on a single specific charge of wrongdoing. Nor is the objective to redo the excellent research of dedicated scholars that has made it much easier to understand the financial world in which Fouquet and his contemporaries operated.

There is also no need to write another biography of Fouquet, although the opening chapters here will provide the reader with the personal and institutional setting in which Fouquet's trial unfolded. Both Dessert and Petitfils have done outstanding biographies of Fouquet, and in them they are dismissive, not surprisingly, of the case against Fouquet. While their studies by implication exonerate Fouquet, neither they nor any other modern scholars have focused on the trial itself. An interesting question therefore remains unaddressed: how did Fouquet convince his judges, and a large segment of the elite in France, of his innocence? The answer goes beyond Fouquet's formidable legal skills and powers of persuasion. Determining how Fouquet achieved his moral victory also requires an investigation of the lingering resentments in judicial and other circles stemming from the Fronde (1648–1652), the legal culture of the period, and the personal beliefs and legal and professional ethics of some of the key judges involved in Fouquet's trial.

This book therefore focuses on the process itself and the political context in which it occurred. It explores the successful attempts of Fouquet and his defenders to transform the trial into an indictment of the financial practices of the French crown in the preceding decades. By doing so, Fouquet not only turned public opinion, but he also swayed his judges enough to inflict on the crown a moral defeat that resonated for decades and still taints the image of the Sun King's reign. How and why this happened are the subjects of this book.

The Prelude

September 5, 1661

The lieutenant was worried. His orders had been explicit, conveyed by the king in person the previous day, but he was not free to execute them until they were confirmed by the minister of war. That minister, Michel Le Tellier, was speaking with the duc de La Feuillade. The lieutenant, Charles d'Artagnan of the royal musketeers, dared not interrupt for fear of betraying his mission. If he did not receive the necessary confirmation soon, it would be impossible to follow his instructions. And the king was not accustomed to hearing the word "impossible."

It was Monday, September 5, 1661, Louis XIV's twenty-third birthday. The court was in residence at Nantes, staying in the old ducal château in the center of town. The king had come on a royal progress to visit his good people of Brittany and to obtain a "free gift" from the provincial representative body, the Estates of Brittany, assembled at the nearby hôtel de ville. This gift was expected to be in the range of 3 to 4 million livres, a tidy sum, of which the cash-strapped monarch could make good use. But there was another unannounced objective as well. D'Artagnan had learned of it the previous afternoon.

Taking him into his private office, Louis had charged d'Artagnan with the mission of arresting the superintendant of finance, Nicolas Fouquet, one of the most powerful men in France. D'Artagnan was instructed to act after a meeting of the royal council scheduled for early Monday morning. He was not, however, to detain the superintendant on the premises of the château: that would infringe on the prerogatives of the commander of the royal bodyguards, the marquis de Gesvres. There was more than court etiquette at stake here. Gesvres was a friend of Fouquet's, and Louis and his adviser Jean-Baptiste Colbert had been unwilling to entrust him with Fouquet's arrest. Should d'Artagnan attempt an arrest within the precincts of the château, Gesvres might intervene and object, perhaps allowing Fouquet to escape in the confusion. So the arrest had to occur off premises. After taking Fouquet into custody, d'Artagnan was to escort the prisoner under guard to the château of Angers and to remain there pending further instructions. D'Artagnan called on Le Tellier later in the day to receive his instructions in greater detail. While he was authorized to make all of the necessary preparations, he was also admonished—it is not clear whether by Louis or Le Tellier—to reconfirm the order with Le Tellier before initiating the arrest.

This last injunction almost undid the precautions taken by Louis and his collaborators, Colbert and Le Tellier. The council meeting was scheduled earlier than normal, under the pretext that the king would go hunting immediately afterward. At four in the morning d'Artagnan had swung into action. Troops were stationed along the main roads out of town to intercept any couriers other than royal messengers leaving the Breton capital. At six o'clock a detachment of musketeers fanned out to cover all of the entrances to the château. Meanwhile, the council convened to conduct routine business. As the assembly rose, Louis detained Fouquet on a pretext, long enough to determine with a hurried glance out the window that d'Artagnan was waiting in the courtyard.

In the meantime, the other ministers made their way out of the château. D'Artagnan hurried over to Le Tellier to confirm his orders, but Le Tellier had been buttonholed by the duc de La Feuillade and was engaged in an interminable discussion. Neither Le Tellier nor d'Artagnan wished to rush La Feuillade, for fear of attracting attention. Finally Le Tellier was able to get away, and with a quick word authorized d'Artagnan to proceed. Indeed, another royal official was already on the way to the hôtel de Rougé, where Fouquet had been staying, to seize Fouquet's papers and records.

But when d'Artagnan turned to find Fouquet, the minister had already disappeared, borne away in his sedan chair by his servants. Followed by a dozen musketeers, d'Artagnan raced down the nearby streets looking for him. Not far from the château he caught up with the superintendant's party, in the square in front of the cathedral: the superintendant was apparently on his way to Mass. D'Artagnan stopped the bearers and approached the sedan chair, telling Fouquet he had to speak with him. When Fouquet got down, d'Artagnan blurted out that he was under arrest. A stunned Fouquet asked if d'Artagnan was mistaken. Was the order really for him? He asked to read it, and then, finally convinced, asked d'Artagnan to be discreet. D'Artagnan took Fouquet into the nearest house, belonging to a canon of the cathedral, where he searched Fouquet's pockets before hustling him into a waiting carriage. With an escort of one hundred musketeers, the cortège set out for Angers. Pending further instructions, Fouquet would be lodged there in a small humid cell in the ancient fortress that still dominated the town, guarded day and night by d'Artagnan and his musketeers and cut off from all communication with the outside world.[1]

Ten days earlier, Fouquet had been greeted at Angers as a minister of state. Now he was a prisoner of state, awaiting the king's pleasure, and uncertain of his fate.

What had led to this extraordinary turn of events?

CHAPTER 1

The Long Reach

The self-made man did not exist in seventeenth-century France, at least not in the rarefied circles of state power. What did exist was the self-made family, rising steadily over generations from non-noble roots, amassing wealth through commercial activities as a basis for a shift in the family's social status. Such wealth was used to obtain landed property and high royal office, "the soap of serfs" as this last was called. Landed property and state service gave the family an assured social position and noble rank while conveying many of the traditional privileges accorded to the "sword nobility," whose status rested on landholding and military service. The majority of these newcomer families remained at the level of regional notables, but a few were able to play on the national stage by acquiring places in the senior judicial, financial, or administrative apparatus of the crown. The combination of wealth, office-holding at a visible level, and family connections and alliances built over time positioned talented and ambitious scions to ascend to the highest nonmilitary offices of state. Such was the background of Nicolas Fouquet.

Like many of the other families that became prominent in the judicial and administrative hierarchies of the French state in the seventeenth century, the Fouquets were of provincial origin. The family had its roots in the Loire countryside around Angers, about 200 miles southwest of Paris. The rise of the Fouquets out of the mercantile class of Angers into the ranks of the judiciary and royal bureaucracy over several generations was hardly unusual. Many of the judicial dynasties of the sixteenth and seventeenth centuries, families such as the de Thous (from Orléans), the Séguiers (from Saint-Pourçain), or the Lamoignons (from Nevers), came from towns and villages along the Loire and the Allier from Touraine to the

Massif Central. The presence of the Valois court along the Loire in the fifteenth and sixteenth centuries facilitated the rise of these families, as did the great ducal courts in the same regions: the Bourbons at Moulins, the Orléans at Blois, and the Anjou princes at Angers.[1] These courts would have been important sources of patronage for merchants and artisans dealing in fine textiles, jewelry, arms and armor, or other luxury goods. Spendthrift aristocrats were always looking to borrow money to finance their expensive bouts of warfare and extravagant lifestyles, often from these selfsame mercantile families turned financiers. The ties created between great aristocrats and their commoner creditors would have facilitated the entry of some of the sons of those plebeians into royal or princely service.

In the dialect spoken along the lower Loire, *fouquet* or *foucquet* means "squirrel," suggesting perhaps a remote rural origin, or perhaps the characteristics of a squirrel: industrious, frugal, adept at climbing to high places. The surname "Fouquet" was not rare in that region, and thanks to forged documents assembled by a great-uncle, Nicolas Fouquet believed himself descended from a younger son of an otherwise extinct noble family of the same name, formerly the lords of Moulins-Neuf on the Loir; the superintendant even bought that estate to reinforce this identification with his supposed ancestors.[2] Here too was a common pattern among prominent seventeenth-century families of plebian origin: the myth of a noble ancestor ruined financially and forced to enter commerce to rebuild the family fortune. Similarly, the Séguiers claimed a tie to a noble clan of the same name in Languedoc, while the Colberts managed to find ties to the Scottish royal house to hide their own commercial antecedents.[3]

The authentic forefather of Nicolas Fouquet, the first of whom there is any record, was a prosperous sixteenth-century merchant of Angers named Jehan (Jean) Fouquet. The Fouquets were dealers in silk and woolen textiles, and the ducal court at Angers would have been a good customer for such goods. Jehan's eldest son, François, also a dealer in fine textiles, became a beadle and purchasing agent for the university of Angers in 1539.[4] The fortune slowly accumulated through commerce and advantageous marriages was used to buy landed estates, to invest in royal obligations secured on tax revenues, and to educate sons of the family for careers in law and service to the crown. After legal studies, perhaps at the local university, several members of the Fouquet family purchased offices in the royal judiciary or elsewhere in the royal administration, usually as financial officials. Two lines of Jehan's descendants, known respectively as the Fouquets de la Bouchefollière and the Fouquets de Chalain, later became prominent magistrates in the Parlement of Brittany at Rennes and political allies of Nicolas Fouquet. But Nicolas's grandfather, François III Fouquet (d. 1590), left his native

Angers and moved to Paris where he became a judge (*conseiller*) of the Parlement of Paris in 1578. A suitable marriage into an established family of the Paris bourgeoisie augmented the family finances, while François distinguished himself by his allegiance to Henri III during the religious wars of the 1580s. He was named an executor of the will of Catherine de' Medici, a great honor and mark of high favor for a newcomer to the ranks of the most prestigious court in France.[5]

The father of Nicolas, François IV Fouquet (1587–1640), raised in part by a Breton uncle after the death of his mother in 1600, assumed his father's post as a member of the Parlement of Paris in 1609. In the following year, he married Marie de Maupeou, whose family had occupied important positions within the judiciary and royal bureaucracy for several generations. Marie's father, Gilles de Maupeou, held the position of controller general of finance in the royal government and was an able collaborator and political ally of Henri IV's great minister Sully and, after 1617, of Sully's successor, Pierre Jeannin.[6]

This connection with the Maupeous may have facilitated the next step in the rise of the family. In 1615, François IV Fouquet sold his office as a member of *parlement* and acquired another, that of *maître des requêtes*, an office that made him a part of the royal power structure. There is no exact or close counterpart to this office in modern state bureaucracies; its function straddled both the judicial and royal administrative worlds. The corps of maîtres, 42 strong in that period, were attached to the royal councils and to the chancellor's office and in effect functioned as the "staff officers" of those organs of government. As such, they prepared the dossiers on matters coming before the king's councils, drafted decrees, and sometimes sat in on council meetings to provide expertise or additional information as required. These responsibilities gave them exposure to the king and to senior royal officials. Maîtres were often sent on special assignments into the provinces to deal with some aspect of royal concern, such as tax gathering or the provisioning and discipline of royal armies in the field, or to investigate complaints of abuse of authority by local officials. In these special functions, they were usually given the title of "intendant" and enjoyed exceptional temporary authority conferred by royal commission. Good performance on such missions could be the stepping stone to even higher office. At the same time, the maîtres retained their status as members of the judiciary, because the corps had originated in the Middle Ages as part of the royal judicial apparatus. As such, they sat as judges in certain specialized cases, especially those involving royal administration, or presided over cases referred to them by a royal council. They also sat in the Parlement of Paris in rotation.[7]

This purchase of the office of maître des requêtes by François IV Fouquet was to prove critical in the ascent of his son Nicolas because it brought him into proximity with the world of high policy and its makers. In addition to his professional achievements, François and his wife were known for their exceptional piety and were active members of the Catholic renewal of the first decades of seventeenth-century France. This tie to "devout" circles (*le parti dévot*) may be the way François first established contact with the young bishop of Luçon, Armand du Plessis de Richelieu, who in his early career had links to the same groups.[8]

However they initially crossed paths, François Fouquet soon became a close collaborator and "client" of Richelieu's and shared in his rise. In 1624, Richelieu, having triumphed over his rivals, became the head of the royal council (prime minister). In that same year he created the overseas council (*conseil de la Marine*) to encourage overseas trade and colonial ventures, often granting commercial or colonial monopolies to various mercantile companies in which he himself sometimes held a stake. François Fouquet was made a member of this council, serving along with ministers of state such as Antoine d'Effiat, the superintendant of finance. This interest in the potential of the sea as a source of power and wealth for France was to form part of the heritage of Nicolas Fouquet and, ironically, to be used against him in his trial.[9]

In 1626, Richelieu appointed François to serve on the special court set up to try the hapless Henri de Talleyrand-Périgord, comte de Chalais, a foolish young courtier lured by aristocratic friends such as the duchess de Chevreuse into a conspiracy to assassinate Richelieu. Richelieu wished to use the occasion as a warning to the grandees of the kingdom, and Chalais was duly tried before a court at Nantes largely drawn from the Parlement of Rennes: the prosecutor was Christophe Fouquet de Chalain, one of the Breton cousins of François. The verdict was foregone, and the sentence as well: Chalais met a cruel death at the hand of an amateur executioner.[10]

Participation in this trial marked François Fouquet irrevocably as a client of Richelieu. In 1627 he was appointed a "councilor of state" (*conseiller d'État*), a post that enabled him to sell his prior office of maître des requêtes.[11] Until his death, in 1640, François worked as a close collaborator of Richelieu on matters of state. He also tended to the redeployment of his own fortune and to the nourishing of his maritime interests, and he saw to the future of his large family, of whom six sons and six daughters survived to adulthood.

Nicolas Fouquet, the third child and second son of François IV Fouquet and Marie de Maupeou, was to become the family standard bearer in the next generation. He was born in January 1615, at the Fouquet residence on the rue de la

Verrerie in the Marais section of Paris. Some time thereafter, the family moved to more spacious quarters on the rue de Jouy, also in the Marais. As a boy, Nicolas would have benefited from his father's copious and rich library, containing an impressive 15,000 volumes, as well as an assortment of globes and "curiosities," meaning antique coins and other artifacts of various sorts. These collections were to form the foundation of Nicolas' own extensive library in later years.[12] In addition, Nicolas obtained what was then considered the best education available, at the Jesuit Collège de Clermont in the Latin Quarter, the institutional ancestor of today's Lycée Louis-le-Grand. No doubt he received supplemental tutorials at the hands of his father, who offered a model for service to the state and whose network of friends and connections provided a means of entry into the circles of power.[13]

Initially, Nicolas was intended for the church. It was assumed that his older brother, François, born in 1611, would carry on the family tradition of state service. Nicolas was tonsured at 16 and shortly thereafter had several church offices conferred on him as the successor to an elderly relative. But by an odd quirk of temperament, the older brother, François, who had begun a promising legal career in 1631 and had joined the Parlement of Paris in 1633, developed a vocation for the priesthood, while Nicolas had no inclination at all for an ecclesiastical career. In 1635, François announced his intention of entering the Church, a development his devout parents welcomed. With the help of both Richelieu and his clerical friends, in particular the saintly Vincent de Paul, the young former magistrate moved quickly into the clerical establishment and was consecrated bishop of Bayonne in 1639.[14]

After resigning his clerical appointments to his brother, Nicolas was free to pursue a future in the law. There is a tradition that Richelieu himself, struck by the young man's intelligence and drive, encouraged him to do so.[15] To start him on his way, his father had already bought him a seat in the newly created Parlement of Metz. At age 18, Nicolas was technically too young for a magistrate's post, but the requirement was waived in consideration of his father's services—and devotion—to Richelieu.[16] Richelieu intended to use this newly created parlement as a vehicle for increasing French jurisdiction over the "three bishoprics," the enclaves of Metz, Toul, and Verdun, within the duchy of Lorraine. These territories had passed into French hands in the prior century, but the rights and powers of the crown within them were not well defined.

As a young magistrate, Nicolas and a colleague were sent to examine ancient documents in the monasteries and episcopal archives in the vicinity of Metz to identify former imperial or ducal rights that now belonged to the crown of

France. Some of Fouquet's research was to be used a generation later by the agents of Louis XIV to justify the crown's claims after the incorporation of Alsace into France,[17] but in the meantime Fouquet's mission was interrupted by another commission from Richelieu. He was delegated to write a long royal declaration accusing duke Charles of Lorraine of hostile acts in order to justify the invasion of Lorraine by French troops, a step actually motivated by Richelieu's decision to intervene directly in the Thirty Years War. Once French troops had occupied Lorraine, Fouquet was sent on another mission to Nancy, to join the French officials there in administering the province. Richelieu rewarded Nicolas's efforts in 1636 by waiving an age requirement to allow him to assume his father's office of maître des requêtes.[18]

The beginning of a new decade also brought significant changes to Fouquet's private life. It was time to marry and continue the Fouquet lineage. A suitable match was arranged with Louise Fourché, whose late father had been a member of the Parlement of Brittany and whose relatives were prominent in administrative and judicial roles there.[19] The couple married at Nantes in January 1640. Louise brought her groom a substantial dowry as well as some landed property in the vicinity of Nantes, and before the year was out she presented Fouquet with a daughter, Marie. But their happiness was overshadowed by the death of François IV Fouquet in late April of that same year. In his will, the senior Fouquet left his books and "curiosities" to Nicolas, as well as a substantial fortune. Scarcely a year later, in February 1641, Nicolas's maternal grandfather, the aged Gilles de Maupeou, also a family mainstay, passed away.[20]

Another terrible blow awaited Nicolas in August 1641, when Louise died suddenly, perhaps of complications from her pregnancy. Fouquet was now left to care for his widowed mother, orphaned daughter, and twelve siblings, for whom he was in effect the patriarch of the family. Fouquet's sisters were all to enter religious life, with five of the six joining the fashionable Convent of the Visitation at Paris. Nicolas's older brother, François, was already a bishop, but the younger brothers had to be launched on suitable careers.[21]

At precisely a moment when the continued patronage of Cardinal de Richelieu would have eased the burdens on Nicolas, the chief minister also departed the scene, dying in December 1642. The formidable cardinal was followed in May 1643 by his master, Louis XIII. The government of France now fell into the hands of the king's widow, the Spanish-born Anne of Austria, governing on behalf of her young son, Louis XIV. While Anne dispensed favors to aristocrats who had long been identified with her "cause" during the time of Richelieu, she also kept many of Richelieu's close associates in power, including his most trusted lieutenant, Cardinal Jules Mazarin. This augured well for Nicolas and others identified with Richelieu; in addition, the Fouquets had ties to the regent. François IV Fouquet had served on the queen's private council, and Fouquet's mother was known to the queen through the network of pious aristocratic ladies associated with the "devouts" in Paris.[22]

In the spring of 1644 Fouquet was sent to Grenoble, the provincial capital of Dauphiné, as an intendant, with authority to look into abuses by local officials. He was also charged with distributing the heavy tax known as the *taille* among the various subdivisions (parishes, towns, and so forth) against which it was levied in a kind of quota system, and with improving the actual collection of funds.

In Dauphiné, Fouquet found a province stumbling under the weight of taxation, necessitated by years of continuous warfare, and seething with deep anger among ordinary peasants and artisans at the maldistribution of those taxes. The taille was levied there on all landed property that was non-noble in origin, even if currently owned by noblemen who were otherwise exempt from the taille (see chapter 2). But in practice noblemen, officials, and well-to-do bourgeoisie had managed either to evade taxation of their landed holdings altogether or at least to obtain ludicrously low evaluations on properties subject to the levy. The effect was to shift most of the burden on those least able to afford it. Fouquet reported all this to Paris and suggested the portion of the taille allocated to the province be lowered in the coming year. This proposal was welcomed in Dauphiné but caused consternation in Paris. Pierre Séguier, the chancellor, brought this troublesome recommendation to the attention of Mazarin and the regent, and Fouquet was promptly recalled. Mazarin even disavowed his agent: both Fouquet's initial appointment and subsequent recall, the cardinal insisted, were entirely the work of the queen.[23]

Fouquet left Grenoble for Paris in August 1644. He stopped en route in the town of Valence to help quell an uprising there by listening to local complaints and promising to investigate alleged injustices. As he attempted to depart, his party encountered a mob of angry peasant and artisan women in the suburb of Bourg-lès-Valence. They attacked his unescorted coach and pulled its occupants, Fouquet and three other officials, out of the cab. Two of the officials were separated from Fouquet (one was later found murdered), and the one remaining with Fouquet attempted to draw his sword. Not wanting to enrage the mob further, Fouquet had his companion put up his sword. Instead, Fouquet advanced toward the crowd, braving a fusillade of projectiles and curses, and began to address them. He continued to speak over the din, asking what the grievances were, and promising to rectify abuses. Those in the front ranks began to listen, and in a shift of mood, formed a protective cordon around Fouquet and his colleague, eventually moving them into a nearby house. Shortly thereafter, Fouquet and his companion were rescued by an armed band of noblemen and taken to the bishop's residence. When troops from Grenoble arrived, Fouquet used them to restore order, but he also took some measures to appease public anger even as he turned over those accused of murdering his colleague to the local authorities for prosecution.[24]

However harrowing, the incident at Valence illustrated some important characteristics of Fouquet: not simply physical courage and a refusal to be cowed by overwhelming force but also his coolness "under fire" and presence of mind. His eloquence was effective because of his ability to "read" his momentary adversaries. He did not deny the validity of their grievances; rather, he sympathized with them and thereby deflected their wrath elsewhere—to the very system of which he was a part.

The controversy that had led to Fouquet's recall did no permanent damage to his career. In 1646, Fouquet was again commissioned as an intendant and sent to Catalonia to join the army there under the comte d'Harcourt. He was to look into a critical lack of supplies and investigate accusations of irregularities against some of Harcourt's senior subordinates. This mission was followed in 1647 by another, this time sending Fouquet to Picardy, where the army was battling Spanish forces based in the Lowlands. Mazarin made a point of telling Gaston d'Orléans, the nominal commander in chief of French forces, that the queen herself had insisted on this appointment.[25] While with these troops, Fouquet witnessed the fatal wounding of maréchal Jean de Gassion at the siege of Lens. As the senior royal official present, Fouquet rallied Gassion's subordinates and saw to an orderly change of command and to the establishment of winter quarters for the troops at the end of the campaign season. All of this played very well in Paris.[26]

In May 1648 Fouquet was named intendant for the *généralité* of Paris, making him responsible for the peaceful—and effective—collection of taxes, and for the provisioning and discipline of royal troops stationed in the vicinity of Paris. But Fouquet's appointment was overshadowed by the first stages of the lengthy civil war known as the Fronde, which began in early 1648 as a "revolt of the judges" of the Parlement of Paris and its sister high courts against new revenue-raising measures the government was seeking to impose. These included the creation and sale of more offices and the imposition of new taxes that would have fallen heavily on the shoulders of the poorer and less privileged inhabitants of Paris. Opposition to these tax proposals enabled the courts and the judges to pose as champions of the people against a rapacious government.

The high court magistrates certainly had a personal stake in the matter. Several measures initiated by Richelieu and Louis XIII and continued by Mazarin and the regent had alienated the royal officeholders (*officiers*) who were the backbone of the royal government. By the 1640s there were perhaps 37,000 nonmilitary royal officials, mostly judicial and financial officers, divided into many ranks, from the top tiers of members of parlement and royal treasurers down through the ranks of provincial magistrates and local tax collectors and customs officers.[27] Virtually all of these officeholders had purchased their offices, which were in a real sense property, an investment paying a salary (*gages*) that was in functional terms a return on the investment, and which could be resold or assigned like any other kind of property.

In 1635 Richelieu had brought France into the Thirty Years War as an opponent of the Spanish and Austrian Habsburgs. The war had dragged on endlessly, and the crown found itself in an impossible financial situation. Virtually all money reaching the government's coffers was diverted to the war effort, so that the officeholders' salaries were either not paid at all or paid at a reduced rate. In addition, new offices were created and sold to raise more money. Increasing the number of available positions for sale as well as the nonpayment of wages had the effect of decreasing the value of existing offices and their investment or resale value. So the crown's own officials were faced with both a cash loss from the nonpayment of wages and a capital loss from the dilution of the investment value of their offices. In addition, these officers were also cowed into subscribing to various forced "loans" to the government, with the threat that failure to do so might result in yet more offices being created, or that the government might withdraw the special arrangement (the *paulette*) that allowed an officeholder to bequeath or transfer an office to another, even at the point of death. Thus, in the provinces, as well as in Paris, many officeholders, from routine tax collectors to the highest magistrates, had serious grievances against the regent and the royal councilors, primarily Mazarin and his superintendants of finance, whom they held responsible for these schemes.[28]

The unrest among the generally well-off and privileged members of society was compounded by the growing bitterness and anger among the ordinary people on whom the bulk of the tax burdens fell. The levels of taxation had risen steadily, both direct taxes, such as the taille and its various surcharges (*taillon*, *crue*), which were mostly paid by peasant farmers and the small artisans living in the countryside or small villages, and the various kinds of indirect taxes, such as the salt taxes, sales taxes, and "customs duties" on goods and foodstuffs moving from one area to the other. These indirect taxes affected the price of food and drink and other basic necessities in the cities and towns, causing widespread unrest in urban areas.

Even while Richelieu was still alive, there had been peasant uprising and sporadic riots in provincial towns where the anger at taxation levels had reached the boiling point. Local collectors were often chased away or occasionally lynched. Richelieu reacted to these revolts by treating the exasperated taxpayers as seditious and treasonous. Troops were brought in to put down these protests and to inflict exemplary punishments such as hangings and confiscations. The regent and Mazarin continued these measures, but they did little to stop the discontent in the countryside as, year after year, the tax burden grew heavier and disorders became more widespread. By the late 1640s whole districts of France, including some urban areas, were hotbeds of unrest and rebellion: the government was visibly losing control of the countryside. Fouquet had had firsthand experience of this in Dauphiné.[29]

A great deal of anger was concentrated on those perceived to be the ultimate beneficiaries of much of the sacrifice demanded of the public, namely the financiers who had come to dominate the royal financial machinery. The judges of the high courts in Paris shared this resentment. Part of this was out of personal pique, because of the nonpayment of wages and the crown's attempts to create more judicial offices to raise more money. Some of it also may have arisen from a sense of sympathy for the peasants: many judges owned country estates and were aware of rural distress and the peasants' inability to pay both a higher taille and the rents and fees owed to their noble landlords.[30]

Yet part of the anger and resentment of the magistrates certainly stemmed from a more deep-seated institutional grievance. Prior to Henri IV (1589–1610), virtually every form of nonmilitary governance, including the financial and taxation mechanisms, was considered part of the "police powers" of the judiciary, and special high courts, the Chambre des comptes (Chamber of Accounts) and Cour des aides (Court of Excise Taxes), existed to scrutinize and verify all the transactions of royal tax officials. Beginning under Henri IV, and accelerating under Richelieu and Louis XIII, many of the newer kinds of state activities, particularly in the financial area, had been removed from judicial scrutiny and review. Courts and judges were to have no say over these transactions, nor were they to entertain lawsuits brought against financial agents of the crown in connection with their duties. The actions of such officials were to come under the purview of—and if necessary they would receive discipline by—the royal council of finance or some official designated by the council.

The judges resented this challenge to their institutional authority, which they saw as violating the traditions and customs of the monarchy and affecting the older style of consultation and consensus with which the monarchy had governed for centuries. So the parlements, particularly that of Paris, saw themselves as being "cut off" from a traditional role in government, just as the high aristocracy in this same period saw its power diminished by its exclusion from the royal council and the elimination of some of its sources of military and provincial patronage. In effect, the quarrel was about the increasing centralization of monarchical power and the lack of consultation between the crown and traditional constituencies in the exercise of that power. Many of the high court judges sought to return matters, ironically, to the imagined golden age of Henri IV.[31]

All of this dissatisfaction came to a head early in 1648. Mazarin and the regent were determined to find the resources to keep the imperial forces in Germany on the defensive that year, since they expected to conclude negotiations that would bring peace on terms advantageous for France. To this end, they decided to raise more money with another round of higher taxes and sales of offices. Knowing that the Parlement of Paris would balk at registering these measures, a special ceremony called a *lit de justice* was held in January 1648. The boy king appeared in person, together with the regent and Mazarin, before the parlement, and in his presence the judges were ordered to register the decrees. By longstanding tradition, a personal royal appearance of this type should have ended any further discussion.

But this time, breaking all precedents, the judges did not cease their objections. Instead, they continued to protest the measures, demanding that the financiers who lent the crown money and the king's superintendant of finance, Michel Particelli d'Émery, be investigated for "corruption." Because some of these tax measures involved new or increased sales taxes in Paris, the "little people" of Paris (shopkeepers, artisans, and the like) demonstrated in favor of the judges' position. At the same time, conditions in the countryside continued to deteriorate, as rural rebellions became even more widespread. In many districts, tax collectors refused to collect taxes, and royal judges refused to hear cases or exercise their police powers. To some extent, the crown had lost control of the machinery of government.[32]

After "negotiations" with the crown stalemated, the Parlement of Paris took another unprecedented step in late June 1648. It joined with the judges of its sister high courts, the Chambre des comptes and the Cour des aides, to sit as a single body, calling itself the Chambre de Saint Louis (after the hall where it met) to discuss general reforms in the management of the government. Its demands included lowering the taille, forgiving all tailles in arrears, paying the salaries in full of all royal officials, paying past due interest on royal annuities, and abolishing the various special offices and commissions the crown was using to circumvent the authority of the courts. In July 1648, the crown agreed to repudiate all existing loan contracts (see chapter 2) with its financiers without compensation for advances or other sums already received. This precipitated a general if temporary collapse of the crown's finances, the so-called bankruptcy of 1648, requiring a desperate Mazarin and his colleagues to initiate negotiations with the financial community to reopen their purses, often ending with undisclosed compensation arrangements for the losses from the repudiation that were even more costly than the canceled arrangements.[33]

The crown temporized on most of the parlement's other demands, and in late August, after word reached Paris of a major victory in the field at Lens, which the government assumed would sway public opinion in its favor, it attempted to arrest two of the most outspoken judges. The result was comparable to that of the famous "Day of the Barricades" during the Wars of Religion (May 1588). Street mobs and ad hoc groups of town militiamen blocked off the streets, attacked royal troops on patrol, and almost lynched chancellor Séguier while he was crossing Paris (he had to be rescued by a heavily armed body of troops).[34] Crowds surrounded the royal palace, demanding the release of the judges, and a humiliated regent was forced to capitulate. With popular support evidently behind them, the parlement repeated its program in yet another declaration in late October, with emphasis on tax relief for the people.[35]

The royal court temporized once more, and was rewarded for its efforts; the treaties that ended the war with the Empire were signed the same day as the parlement's October pronouncement. It was already the end of the normal campaigning season, and so the government was able to order Louis de Bourbon, prince de Condé, to return with his army to the vicinity of Paris and to be ready for deployment. In early January 1649, the court fled the city for Rueil, a suburban royal château, and once there imposed a blockade on the city.

During all of these disturbances, Fouquet was faithful to his oaths of office and had remained loyal to the crown. Sensing the widespread support the high court judges enjoyed, he counseled Mazarin to take a moderate line and to appease the magistrates.[36] Yet he sided with the royal administration when the quarrel degenerated into open warfare. After the regent and Mazarin used troops under Condé to besiege the city, Fouquet, as intendant for Paris, worked to supply Condé's forces.[37]

But the judges were not intimidated, even by Condé's fearsome reputation.

Parlement responded by declaring Mazarin an "enemy of state" and an outlaw. It mobilized the city militia and authorized the raising of troops.

To lead the troops and defend Paris from royal forces, the parlement turned to the high nobility and soon found that there were many aristocratic malcontents willing to side with the magistrates to advance their special interests. These included some of the king's relatives, such as the prince de Conti, younger brother of Condé; the duchess de Longueville, their sister; and the duc de Beaufort, a grandson of Henri IV. Conti was named commander in chief of the Parisian forces, to protect the city against his own brother.

Conti, however, did not share his elder brother's military aptitudes, and the Parisian forces suffered a sequence of defeats at Condé's hands. Initially, the royal government intended to impose a harsh peace, since it had the whip hand, but all this changed as word reached Paris in the early spring that the Spanish (with whom France was still at war) had invaded to the north. Condé's troops would be needed to stop them, while maréchal Henri de la Tour d'Auvergne, vicomte de Turenne, the only general who was a match for Condé, had gone over to the Fronde. These developments spurred a more conciliatory attitude on the part of Mazarin and the regent.

After more negotiations, the Peace of Rueil-Saint-Germain was signed on March 11, 1649, and seemed to satisfy everyone. Parlement agreed to rescind the decrees against Mazarin, to discontinue meeting with the other high courts, and return the fortresses of the Bastille and the Arsenal to royal control. The crown in turn promised to honor the demands of the parlement in its declarations of July and October 1648, and all rebels were amnestied. There were also promises of pensions and other appointments for the various noble supporters of the Fronde.[38]

On the surface, the Parlement of Paris seemed to have made some impressive gains, especially given the quasi-revolutionary nature of the right it was claiming to modify or annul royal decrees and outlaw royal ministers. But the peace concluding the first episode of the Fronde, called the Parlementary Fronde, turned out to be an illusion. The government soon disregarded its many promises, and both sides, parlement and crown, found themselves overshadowed by the great nobles they had recruited to use against one another.

Violence broke out again early in 1650 after the regent and Mazarin, tired of Condé's endless attempts to dominate the royal council, arrested him, his brother, Conti, and brother-in-law, the duc de Longueville. This sparked a new round of warfare, a deadly cycle that was to last until the beginning of 1653 and is known as the Fronde of the Princes. A constant switching of sides by great aristocrats, military commanders, and even senior officials such as chancellor Séguier, makes the narrative difficult to follow. But throughout it all, Fouquet remained true to the crown. In the course of 1650 he was sent on a mission to Normandy to prevent the seizure of that province by Condé's partisans and then rejoined the court and royal troops in Burgundy, where once more he exercised authority as an intendant over the royal army.[39]

In November 1650, Fouquet reaped the reward for his loyalty. The post of *procureur général* ("attorney general") in the Parlement of Paris was available. The position was one of the most prestigious in the judicial system: the royal procureur général, together with the *avocat général* and their respective deputies, represented the interests of the crown before parlement, and were referred to collectively as the *parquet*. The procureur général was also charged with special administrative responsibilities over the police and judicial apparatus of the kingdom, as well as over matters concerning the Church, the royal demesne, and education. The incumbent, one Blaise Méliand, wished to sell the office. Fouquet was a willing buyer, but this office, although it could be sold, was one that required royal approval of the buyer. Mazarin was delighted with the possibility of Fouquet's becoming the guardian of the crown's interests at the Palais de justice. The deal was closed for 450,000 livres, paid partly in cash and partly with the transfer of Fouquet's office of maître des requêtes, valued at 150,000 livres, to Méliand's son.[40]

In the nearly ten years since the death of his wife, Fouquet's attention had been focused on his career and the care of his siblings. The time had come to remarry to strengthen the family network of alliances and to produce a male heir. His choice fell on a member of a well-established family in the world of high finance, Marie-Madeleine de Castille. Born in 1636, Marie-Madeleine was more than twenty years younger than her fiancé, but her family included prominent financiers and was connected to that of Pierre Jeannin, under whom Fouquet's grandfather Gilles de Maupeou had served. The bride's relatives included the financier and royal treasurer (*trésorier de l'Épargne*) Nicolas Jeannin de Castille; an uncle who served as a senior household officer to the king's uncle Gaston d'Orléans; and a cousin, the maréchal de Villeroy, governor to the young king. Ironically, another cousin of the bride, Charlotte de Castille, had been married to the unfortunate comte de Chalais whom Fouquet's father had condemned to death in 1626.[41] But present interests trumped old grudges, and that memory did not disrupt the wedding, which took place in February 1651. Although the bride's dowry was smaller than that of Fouquet's first wife, she was an only child and heiress, and within a few years of the marriage the death of her parents brought into the Fouquet household a fortune valued at 1.5 million livres. This was almost twice the size of the fortune left to Nicolas by his father, and marked the Fouquets as very wealthy indeed, with holdings comparable to those of the higher ranks of the aristocracy.[42]

The wedding festivities coincided with yet another turn of the wheel of fortune. In the same week as the nuptials, the parlement of Paris again called for the dismissal and exile of Mazarin and the release of Condé and his princely companions. This time Gaston d'Orléans sided with the magistrates, as did the coadjutor archbishop of Paris, Jean François Paul de Gondi (the future Cardinal de Retz). All this sparked renewed popular uprisings in Paris, and a mob actually invaded the Palais-Royal demanding to see the young king. Mazarin fled the country, stopping only briefly at Le Havre to "liberate" Condé and his fellow prisoners, before continuing on to exile in the territories of the elector of Cologne.

For the moment, the rebel princes and Gaston were triumphant, once more dominating the royal government and forcing the regent to dismiss some of her ministers—including Hugues de Lionne, who was hidden by the Fouquets on one of Madame Fouquet's country estates.[43] While these new masters of the kingdom fell to quarreling among themselves in the months that followed, Fouquet did his best to mitigate the damage to Mazarin. He attempted in vain to prevent the parlement from seizing and dispersing Mazarin's famous art collections, and he tried to build within the high court a coterie of magistrates devoted, if not to Mazarin, then at least to the principle of a royal government devoid of princely bullies. His efforts were known to Mazarin, who expressed his gratitude on multiple occasions.[44] Nicolas was seconded by his younger brother Basile, known as the abbé ("abbot") because he enjoyed the revenues of several abbeys without in fact being a clergyman. Basile, seven years younger than Nicolas, had entered Mazarin's service during the Fronde and served as a kind of agent or courier, negotiating privately on Mazarin's part with various self-interested grandees, running networks of spies and informers for the cardinal, and trying, like his brother Nicolas, to create a submerged base of support for the former minister that could play an important role at the right time.[45]

In September 1651 the king reached his thirteenth birthday and his majority was proclaimed. This event undercut an important Frondeur objection to the measures previously taken by the regent: that only an adult king could exercise the plenitude of the royal authority.[46] Now the king could issue decrees in his own right to confirm what had been ordered by his mother or the cardinal. While this distinction appealed to some of the magistrates in parlement, it did not sway the princes. In September 1651 civil war broke out anew between Condé and his partisans of the moment on the one hand and the government on the other. This time several important actors, including Turenne and some high-ranking parlementary officials, sided with the king's party, thanks in part to the efforts of the Fouquet brothers.[47]

In December 1651 Mazarin reentered the kingdom, causing parlement to outlaw him and to seize and sell his assets, including his magnificent library, in a senseless act of cultural vandalism Fouquet was unable to stop.[48] Condé and his partisans soon regained control of Paris, and in May 1652 Fouquet formed part of a parlementary delegation that once more demanded Mazarin's exile as a condition of peace. Fouquet let it be known privately that he saw this as a temporary but necessary expedient. But Mazarin refused to go, convinced that if he left he would never be called back.[49]

Fouquet's true allegiance could never have been in question. In July 1652, Condé's army was camped outside the walls of Paris. The local authorities had refused it entry, but Condé began a march around the walls, hoping to enter the city by the Porte Saint-Antoine on the east side of Paris, which was guarded by the Bastille. Fouquet managed to get a messenger to the nearby royal army under Turenne, advising Turenne of the maneuver and of the strength of Condé's forces.[50] Making use of this information, Turenne trapped Condé and would have crushed his armies against the walls of the city had not Gaston's daughter, the duchess de Montpensier, persuaded Gaston to order the gates opened to Condé's army. Its retreat was covered by the guns of the Bastille, firing at the royal troops on the orders of the duchess.[51]

Paris itself was once more under Condé's sway. Nicolas slipped out of the city and rejoined the court, where he argued again that Mazarin should step down temporarily. When the Parlement of Paris proclaimed the king a prisoner of Mazarin's and appointed Gaston d'Orléans the lieutenant general of the kingdom and Condé the head of its armies, the royal government responded by ordering parlement to vacate Paris and reassemble temporarily at Pontoise, a measure supported by Fouquet.[52] Only a handful of judges obeyed, although their number included the first president, Mathieu Molé, as well as the procureur général, Nicolas Fouquet.[53] There were now two rival Parlements of Paris, one meeting in Pontoise and the other, larger one sitting in its ancient headquarters in the capital under the thumb of the princes. One of the first acts of the Pontoise parlement was to petition the king to exile Mazarin.[54] This time the cardinal yielded, withdrawing in August 1652 to the territories of the duc de Bouillon, which were part of the Empire. While the royal court established itself at Compiègne, Fouquet remained at Pontoise, a useful vantage point for keeping an eye on events in Paris. He and his brother Basile, who acted as Mazarin's eyes and ears in Paris and Compiègne, reported on developments in correspondence with Michel Le Tellier, the minister for war, and also with Mazarin.[55]

In Paris, however, the parlement and princes had dissolved into irreconcilable factions. Many entered into secret negotiations with the crown. Condé, unwilling to yield and lacking the resources to continue, left Paris in October, bound for a self-imposed exile in the service of the king of Spain. Scarcely ten days later, the young king made a triumphant entry into Paris. In the following weeks, some leaders of the rebellion who lingered, such as Gaston d'Orléans and his daughter the duchess de Montpensier, were ordered to leave Paris, while others, notably Gondi, were arrested.

Mazarin returned from exile in February 1653. If rebels were to be punished, the faithful looked to their just rewards. Fouquet had his in mind. In early 1653, Charles de La Vieuville, superintendant of finance, died. The office of superintendant of finance was one of the most important posts in government, and one held by royal commission rather than by purchase. Nicolas Fouquet had no hesitation about recommending himself, stressing the importance of choosing someone with a reputation for integrity, who enjoyed credibility with the public, and who had demonstrated "unshakeable [*inviolable*] loyalty to Your Eminence."[56] There were many other interested parties, including such luminaries as Abel Servien, one of the principal negotiators of the Peace of Westphalia, who had also remained faithful to the crown and Mazarin during the Fronde; Mathieu Molé, one of the most respected members of the Parlement of Paris; and Madame Fouquet's cousin, the well-connected maréchal de Villeroy. In the end, Mazarin decided on a joint appointment, naming as dual superintendants Servien and Fouquet.

By virtue of this new position, which included the additional title of "minister of state," Nicolas Fouquet, a fifth generation descendant of a provincial textile merchant, would now take his place in the king's council chamber.[57]

CHAPTER 2

The Superintendant at Work

As a minister of state, holding simultaneously two of the most visible positions in the royal administration, Nicolas Fouquet was at the center of public life in the 1650s. Although the decade following the Fronde is often passed over by historians anxious to move on to the beginning of Louis XIV's "personal reign" after the cardinal's death in 1661, the events of this second part of Mazarin's tenure in office were critical to what followed. France had been a signatory of the Peace of Westphalia (1648), but the country was still at war with her chief foe, Spain, and would remain so for the balance of the 1650s. As the decade continued, the conflict's final outcome was by no means certain. Spain was still able to field powerful armies, and benefited from the talents of Condé, now based in the Spanish Low Countries, who preferred to fight on as a quasi-independent ally of the Spanish king. The struggle with Spain meant additional financial strain on a system overburdened with the enormous debts already incurred to support the war and on an economy that had been weakened by the violence of the years of the Fronde.

While the Fronde had ended with the return of the court to Paris in late 1652, France was by no means pacified. With no real relief possible for the peasants and artisans who bore the brunt of the tax burden, sporadic uprisings broke out from time to time in the countryside or in provincial towns. At the same time, the high court judges of the Parlement of Paris and its sister courts continued to criticize the financial measures put into place by Cardinal Mazarin and his colleagues.[1] A reading of Mazarin's correspondence for those years gives the impression that until the achievement of peace with Spain in 1659, the king's ministers functioned in an environment of perpetual crisis, seemingly only one battle or one bankruptcy away from catastrophe.

When he assumed his new responsibilities, Fouquet was by no means a stranger to the complicated fiscal and financial structures that supported the French state. As intendant in Dauphiné and Paris he had had firsthand experience of the vagaries and inequities of the system. His wife's family, the Jeannin de Castille clan, were prominent members of the financial community, and the Fouquets, like most other wealthy French families, would have had investments in state obligations. Yet such tangential involvement would hardly have provided him with the mastery of an intricate system that was scarcely understood by its own practitioners.

Fouquet and his ministerial colleagues knew that at the end of the day, the tax system did not provide the crown with adequate resources to meet its obligations. It had to be supplemented with both short-term and long-term borrowings. For the modern reader, a brief survey of this system and the related financial mechanisms used to bridge the gap between revenue shortfalls and cash requirements is essential to understand Fouquet's role as superintendant and the background to his trial.[2]

Since the late Middle Ages, the most important direct tax in France was a levy known as the *taille*. The taille was imposed on the individual household at a level that supposedly reflected that household's wealth subject to the tax. But like everything else in the ancien régime, nothing about the tax was simple in practice or uniform throughout the kingdom. The total revenue target for the taille and certain other direct taxes and surtaxes (*taillon*, *crue*, and so forth) was set annually by the king and payable by those who were neither noble nor churchmen. There were other reasons for exemption, too: for example, most towns had purchased a collective exemption for those who dwelt within their walls, and many non-noble individuals were exempt by reason of office holding, such as royal treasurers (*trésoriers de France*), or held personal exemptions granted by the king. In some provinces, like Dauphiné, the noble exemption was attached to land classified as "noble" centuries earlier, not to individuals. If a noble held "non-noble" land, he was required to pay the taille on the assessed value or wealth of that property—in theory because in such circumstances nobles or wealthy bourgeois landlords usually found a way to evade the tax. In practice, the myriad exemptions available to the wealthy and powerful meant that the burden fell largely on peasants and artisans.

The method of collection and the obligations of individual households also varied greatly from one part of the country to another. In the center and northeast regions of the country, which no longer had provincial representative bodies, or Estates (*États*), the crown determined for each tax district (*généralité*) the sum to be collected. This gross assessment was reapportioned several times until finally it was levied against the individual household. Collections were normally performed by royal officials known as *élus*, and the parts of France using this mechanism were known as *pays d'élections*. Parts of France where Estates had survived—such as Brittany, Burgundy, Provence, and Dauphiné—were known as *pays d'États*. In those regions the crown and the respective assemblies negotiated the amount that the province would pay, and the collections were left largely under their supervision. Not surprisingly, the contributions of the pays d'États were considerably lower in the aggregate than those of the pays d'élections. A few areas, such as Languedoc, because of historical circumstances of their acquisition had their own separate tax system, and the crown negotiated with the local Estates on a contribution in lieu of the taille.

The second major form of taxation consisted of excise taxes, for instance, taxes on the sale of commodities such as wheat or wine, generally known as *aides*; the notorious *gabelle*, or salt tax, which not only taxed consumption but also required minimum household purchases of salt at government-controlled warehouses, and from which nobles and clergy were also exempt; and tolls and internal customs duties, known as *octrois*. Once again, the burdens placed on different districts varied enormously, often as a function of the historical circumstances at the time a given province came under the crown's direct control. Most of the northern parts of France paid the heaviest rate for the gabelle (the tax was known as the *gabelle de France*) while there were separate and lower rates for provinces such as Languedoc, Dauphiné, or Provence. The Bordeaux region was subject to a special tax on wines known as the *convoi de Bordeaux*, which had originated as a tax to pay for protection against English pirates during the Hundred Years War.[3]

The taille and the various indirect excise taxes provided most of the royal revenues, although the percentages of revenues derived from each category varied significantly from year to year. The rest of the crown's revenues was provided by a miscellany of sources classified as "extraordinary" revenues, to distinguish them from those provided by the taille and the indirect sales taxes and tolls. For example, those entering certain trades or professions had to pay a kind of entrance or initiation fee before taking up their occupations, a payment known as the *marc d'or*. Another important form of extraordinary revenue was the capital raised by selling annuities (*rentes*) secured on future defined tax revenues, for example, on sales taxes collected in Paris (known as *rentes sur l'hôtel de ville*). One of the most important sources of revenue, quite alien to modern concepts of government, was the creation and sale of royal offices, chiefly within the judicial and financial apparatus of the monarchy. As noted above, buying an office was a form of investment, since royal offices paid a salary or wage (usually a small percentage of the purchase price), so they also were a form of annuity. They conveyed both prestige, as in the case of a judgeship, and privileges, like exemption from taxation and sometimes noble status, as well as the ability to make money indirectly from one's duties—bribery was endemic among judges and tax collectors. Moreover, an office could be sold, although sometimes the purchaser had to make an additional payment to the royal treasury when assuming the office (the marc d'or mentioned above). If the king wanted to dismiss someone from an office, he had to refund its purchase price or find a buyer for it because it was a piece of property like any other. As kings grew needier, the expedient of creating more offices grew until by the seventeenth century it had become a major source of royal revenues.

The Church was exempt from taxation but routinely consented to grants or gifts (*décime, don gratuit*), intended in principle to help defend the realm against foreign enemies and domestic heretics. The amounts were subject to negotiation between the parties and varied from one period to the next.

Few aspects of the old regime were more hated and disliked than the tax-collecting system, even by those who were largely exempt from its exactions. Crown officials were often brutal in their collection and enforcement methods, seizing the livestock, the land, or any other possessions of hapless peasants who could not pay, even when the underlying reason for delinquency was a bad harvest or some other natural calamity. There were no avenues of appeal.

Whatever the source, all of these revenues passed through many hands before reaching the royal coffers. When funds collected locally arrived at the regional royal treasuries scattered throughout the kingdom, they were first tapped to pay the wages of local officials and of troops billeted in the district, and also to pay royal obligations secured by pledges of those revenues. After these deductions, what was left, if anything, found its way to the central treasury in Paris. Such practices provided any number of opportunities for corruption, peculation, and delay. The endless accusations of fraud and dishonesty directed at royal officials, financiers, and tax farmers at every representative gathering and in the satiric literature of the period no doubt had a firm basis in fact and reflect the resentment of almost everyone subject to taxation.[4]

As a result of these practices, neither the timing nor amount of revenues reaching Paris could be predicted with any accuracy. The crown was always short of cash, which it needed "up front" to compensate the troops during times of war, to pay for their munitions and supplies, and to cover the household expenses of the king and other necessities of state. Since tax revenues came in erratically, the crown resorted to borrowing money from a small number of financiers, called *partisans* or *traitants*, who could supply cash for pressing needs. Such loans were often secured on the anticipated returns from uncollected taxes, which were pledged several years in advance (e.g., borrowing in 1648 on the taille of 1651). Sometimes the crown leased the right to collect indirect taxes, say a customs tax, to the financiers for a given number of years. This practice, known as "tax farming," was offered in return for a fixed upfront payment and periodic payments thereafter. In these instances, wealthy merchants or bankers would form a syndicate and provide the king an estimate of the amount that a given tax was expected to provide over a the life of the contract, less fees and discounts up front. In return, the king authorized the individuals to collect the taxes and use the proceeds to repay themselves. The financiers would then have the right to use their own agents to collect the tax and to keep the difference between the amounts advanced and the amounts collected. Given the tenuous nature and uncertainty of these arrangements, the deals were often "sweetened" with special fees and allowances for collection costs and then subjected to deep discounting, so that very often the crown received less than 50 percent of the nominal purchase price. There was nothing to prevent these private collectors from squeezing as much as they could out of the taxpayers, and they could call on the royal authorities if necessary to help with their efforts.

In addition to enabling the crown to borrow against established sources of revenue, the financiers often proposed some new levy or fee, or an upward modification of an existing fee: for example, requiring a class of officeholders to pay some supplemental sum for the right to nominate a successor, thus making an office more marketable. If the crown accepted the proposal, the financiers would advance an agreed-on sum, sometimes to be paid in installments, based on estimates of the revenue the measure would raise, in return for the right to collect the new levy for a set period of years. Such arrangements, called *traités* ("contracts"), hence *traitants* ("contractors") were often wildly oversubscribed by the wealthy investors who formed the funding base for the more visible layer of financiers.

Who exactly were these contractors, these financiers who trafficked in the state's revenues? The term "financier" was used to mean anyone who "collected, spent, invested, or otherwise managed royal funds."[5] In effect it was an umbrella term that incorporated all those who acted as tax farmers, accountants, traitants, partisans, and so forth in the business of raising money for the crown. These roles were interchangeable and often overlapped with official ones, as many financiers also held offices in the financial apparatus of the state—treasurers or financial counselors, for example—which increased their hold on the state's financial mechanisms.[6] By Fouquet's time, the financiers had become a separate, powerful interest group in the monarchy, and they were often at loggerheads with the parlementary aristocracy that sometimes used judicial inquiries to attack their power base since, in theory, many of these techniques were illegal. Not surprisingly, given the public distaste for these transactions, those involved often hid their identity by using assumed names or "straw men," a valet or servant or client who would be the contractor or participant of record.[7]

These methods of raising funds offered an enormous reward for financial "entrepreneurs," one that came at the expense of those who paid the taxes; of those officeholders (including high court judges in *parlement*) whose wages were unpaid because all the available tax money had been pledged; and of those holding more traditional royal annuities (rentes), which went unpaid for the same reason. Nor were these methods especially effective. Very often, tax farms delivered less than what was promised to the crown, due to bad harvests, the damage to the countryside caused by the endless troop movements during the struggle with the Habsburgs or the Fronde, and the inevitable peasant uprisings.[8] When this type of shortfall occurred, the arrangement could be canceled, and royal officials had to scramble to find a substitute.[9]

Many of the irregularities in the financial system, including the creation of false or overstated expenditures to cover discounting above the legal interest rate of 5.5 percent, were concealed by the means of an order, called an *ordonnance de comptant*, signed by the superintendant of finance. This order authorized an expenditure for which no explanation was provided, and which was not subject to audit by the Chambre des comptes or other financial officials. The justification was that the expenditure was for purposes of state too secret to reveal: for example, subsidies to friendly foreign princes. What had been a relatively small percentage of such expenditures under Henri IV and the duc de Sully (for bribes or pensions in most instances) mushroomed under Richelieu and Mazarin to more than 40 percent of total governmental outlays by the 1640s.[10] Most of it was used to hide interest and financing costs above the legal limits.[11]

By the seventeenth century, tax farming and money lending secured on tax revenues or collected by syndicates, with the true terms and costs often disguised as indicated above, had become a routine and indispensable part of the financing of the state. But through these practices the crown had created a new element in society that had to be conciliated. The state was in fact hostage to these purveyors of capital, and public anger arising from the looting of the state's coffers was also directed at those, namely the regent and Mazarin, deemed responsible for allowing such "corruption" to continue.

This system functioned poorly in peacetime and almost not at all in periods of stress, particularly those caused by war and civil war, when the state's needs grew exponentially as it tried to raise and maintain armies. These strains increased dramatically with the coming of the Thirty Years War. Even before France formally entered the conflict in 1635, Richelieu's policy of subsidizing foreign princes and powers already engaged in the conflict against the Habsburgs had begun to undermine state finances. Beginning in the mid-1630s, the amount of both direct and indirect taxes rose sharply. Surviving figures must be used with great caution, but they suggest the magnitude of the change in resources required to pursue these policies. In 1624, the year Richelieu took office, the total revenues of the monarchy from all sources were about 34 million livres, and its expenditures about 33 million livres. By 1635, both revenues and expenditures totaled nearly 108 million, and in subsequent years through the 1650s that figure never dropped below 85 million. In many years, expenditures reached as high as 147 million livres.[12] The increases in direct and indirect taxes needed to support this effort could not be sustained, and the gap between the revenues required and what the taxation system would bear was bridged by borrowings and alienations of royal "rights" such as future tax revenues, or tolls. This was further supplemented by whatever expedients the royal officials charged with raising the money (chiefly the superintendant) could devise, often with the "help" of the financiers he was expected to cultivate. By the late 1630s, the "extraordinary revenues" from the sale of rentes, offices, and the like accounted for more than 50 percent of total revenues; by the early 1650s, it had reached over 60 percent.[13]

Such figures need to be used with reservations because of the peculiarities of the accounting systems used, which masked true cash flows in the modern accounting sense. Revenue estimates were usually provided gross and do not reflect deductions at the point of collection by local authorities to pay local crown expenses (wages of office holders, collection expenses, military garrison expenses) or the amounts deducted by tax farmers or assigned to financiers for interest payments. Expenditures recorded for a given year often included unpaid sums due in prior years to contractors or financiers and other state creditors and simply rolled over.[14]

Records of a meeting of the council of state to discuss royal finances in the spring of 1651 suggest the difficulties faced by royal ministers: the council was advised that of a total of 40 million livres in direct taxation anticipated for 1651–1652, only about 23 million would ever reach the royal treasury; the rest, more than 42 percent of the total, would be consumed by finance charges. At the same time, expenditures for garrisoning troops during the winter months, previously estimated at 7 to 8 million livres, would actually cost about 24 million (that is, more than the net available funds from direct taxation), and, of course, there would be no money for any other expense or expenditure.[15] For the year 1653, Richard Bonney has estimated that no more than about 17 percent of the nominal 110 million livres in royal revenues was actually available; the balance had been drained by deductions to pay for military garrisons. Yields from the existing tax farms were disappointing, and there were few offers on the table for new tax contracts: this last was a pressure tactic by the financiers to force the government to compensate them for their losses from the bankruptcy of 1648. The government had little choice but to accept whatever terms it was offered.[16] In effect, throughout these wartime decades, the officers of state, particularly those charged with managing the crown's finances, functioned in a crisis atmosphere, lurching from one emergency to the next, and improvising with one expedient after another.

The duties of the superintendant of finance included raising revenues and authorizing their disbursement, but not the actual handling of funds. Proceeds from tax revenues or loans were deposited with the central treasury (*Épargne*), and the royal treasurers were responsible for their disbursal when presented with a proper authorization from the superintendant.[17] Initially, Fouquet and Abel Servien had equal authority over both sides of the financial administration, but this proved unworkable in practice, and in December 1654 their functions were formally divided. Servien would be responsible for verifying and authorizing all expenditures and payments. Fouquet was given the more onerous task of raising money, an arrangement that helped minimize friction between the co-superintendants. At the same time, Barthélemy Hervart (or Hervarth), one of Mazarin's own bankers and business partners, became a controller with responsibility for assigning and recording the fund from which bills or loans would be paid.[18]

Given the co-superintendants' respective backgrounds, and Fouquet's connections to the financial community through his ties with the Jeannin de Castille family, the division of labor made some sense.[19] In accepting his new mandate, Fouquet made clear to Mazarin that to succeed in borrowing the 25–30 million livres required every year at the beginning of the campaign season, the state would have to keep faith with its creditors; repudiations and forced renegotiations as in 1648 were out of the question.[20]

Fouquet's insistence on this last point was not surprising. As superintendant, he would need to create and maintain a network of willing financiers prepared to advance funds for the crown's use, but with the backstop of a claim on the superintendant himself. In practice, transactions were frequently structured as advances to the superintendant personally, who would then pass the funds to the crown. If the crown repudiated its obligations, the superintendant would still be answerable to the lenders. The superintendant was liable to suit by his creditors; the crown was not.[21]

Fouquet very quickly built a financial circle (*clientèle*) out of which he was to fashion the various transactions used to fund the state. As noted above, these prominent and wealthy individuals usually had clients of their own who took part in these financings, sometimes secretly under the "cover" of their patron's names, or by use of a false name or some proxy or surrogate, normally a servant or clerk. Not surprisingly, many of the financiers were close to Mazarin and were also active as suppliers to the army (often in partnership with the cardinal), men such as Claude de Boislève, the Gruin brothers, and François Jacquier; others, such as Nicolas Jeannin de Castille or Hervart, held offices within the royal financial administration that allowed them to manipulate transactions and accounts at will.[22]

On a day-to-day basis, Fouquet relied on his "senior clerks" (in effect, senior administrators) to assemble the borrowing syndicates and work through the transaction details. All three of them—Charles Bernard, Jacques Delorme (1654–1657), and Louis Bruant (1657–1661)—were also participants in the system, with clients of their own.[23] As one leading scholar on the subject, Julian Dent, has put it, this system was "a closed shop in which everybody knew everybody else and cooperated in each other's financial deals."[24] Another commentator, Daniel Dessert, has identified a controlling group in the syndicates of the period, all close associates of Mazarin: the brothers Claude and Pierre Girardin, Robert Gruyn (or Gruin) du Bouchet, the brothers Nicholas and Pierre Monnerot, Claude de Boislève, and François Jacquier, all of whom had satellite pools of investors. The sums involved were enormous. Dessert has calculated that for the years 1653–1661 loans to the crown aggregated about 216 million livres, and tax-farm treaties about 208 million livres. So the financiers provided total funding of about 424 million livres, before deductions and discounts, to the state during Fouquet's time in office.[25]

Fouquet soon became a full participant in this fun-house world of distorting mirrors, where the private and public obligations seemed to blur. At one point in the 1650s, he mortgaged his wife's properties, valued at 2 million livres, to provide 1.2 million livres for the crown, and he raised additional funds by selling one of her estates.[26] By one modern calculation, Fouquet borrowed an aggregate of more than 30 million livres under his own name for on-lending to the crown during his tenure as superintendant; at the time of his arrest in 1661, he owed about 8 million livres on behalf of the crown and 4 four million for his private affairs. His creditors, more than 500 strong in 1661, included not only prominent financiers and his own relatives but many prominent magistrates and other officials of the legal and financial hierarchies of state.[27]

Fouquet's responsibilities also included supplying Mazarin directly on a monthly basis with large sums of money intended to pay for ongoing military expenses, as well as those of the royal household. Fouquet was to furnish the sums in question in gold or silver coin. Mazarin would see to the precise disbursements, with no accounting detail for Fouquet.[28] This arrangement allowed Mazarin to conceal considerable self-dealing. In May 1655, for example, the contract to collect the gabelle was awarded to a syndicate headed by Claude Girardin. Girardin also had personal dealings with Mazarin, and had acted as a tax farmer for Mazarin's private revenues from his ecclesiastical appointments and offices. In 1654, Girardin had headed a syndicate that successfully bid for the tax farm on the aides, after it provided Mazarin with a bribe of 50,000 *écus* (150,000 livres). For this new transaction on the gabelle, the syndicate was now required to agree to a "pension," a share of the proceeds of the tax farm, of 120,000 livres per annum, for the life of the contract, payable to an unnamed person. It was clearly understood by all, including Fouquet, that the cardinal was the beneficiary.[29]

At the same time that Mazarin was seeing that his own coffers received their share of state borrowings, he inundated Fouquet with unceasing and frantic demands for funds to support the troops in the field and to pay for necessary military supplies (some of which the cardinal furnished as a contractor) or for other urgent and time-sensitive needs of state.[30] On some occasions, funds had to be raised on the spot, and Fouquet was forced to borrow on his own account for on-lending to the crown. In November 1655, for example, maréchal d'Hocquincourt, the royal governor of Ham and Péronne, threatened to surrender those important fortress towns to nearby Spanish troops, or to Condé. To dissuade him, Fouquet had to find 200,000 écus (600,000 livres), almost overnight and on his own signature, and turn it over to the maréchal's emissaries—along with a royal pardon for the attempted treason.[31]

The following summer, in July 1656, Fouquet once more proved his fund-raising capacities. In the field, Turenne and the maréchal de La Ferté had laid siege to the Spanish-held city of Valenciennes. In a daring maneuver, Condé, leading Spanish relief forces, attacked La Ferté's troops, who were camped on the left bank of the Scheldt, routing this wing of the French army and taking La Ferté prisoner. Turenne, based on the opposite bank, could do little to help and instead withdrew with the rest of the French forces toward Quesnoy. A desperate Mazarin, headquartered at La Fère, appealed frantically to Fouquet for funds to pacify the remaining troops, whose wages were months in arrears, and continue the struggle. Once again, Fouquet rose to the occasion, amassing 900,000 livres from his circle of financiers and arranging for a well-escorted convoy of wagons to bring the treasure to the cardinal. The cardinal could scarcely contain his joy and relief, writing Fouquet that he had brought this great service to the attention of the king and the queen mother, who sent their gratitude and promises to remember his help in their hour of need.[32]

Despite this glowing tribute, Mazarin complained frequently to Fouquet that he was not receiving reimbursements for sums he had advanced to the crown or for supplies he had furnished—in this case, troop rations. Mazarin often complained that the superintendant put other creditors of the crown ahead of him while he "didn't know what it was like to have a penny's worth of interest."[33] These caustic comments were usually conveyed through Jean-Baptiste Colbert, the trusted servant who handled many of the cardinal's private affairs.[34] This last exchange, in June 1657, provoked an angry response from Fouquet, who denied that other creditors were receiving any preference and noted that he himself was out another 300,000 livres beyond what had been owed him at the beginning of the year. He reminded the cardinal that the treasury was empty and that the only payments he was making were in paper (i.e., the exchange of old notes for new ones), and alluding to the episode of Valenciennes, he added, "One does not send paper in wagons."[35]

In spite of this friction, Fouquet continued to furnish astonishing sums to the crown. In the late fall of 1657, working with Jeannin de Castille and Hervart, Fouquet managed to raise 10.2 million livres (after a 1.6 million livres discount from the face value of 11.8 million livres) to keep the royal armies in the field and to begin a campaign that ended with the decisive Battle of the Dunes in June 1658. Much of this money had to be personally guaranteed by Fouquet.[36]

Sometimes the actual benefit to the crown was difficult to see. During that same year, 1657, Fouquet and Servien worked on a suggestion of Mazarin's that additional revenues might be raised by expanding the marc d'or, a required fee payable by some office holders at the moment they assumed their functions. This fee, following a royal order issued in December 1656, was now payable by the purchasers of many more kinds of office. It was further decreed that the proceeds derived from this enlarged base would not belong to the royal Order of the Holy Spirit (the traditional recipient) but would benefit the crown. The income from the expanded levy was estimated to be 140,000 livres per annum and given a capital value of 2 million livres.

Monetizing this transaction proved to be a challenge: it was difficult to find a buyer for a new and untried measure. Finally a buyer was found whose identity was concealed by the use of one of Servien's clerks, Duché, as the front man, or acquirer of record. In its final form, the transaction provided the purchaser a discount for collection costs of one third of the notional price, or 666,000 livres. So the actual purchase price was reduced to 1,334,000 livres. But a certain M. Boulin, who held the rights to the existing revenues from the older form of this tax, had to be compensated with 300,000 livres. The balance due to the crown was therefore 1,034,000 livres, payable per terms of the contract in eight installments over two years. After applying an additional 10 percent discount from the remaining proceeds (134, 000 livres), the crown was left with 900,000 livres in notional proceeds.

This last sum was approximately what Fouquet had advanced at Valenciennes, and he was now permitted to retain the balance for himself as a reimbursement. Since the new transaction had not really been monetarized, Fouquet received treasury bills for the amount in question, which would be eventually paid down with proceeds from the installment payments. Fouquet then sold one-third of these bills to Jérôme de Nouveau, the royal postmaster (and, like Servien, an officer of the Order of the Holy Spirit), who paid by exchanging existing (and probably worthless) treasury notes for these new ones; the superintendant also sold another small portion to a friend, Madame du Plessis-Bellière, for 100,000 livres. Fouquet used the remaining notes in his possession to repay the creditors from whom he had borrowed to support the operation at Valenciennes. The only tangible benefit to the crown in all this was the refinancing of some indirect debt, the sums Fouquet had borrowed for Valenciennes. In terms of new money, not a sou seems to have found its way to the treasury. Nevertheless, Fouquet, Servien, and Pierre Séguier, sitting as the council of finance, approved the transaction in January 1657.[37]

In the summer of 1658, Fouquet took part in another operation that again illustrates how complicated such financing schemes could be. In form, the transaction was to be an annuity of 400,000 livres secured on future tailles. In practice, however, the crown would withhold two quarterly installments per annum so that the annual yield to the purchasing parties would only be 200,000 livres. This 200,000 livres payout would be further reduced by 50,000 livres payable to the treasury agents and others through whose hands the funds would flow. So the net yield to the holders of the annuity after deductions would be 150,000 livres. The bid for this annuity was 800,000 livres, meaning that the crown was paying a true interest or annuity rate of 18.75 percent on the transaction (150,000/800,000 = 18.75%). But, legally, the crown was not supposed to pay more than 5.5 percent for such transactions ("*le denier dix-huit*"). Since the nominal or face amount of the annuity was 400,000 livres, the crown should have received 7.2 million livres as the purchase price of the annuity (400,000/5.5% = 7,272,727). The investors, however, were only prepared to pay 800,000 livres. To cover the illegality involved in so low a purchase price, the superintendant provided the purchasers fictitious receipts for the sum of 6 million livres, which were later forwarded to the Chambre des comptes, whose duties included examining and verifying the crown's financial operations. In theory, the holders still owed the treasury a balance of 1.2 million livres. This sum was further reduced by an allowance of one-third, or 400,000 livres, for "collection expenses," a typical discounting in this type of transaction. So the net due was 800,000 livres, the amount the investors had actually bid. Although the transaction was illegal in principle and required fraudulent accounting entries to record it, the transaction was authorized by Fouquet and Servien, the co-superintendants, by Hervart, and by chancellor Séguier, the crown's chief legal and administrative officer.[38]

The death of Servien in mid-February 1659 brought with it the possibility of still more power for Fouquet. For several days, there was speculation on whether Fouquet's colleague would be replaced. There was no shortage of candidates, and Mazarin toyed with the idea of assuming the office himself. On reflection, the cardinal realized the utility of having a buffer between himself and the many irregular transactions used to fund the operations of state. A review of the financial situation with Fouquet, Colbert, and Hervart made it evident that such practices were likely to continue indefinitely: virtually all of the state's revenues, of whatever nature, had already been pledged in advance for the next two years. Any superintendant would be incurring heavy personal liabilities in the course of exploiting the usual mechanisms to keep the state afloat. So Mazarin announced that Fouquet would be the sole superintendant in the future, a decision ratified by a royal decree praising Fouquet for his "prudence" and "zeal" and many valuable services in the past.[39] As evidence of his zeal, Fouquet might have cited the more than 5 million livres the crown owed to him, which he had borrowed in his own name from various financiers.[40]

Fouquet's official duties did not preclude his private business activities, particularly since his private interests and public responsibilities sometimes complemented one another quite well in an era when the notion of "conflict of interest" was rarely acknowledged by the powerful. Fouquet had inherited his father's holdings in the various trading ventures set up in Richelieu's time to develop trade with the Americas, Africa, and Asia. Many of these activities were based in Breton ports, and they continued long after Richelieu's death. Fouquet also invested in newer commercial enterprises based in Brittany. In addition, beginning in the 1640s and accelerating through the 1650s, he began to purchase large estates in Brittany, where he had a natural constituency, given the prominence of the Chalain branch of the family there, who were often partners in his businesses. These commercial ventures often overlapped with privateering. From the late 1640s on, the Fouquets operated a fleet of well-armed privateers, nominally commissioned by the Portuguese crown, which preyed on English, Dutch, and Spanish shipping off the western coast of France. These ships, privately owned and armed by the Fouquets, sailed out of several local ports, including Concarneau, the governor of which was one of the Fouquets de Chalain, and the isle of Yeu, which belonged to the noble Breton family of Rieux d'Assérac, also close associates of the superintendant. Fouquet was hardly alone in these activities: Mazarin, Hugues de Lionne, and Abel Servien were also engaged in privateering.[41]

In 1658, an opportunity arose for Fouquet to acquire the island of Belle-Isle, which guards the approaches to the Bay of Quiberon on the south coast of Brittany and which was ideally located for such ventures. Its purchase was a fortuitous overlapping of Fouquet's private interests with those of state. Belle-Isle had been owned by the Gondi family since the sixteenth century. The family, headed by the duc de Retz, had fallen on financial hard times, as well as political disgrace because of the activities of Jean François Paul de Gondi, Cardinal de Retz, during the Fronde. Seeking to raise cash, the Retz family put the island up for sale. Given its strategic position, Mazarin wanted to see the island in "safe" hands, and encouraged Fouquet in the summer of 1658 to buy the property. There may have been an understanding that at some future date the property would pass into the hands of one of Mazarin's heirs. A royal decree issued in August 1658 approved its acquisition and gave Fouquet the authority to name a governor for the island and to fortify and garrison the place.[42]

These last provisions were hardly unusual. Fortified harbors and garrisons were part and parcel of the privateering business, and Fouquet earlier had engaged in similar activities at Concarneau and the isle of Yeu. But the opportunity to acquire Belle-Isle was especially welcome because Fouquet's partners, the Assérac family, were seeking to dispose of Yeu. Belle-Isle offered an even more attractive base for operations, and Fouquet happily provided the purchase price, 1.3 million livres, raised partly by the sale of other holdings.[43]

In authorizing and even promoting this transaction, Mazarin may have had personal motives as well. Fouquet's privateering ventures based on the island of Yeu, directed at Dutch shipping, had the side effect of diminishing port taxes and revenues in other parts of Brittany in which Mazarin held financial interests.

Mazarin seems to have spoken to Fouquet about this, and Fouquet extricated himself by acquiescing in the sale of Yeu and the transfer of his activities to Belle-Isle.[44]

Fouquet enjoyed a very large income from his two high offices of state, perhaps as much as 200,000 livres per annum; these were supplemented by revenues from his landed properties, his maritime activities, and his participation in loans and advances to the crown. One modern scholar has concluded that his aggregate income in the 1650s probably approached 500,000 livres per annum. This was a greater income than that enjoyed by most dukes in that period and was comparable to the revenues of the Condé family, the king's cousins and senior princes of the blood.[45] Like other great aristocrats and high officers of state, Fouquet lived on a scale that befitted his status. Wherever he was in residence, Fouquet was expected to keep an open table and to entertain frequently and lavishly. François Vatel, the maître d'hôtel who later served the prince de Condé, had charge of Fouquet's household and presided over the various receptions and fêtes that Fouquet hosted.[46]

At his trial, Fouquet was to argue that an opulent style was essential to maintaining the trust of royal creditors, who looked to the superintendant, rather than the crown, for the repayment of their advances.[47] There was certainly precedent for such behavior on the part of other high officials, of whom both Mazarin and Richelieu offered obvious examples. Mazarin's collections of paintings, tapestries, jewelry, and objets d'art were widely admired and envied. Richelieu had built a Paris residence that was grand enough to pass into the crown's hands and became the Palais-Royal, and his château at Richelieu was lavish enough to astound the king's cousin, the fabulously wealthy duchess de Montpensier, who had been raised at the Tuileries.[48]

Like Richelieu, Fouquet was also a patron of the literary community. By the late 1650s, he had become a familiar figure in the salon society of Paris, where gifted and aristocratic amateurs mingled freely with "professional" writers who relied on the commissions and pensions from élite sponsors to make their way in the world. Madame Fouquet, who shared many of her husband's tastes, hosted her own salon, and there as elsewhere in the capital Fouquet could mingle with aristocratic amateurs such as the duc de La Rochefoucauld, Madame de La Fayette, Madame de Sévigné, and Madeleine de Scudéry, as well as professional literary craftsmen such as Jean de La Fontaine, Thomas and Pierre Corneille, Molière, Charles Perrault, Isaac de Benserade, and Valentin Conrart, the founder and longtime secretary of the Académie française, which Richelieu had taken under his wing.[49]

Conrart was a Huguenot and may have introduced one of his protégés to Fouquet, a young Huguenot from a prominent legal family of Castres, Paul Pellisson. A humanist by inclination, Pellisson had a firm grounding in the classics and had studied law at the University of Toulouse. In 1656 he joined Fouquet's official household, becoming his senior clerk (*premier commis*) in 1657.[50] Pellisson also acted as the superintendant's liaison with the world of letters, assembling around Fouquet what Marc Fumaroli has called "a great encyclopedic academy . . . worthy of those of the Italian Renaissance or the Valois."[51] These aristocratic literary friends and nonaristocratic clients repaid Fouquet in the coin of their realm. La Fontaine, who was to remain one of Fouquet's more devoted followers, dedicated a long lyrical poem, *Adonis*, to the superintendant in 1658,[52] while Pierre Corneille paid homage to Fouquet in the preface to his *L'Oedipe* (*Oedipus*), which opened in Paris in February 1658.[53] The wildly fashionable Madeleine de Scudéry, whose salon was one of Fouquet's haunts, provided posterity with a vivid description of Fouquet's magnificent country house at Vaux (see below), as well as a "portrait" of the superintendant under the name "Cléonime" in her astonishingly long romance, *Clélie*.[54] With Madame de Sévigné, Fouquet struck up a deep friendship, perhaps hoping for more: an early surviving letter from the marquise suggests the ambiguous nature of this tie.[55]

The superintendant and Madame Fouquet received their many guests and clients in the superb residences that he had acquired and embellished over the years. In Paris, Fouquet changed his abode several times, finally coming to reside in the former mansion of his predecessor, Michel Particelli d'Émery, on the rue Croix-des-Petits-Champs, a stone's throw from the Palais-Royal; its gardens extended over part of the present Place des Victoires. As superintendant, he also disposed of an official apartment at the Louvre.[56]

Fouquet spent a great deal of time at his manor house at Saint-Mandé on the outskirts of Paris, where his gardens abutted on those surrounding the royal residence of Vincennes. Mazarin had a preference for Vincennes, and the court was there frequently in the 1650s, even while the two pavilions designed by Le Vau, the Pavillon de la Reine and the Pavillon du Roi, were under construction. Fouquet had bought the Saint-Mandé property in 1654 and over the next few years improved the gardens with rare plants and an orangery. He also expanded the buildings, partly to house his library, reputedly more than 30,000 volumes, the core of which he had inherited from his father. The library was available to the scholars and men of letters of the time, and Fouquet engaged a full-time librarian to look after his collection, part of which eventually was added to the Royal Library.[57] If the men of letters appreciated the books and manuscripts, the court had a chance to admire the gardens and artistic treasures on display there—tapestries, paintings, statues—when the royal family and Mazarin honored Fouquet with a brief visit in November 1657.[58] Fouquet's collections, which are now scattered in various French museums, included paintings by Nicolas Poussin, Lambert Sustris, Anthonis Mor, and Paolo Veronese, and many other works selected by his brother Louis, the future bishop of Agde, during a visit to Italy in 1655.[59]

Not all of these works were at Saint-Mandé. Some would have been on display at Fouquet's Paris hôtel and some at his most magnificent property, the château of Vaux-le-Vicomte. It was there that Fouquet was to marshal all of the literary and artistic talent at his command to host the famous fête given in honor of Louis XIV in the summer of 1661.

The territory of Vaux lay just to the east of Melun, about 20 kilometers from the great royal château of Fontainebleau, which was still the favorite country residence of the kings of France. Fouquet purchased Vaux in 1641 and added to it part of the adjacent viscounty of Melun. When acquired, Vaux consisted of little more than a rundown château and several neglected country villages as dependencies. For several years Fouquet poured money into restoring the old buildings and grounds, but in 1656 he decided to raze the existing buildings and modify the landscape to create a magnificent estate that would immortalize his reputation and fix his status as a landed grand seigneur of the first rank. Here again, one is reminded of Richelieu's efforts at the château bearing his name. But the cardinal's château lay in remote Anjou, unseen by most and rarely visited, even by its owners. Vaux, by contrast, would be in the line of sight of the royal court whenever it moved between Paris and Fontainebleau.

In the years after 1656 Fouquet lavished not just money but also the talents of some of the greatest artists and craftsmen of the age on the project. Louis Le Vau was commissioned to design the building, while André Le Nôtre, whose father had laid out the gardens at Richelieu, was commissioned to plan those at Vaux. Expanding the gardens entailed extensive diggings and reconfigurations of the original landscape, as well as the demolition of the outlying villages, a project that was to involve thousands of workmen. In addition to the artisans and laborers employed on the exterior, hundreds of craftsmen of all kinds fashioned the splendid interior under the direction of Charles Le Brun, who had studied in Italy on a grant provided by chancellor Séguier, and who incorporated into the interior styles and techniques learned in Italy but not common in France.[60]

The splendor of the château was mirrored by the astonishing gardens laid out by Le Nôtre. A series of walkways, parterres with formal flowerbeds, strategically placed statues and grottoes and above all, a display of waterworks, fountains, a grand canal, and a pool, all supplied with water from an elaborate series of underground lead pipes feeding from nearby streams, enveloped the château. The cost of all this grandeur has never been determined, although it was to be a point of contention at Fouquet's trial. The total acquisition costs of the combined properties centered on Vaux has been calculated at about 506,000 livres and the contracted construction prices for the château and outbuildings at around 857,000 livres.[61] These figures do not account for the landscaping, the costs of fixtures, or the value of the works of art, furnishings, or other appointments within the château. Contemporary estimates put the total cost at 23 million livres; Jules Lair believed it was between 3 and 4 million livres, and Jean-Christian Petitfils placed it at 4 million.[62]

Whatever the cost, Fouquet got what he paid for. The overall effect, as Anthony Blunt put it, was "triumphantly successful," adding that the "combination of château and gardens has hardly its peer in France."[63] Thanks to a twentieth-century restoration, a modern visitor can easily imagine the astonishment this dazzling ensemble created when it was built, one that was to be imitated several decades later at Versailles by the same team originally assembled by Fouquet. Fouquet's friend Mademoiselle de Scudéry called it a work "completed by a man who only does great things."[64]

Fouquet's great project was hardly a secret. In the summer of 1659 Mazarin stopped there overnight. The cardinal admired the progress of Le Brun's work within the château, examined Le Nôtre's recently completed plans for the gardens, and studied Fouquet's assemblage of works of art with the eye of a great connoisseur. His glowing account prompted a royal but informal visit some weeks later in July 1659 by the young king, his brother Philippe, and the queen mother.[65] Almost exactly a year later, Louis returned with his Spanish bride, Queen Maria Theresa, stopping with the court for a visit and dinner at Vaux while traveling from Fontainebleau to Paris. The king's cousin, the duchess de Montpensier, herself the veteran of several building projects, called Vaux an enchanted place.[66]

In July 1661, the king's brother, Philippe d'Orléans, and his wife, Henrietta of England, visited Vaux at the head of a troop of courtiers. They were received in great splendor, served a grand collation, and treated to a first performance of a new play by one of Fouquet's protégés, Molière, called *L'École des maris* (*The School for Husbands*).[67] This visit was to be a dress rehearsal for the famous fête that the superintendant gave in the king's honor to celebrate the completion of the project in August 1661, and which, according to popular lore, led to Fouquet's downfall. In fact, long before the young king accepted the hospitality of his superintendant, Fouquet's fate had been decided.

CHAPTER 3

Fall of a Titan

Among those Fouquet encountered frequently in the course of his duties was the cardinal's factotum, Jean-Baptiste Colbert. Colbert, four years Fouquet's junior, was a native of Reims, where his family had been prominent wholesale merchants and international businessmen and bankers for several generations. His father, Nicolas Colbert, had relocated to Paris in 1629, where he became a *partisan* (a participant in loan syndications to the crown). He also bought an office (*receveur général . . . des anciennes rentes . . . sur les aides*) with responsibility for collecting excise taxes (*aides*) on certain goods entering Paris, and disbursing the funds to pay annuities secured on those revenues. Other family members also held offices in the financial administration, and some were active in the syndicates that farmed the salt tax (*gabelle*). The Colberts could even boast a family tie to Fouquet's detested predecessor, Particelli d'Émery.[1]

Jean-Baptiste Colbert's introduction to the convoluted world of state finance may well have come from the activities of his father and his father's associates. As a young man Jean-Baptiste was apprenticed to bankers and merchants in Reims, Lyons, and Paris, and then spent some time reading law under several Paris lawyers. Colbert's talents, however, lay with finance and administration, and he does not seem to have acquired any deep understanding of the law. Nor in later life did he demonstrate any respect for the sense of process and adherence to form so dear to the legal mentality.

In 1640, his father bought him a post in the government as a *commissaire ordinaire de guerre*, serving under the secretary of state for war as a kind of inspector charged, among other duties, with verifying garrison strengths, and certifying the availability of munitions and materials. Some of Colbert's family connections were already senior officials in this department, and in 1643 one of them, Michel Le Tellier (whose sister had married into the Colbert family), became the secretary of state for war. Although in later decades the Colbert and Le Tellier families were to be intense, even bitter, rivals, in the 1640s the Colbert clan was allied with the Le Telliers, and young Jean-Baptiste began his rise as a protégé of Michel Le Tellier.[2]

Throughout the 1640s Colbert served under Le Tellier, and, like Le Tellier, was fiercely loyal to the crown during the Fronde. Colbert soon acquired a reputation for hard work, one he would enjoy all his life, and for attention to detail. He also was able to convince the patron of the moment that he was entirely devoted to that person's interests: this was a reputation he enjoyed in succession with Le Tellier, Mazarin, and Louis XIV. In those same years, Fouquet too was acquiring a reputation as a zealous servant of the crown, and the two men seem to have met for the first time in August 1650. Colbert's initial impressions were quite favorable, and he apparently persuaded Le Tellier not to oppose Fouquet's appointment as *procureur général* in the fall of 1650.[3]

Colbert's activities frequently brought him into the presence of Mazarin and the regent. In the early winter of 1651, Mazarin went into exile in the territories of the bishop-elector of Cologne. Desperate to find a trustworthy agent to safeguard his personal possessions and wealth left behind in France, he turned to Le Tellier's aide. While still technically a member of Le Tellier's staff, Colbert became de facto the general agent and confidential secretary of the exiled cardinal. Once again, Colbert was able to ingratiate himself with a patron, soon convincing Mazarin that "Colbert is my man and would drown those he loves for my sake, not excepting Le Tellier."[4] In an early letter to Mazarin, Colbert took the liberty of remonstrating with him for diminishing his fortune by giving away some of his ecclesiastical revenues, offering large pensions to others, and taking out loans "on the king's behalf, which have brought you to your present awkward state."[5] In effect, Colbert was scolding Mazarin for putting the king's interests above his own, an unintentional irony given Mazarin's determination to see that his own interests were not neglected, even at the peril of the state. Working with Nicolas and Basile Fouquet, Colbert did his utmost during Mazarin's exile to save what could be saved from the seizures authorized by the Parlement of Paris.[6]

After Mazarin returned to France permanently in early 1653, Colbert continued to function as his business manager. In theory, his responsibilities extended only to the cardinal's personal finances, but as Inès Murat, a Colbert descendant, admits, the separation was only theoretical "given the incredible confusion between the state's revenues and the cardinal's," a confusion that worked much to

Mazarin's benefit.[7] The cardinal, as noted in chapter 2, rebuilt his fortune by investing in state financings and by serving as a major supplier of commodities to the French armies in the field. He also accepted bribes to appoint someone to an office or to approve the terms of financial transactions (including those he participated in). In addition, Mazarin helped himself to large amounts of cash flowing through the state's coffers, even when the royal armies were on the verge of disintegration in the field because of a lack of supplies or payment for the troops.[8] The amounts involved were staggering. A modern scholar, Julian Dent, has calculated that on average Mazarin took 23 million livres per year from the treasury, much of which went for his personal use. Several of those involved in the royal financial administration, Barthélemy Hervart, Louis Berryer, and probably Jean de Gourville and Paul Pellisson as well, asserts Dent, were Mazarin's agents in these matters.[9]

There can be little doubt that Fouquet and his co-superintendant Servien were aware of these diversions of funds, and that Colbert was complicit in Mazarin's activities. The unpublished correspondence from the Luynes family archives used by Inès Murat in her study of Colbert makes the degree of Colbert's culpability in all of these questionable activities only too evident.[10] The results were extraordinary. In June 1658, according to Colbert's figures, Mazarin's fortune was slightly in excess of 8 million livres. By the time of the cardinal's death in 1661, the value had risen to between 38 and 39 million livres, by some estimates, inclusive of liquid assets of 8 to 9 million livres—well in excess of the sums available in the royal coffers.[11]

Colbert also made sure that his own services were well compensated. In 1647, for example, he was granted estates that had been confiscated from a traitorous relative, and somewhat later he was appointed, without cost to himself, secretary of the queen's household; in 1660 he was able to sell that post for 500,000 livres.[12] At his trial, Fouquet was to demonstrate that Colbert took part in some of the cardinal's shady transactions, and there may have been more than we know from the record. There were also appointments and offices to be provided for relatives through the cardinal's benevolence. By 1657, Colbert was already rich enough to acquire an important landed estate at Seignelay; his son and namesake was to be known as the marquis de Seignelay.[13]

Despite his initially positive interaction with Fouquet in 1650, Colbert evidently concluded that Fouquet was an obstacle to his own ambitions and those of his patrons. When the post of superintendant of finance became vacant at the duc de La Vieuville's death in 1653, Colbert allied himself with Le Tellier, who may have wanted the post for his own, to oppose Fouquet's nomination.[14] Colbert gave a veiled warning to the cardinal about those who "give a great deal cheaply to the subordinates in order to betray the leader more easily."[15]

But Colbert's initiative was premature. In succeeding years, if the cardinal depended on Colbert to manage his affairs, he also needed Fouquet's help, if not complicity, if they were to flourish. So Colbert had to be discreet in his criticisms of the superintendant. Mazarin was preoccupied with his personal affairs, and many of his peevish complaints to Fouquet revolved around the nonpayment or delayed payment of sums due to him. Such payments took precedence in Mazarin's eyes over virtually everything. And as Colbert was the watchdog over these matters, it can be assumed that he was happy to call any delays and delinquencies to his master's attention. Thus, for example, as early as June 1654, Colbert was suggesting that Fouquet was neglecting the cardinal's interests.[16] Similar insinuations in later years may have prompted the testy exchange of letters between Mazarin and Fouquet in the summer of 1657 (see chapter 2).[17]

By mid-1657, Fouquet seems to have been aware that in Colbert he had a critic, if not yet a rival, whom he tried to win over, but apparently to no avail.[18] It may well have been that Colbert, as he was later to insist, was motivated by a desire to bring some order to state finances and to have the superintendant mend his ways.[19] But Colbert's ambition and politics within the cardinal's entourage are just as likely explanations for his actions, perhaps exacerbated by Fouquet's interference in a lawsuit between Hugues de Lionne and the Colberts on a family matter, an incident that provoked Colbert to protest to the cardinal, who intervened to have the matter settled "amicably" and privately.[20]

Colbert, however, had by now embarked on a secret but prolonged campaign against Fouquet, making use of his old ties to Le Tellier and knitting new ones with Hervart, who had access to the financial transactions undertaken by Fouquet. He also began to keep a close eye on Fouquet's other activities, including his Breton-based ventures. When Fouquet drew up proposals for a revival of commerce and industry in 1657, Colbert prepared a rival plan, which he promptly submitted to Mazarin.[21]

By the summer of 1659, Colbert felt his standing with Mazarin was strong enough to move openly against Fouquet. But Mazarin, as always, was hard to read. In July, en route to meeting with his Spanish counterpart, Don Luis de Haro, to negotiate a peace with Spain and the marriage of the Spanish infanta Maria Theresa with the king, the cardinal stopped at Vaux-le-Vicomte overnight to see the progress of Fouquet's renovations there and to discuss the state's abysmal finances with the superintendant once more. He left with promises from Fouquet to find more money.[22] Before setting out, however, the cardinal had asked Colbert to review the royal finances, which in effect meant a review of Fouquet's stewardship.[23]

As the cardinal made his way slowly southward, he obtained the rewards for this initiative: he was bombarded by letters from Colbert denouncing Fouquet's administration and that of the financiers who worked with the superintendant. Colbert summarized his views in a long memorandum, dated October 1, 1659, accusing Fouquet of misappropriation of funds and self-dealing, of trafficking in deeply discounted old state obligations (long since dishonored) and exchanging them for new ones, and of using state funds to build "establishments" for friends, family, loyal servitors, and business partners. The remedy, in Colbert's eyes, was Fouquet's dismissal and the establishment of a *chambre de justice*—a special tribunal—to judge and punish those guilty of pillaging the state coffers, including Fouquet.[24]

Fouquet, however, had his own well-placed spies and confidants. Informed by his sources of Colbert's attempts to undermine him, the superintendant left Vaux abruptly at the very end of September to find the cardinal and make his case to him. Thanks to those same informants, Colbert's memorandum of October 1 was secretly intercepted and handed to Fouquet when he reached Bordeaux. If Jean de Gourville, one of Fouquet's close collaborators, is to be believed, he and Fouquet quickly copied it and returned the original to the courier, who then carried it to Mazarin.[25]

Joining the cardinal at Saint-Jean-de-Luz some days later, Fouquet took the offensive. He complained to the cardinal about false accusations leveled against him, blaming them on Hervart and another rival, Denis Talon, the royal *avocat général*, with whom he shared the "king's bench" in *parlement*. He expressed his surprise to Mazarin that Colbert had joined in such denunciations, since he had always tried to work with Colbert, who was a talented man and entirely devoted to the cardinal's service. Mazarin, who had read Colbert's memorandum, was not prepared to dispense with either Fouquet or Colbert. Instead, he was conciliatory, insisting that Colbert was not hostile to Fouquet, and that this impression of Fouquet's was somehow a misunderstanding. He told Fouquet he needed both of them, and he asked Fouquet to work with Colbert in the future. As Claude Dulong has pointed out, the cardinal could hardly investigate Fouquet's "corruption" without uncovering his own.[26]

The conversation then passed to the sad state of the royal revenues, and for possible remedies (i.e., new ways of raising money). As part of his attempt at conciliation, and as a token of his esteem, the cardinal presented Fouquet to Don Luis de Haro, the cardinal's Spanish counterpart and chief interlocutor in the peace negotiations. When Fouquet returned to Saint-Mandé in December 1659, Colbert, on Mazarin's orders, waited on Fouquet. Many insincere compliments were exchanged, so each could tell the cardinal that, as instructed, they had reconciled.[27]

Fouquet was not blind to the need to improve the terms on which the crown borrowed, nor was he oblivious to the change in mentality that the peace with Spain would bring about: abuses tolerated in times of desperation would not be acceptable in times of peace. On his return to Paris in late fall 1659, he undertook several measures intended to augment royal revenues. Several newly available tax farms were amalgamated to increase the revenue yield and the annual installments payable by the farmers of the *gabelle de France* were increased by 1660 to 14.5 million livres from the prior contract level of 8.6 million; the annual yield from the aides farm increased to 4.5 million livres from 3.2 million, and from the *cinq grosses fermes* from 2.2 million livres to 4.4 million, exactly the kind of reforms for which Colbert was later to claim credit. Fouquet was able to cut the "secret expenditures," a major source of corruption, back to 30.6 million livres in 1660 and 20.3 million in 1661.[28] Nevertheless, royal borrowings remained high, at the level of 40 million livres in 1660, due in part to the large hangover of existing debt, which still required servicing or refinancing. Fouquet, however, did manage to borrow at slightly lower rates. He also opposed the idea of a chambre de justice to force retroactive renegotiating of interest rates through the disgorging of excess profits. Instead, he favored an understanding with the financiers to lend at the legal rate of 5.55 percent (a rare event) on revenues not available until the period 1662–1665, a proposal actually under discussion at the time of his arrest.[29]

Given his roller-coaster relationship with Mazarin, it is not surprising that Fouquet wondered from time to time if the cardinal might at some point dismiss or even arrest him. After one of their caustic exchanges, Fouquet sat down in his study at Saint-Mandé in late June or early July 1657 and drafted a plan to resist in such an eventuality.

Assuming Mazarin's domination of both the queen mother and the young king, Fouquet envisioned a threat of armed rebellion and pressure from sympathizers as the means to secure his release. He postulated three likely scenarios for a future detention. The first assumed that he would be arrested alone; in that case, his brother Basile would coordinate the efforts to free him; in the second, he and Basile would both be arrested but would find some way of communicating with the outside world. In both of those circumstances, they would be able to convey instructions to their supporters. Finally, Fouquet imagined a third scenario in which he and Basile were held incommunicado. In those circumstances,

Madame du Plessis-Bellière, a Breton aristocrat, business partner, confidante, and possible mistress, was to take command.

But what were to be the next steps? Fouquet expected that his friends and clients who commanded strategic military outposts would close their gates to royal troops. Since Fouquet's eldest daughter was married to the son of the comte de Charost, who was the governor of Calais, Fouquet saw Calais as a place of refuge for his wife and other family members; Amiens, Arras, and Hesdin were also in friendly hands. All of these, as Jean-Christian Petitfils points out, were in the strategic northeast of France, close to the Spanish Lowlands. Implicit in this strategy was the possibility of opening these towns to Spanish invaders if Fouquet were not freed. On the western coast, Concarneau and Tombelaine (near Mont-Saint-Michel) were also assumed to be in the hands of Fouquet's supporters.[30]

Influential friends such as the duc de La Rochefoucauld and Gourville were to intercede on Fouquet's behalf, and Fouquet's Maupeou relatives and Achille de Harlay would be asked to sway the Parlement of Paris to protest the arrest of the procureur général. Overall strategy would remain in the hands of Madame du Plessis-Bellière "in whom I place all my faith," and with whom "I have never had any secrets or reservations [*réserve*]."[31]

Beyond this rather sketchy outline, Fouquet gave no instructions for any specific actions. The plan lay in this unfinished state for many months, as Fouquet's relationship with the cardinal waxed and waned. In late December 1658 or in early 1659, Fouquet took up his pen once more. By now, he and his brother Basile had broken with one another for reasons that are still not clear, and Fouquet had also acquired Belle-Isle. So his revisions to the plan reflected these important changes of circumstances. With Basile estranged, the fortress of Ham (controlled by Basile) was out of the equation, as were Hesdin and Tombelaine, which had changed governors. This time Fouquet preferred to rely on strategic harbors at Calais, Le Havre, Concarneau, and Belle-Isle, not surprisingly, given his private maritime fleet. His brothers Louis and François, now respectively bishop of Agde and archbishop of Narbonne, were entrusted the task of organizing protests in parlement and among the clergy. Guillaume de Lamoignon, first president of the Parlement of Paris, "who owes his office to me," was counted as an ally, as were several other *parlementaires*. Pellisson would draft manifestoes and proclamations. Other possibilities included the abduction of Le Tellier or some other major figure, or trying to stir up the Huguenots. In all of this, Madame du Plessis-Bellière was to play a coordinating and directing role.[32]

Years later, Gourville claimed that Fouquet had shown him the draft of the project, apparently in 1660, and that he had so ridiculed the idea that Fouquet decided to destroy the draft, even sending for a candle to set it afire. But at that moment, an unexpected visitor caused Fouquet to put the draft behind a mirror in his study. Distracted by other matters, the superintendant let it slip out of mind, and the draft was later discovered where Fouquet had placed it.[33]

Gourville's story often finds its way into popular histories, but it is most likely an embellishment by that gossipy and not entirely reliable witness. The more interesting question is how seriously to take the plan. Historians since the nineteenth century have disagreed vehemently, as do contemporary ones. For Fouquet's judges, of course, this question was to be of capital importance in determining his fate. Although the redraft of the plan in 1658 and its strategic implications are certainly telling, no evidence has ever emerged that anyone other than Gourville saw it or discussed it with Fouquet. If Fouquet made no attempt to lay the groundwork for its possible implementation by taking into his confidence the people he depended on to act on his behalf, it is not unreasonable to conclude that he never intended to make use of the plan at all.[34]

At the time Gourville supposedly saw the plan, Fouquet's concerns had shifted from Mazarin's intentions to Mazarin's passing. By 1660 the cardinal's health was failing, and it was obvious that he would not have long to enjoy the triumphant outcome of so many years of war and diplomacy. Early in 1661 he was warned by his physicians that he must prepare himself for the end, and in February the court moved to Vincennes, where the cardinal wanted to await his doom, and speculation mounted about his successor as chief minister.[35]

During his waning days, much of the cardinal's time was spent on his private affairs. In early March, he went through the motions of offering to the king his entire fortune, which the king, after making the cardinal wait three days for an answer, refused in a show of royal magnanimity—and naïveté—on March 6.[36] With his mind at ease, knowing that his enormous wealth would pass to his heirs, Mazarin was now free to contemplate his demise, and the final advice he should leave for the young Louis. The following day, after receiving the last sacraments, Mazarin turned his attention to matters of state. He held a council meeting in which he praised all three of his chief subordinates—Le Tellier, Lionne, and Fouquet—and recommended them to the king.

Supposedly on the next day, however, he modified his stance by warning Louis of Fouquet's ambitions and recommending his dismissal. At the same time, he is said to have told Louis that while he owed him everything, in leaving him Colbert, he was balancing the account. But for this volte-face we only have the word of Colbert and his supporters, so one should perhaps be skeptical.[37] Such advice is certainly not consistent with Mazarin's nomination of Fouquet at the same time as one of the executors of his will, along with Le Tellier, Colbert, Lamoignon, and another confidant, Giuseppe Zongo Ondedei.[38]

One might argue that Mazarin was hedging his bets on the future, but if so, revealing that Fouquet was guilty of irregularities in the management of the state's finances would hardly have protected his own fortune, the cardinal's chief preoccupation in his final days. If Fouquet were guilty of improprieties, the best protection for Mazarin's wealth would have been Fouquet's continuance in office, since, as the cardinal well knew, that fortune was tainted by the same activities ascribed to Fouquet. So it is likely that no such warning emanated from the dying prelate. A modern scholar has also suggested, based on Fouquet's trial testimony, that he was named an executor of the cardinal's will because of his authority as procureur général to block any inquiry by the Parlement of Paris into the cardinal's personal finances.[39]

In the months following the cardinal's death, on March 9, Fouquet may have paved the way for his own destruction by badly misreading the character and intentions of the young monarch. Throughout the 1650s Louis had left the cares of state largely to the aging cardinal and his subordinates. The young king of the 1650s, as described by contemporaries such as his cousin the duchess de Montpensier, was a typical princely wastrel, amusing himself with the endless round of balls and receptions of post-Fronde Paris and with the conquest of a string of aristocratic young women.[40] But in the wake of Mazarin's demise, a different monarch seemed to emerge. Summoning his chief councilors and secretaries of state on the morning of March 10, Louis advised them that it was time that he "governed on his own" and commanded his ministers and secretaries of state to report directly to him for instructions. Orders were not to be signed, nor funds disbursed, without Louis's personal authorization. He would be, in effect, his own chief minister.[41] At the same time, Louis reorganized the structure of his councils. In the future, the highest council, the Conseil d'en haut, was limited to the ministers for war (Le Tellier), foreign affairs (Lionne), and finance (Fouquet). Breaking with centuries of tradition, the chancellor, Séguier, was not to be a member of this body but was to confine his efforts to the areas of justice and royal administration (i.e., the sealing and verification of royal edicts). Close members of the royal family who traditionally sat on the royal council—such as the queen mother, the king's brother Philippe, and Condé as first prince of the blood—were removed from it and from any share in the public authority. Those excluded, including the king's mother, were vocal in their dismay, and none more than Séguier, who supposedly blamed Fouquet for his relegation to more mundane duties.[42]

Like many others, Fouquet seems to have believed that these new arrangements, which placed most of the burdens of government on the king himself, would be a short-term experiment, and that the king would soon tire of this self-imposed yoke. But Fouquet was deeply mistaken. As Louis was to say in his *Mémoires*, "It was not my intention to share my authority" with the ministers.[43] Above all, Louis was determined to be master in his own house, to be the center of all attention. Those of his collaborators such as Colbert or Le Tellier (and his son Louvois), who understood the character of the young king, who sensed the pent-up frustration and wounded pride of a man who had endured the humiliations of the Fronde and the post-Fronde domination of Mazarin, were to have long and successful careers. But Fouquet continued to behave with the flamboyance of the Mazarin years, living extravagantly and perhaps, within the confines of the council (for which there are no minutes), being openly dismissive of the king's competence in matters financial.

Initially, however, he continued to function as one of the king's senior ministers. In April 1661 he was commissioned to set up, or revive, a council for commerce, whose members were to include Colbert and Fouquet's former fellow intendant Olivier d'Ormesson.[44] He was also entrusted with important diplomatic responsibilities. Bypassing his regular ambassador in London, Louis had Fouquet make the arrangements to bribe Charles II of England and his ministers to align themselves with the Portuguese in their ongoing struggle with Spain and for Charles to take Catherine of Braganza as his queen in token of this policy. Fouquet also worked on an unsuccessful effort to secure the elective throne of Poland for Condé's son (the duc d'Enghien), and on several matters involving Sweden.[45]

At the same time, and in spite of these achievements, Fouquet's credibility with the king was fast eroding, thanks to Colbert. In the months following Mazarin's death, Colbert was able to arouse Louis's suspicions about Fouquet's conduct of state finances, resurrecting some of the same charges against Fouquet that Mazarin had dismissed in 1659.[46] Louis himself, in the memoirs written in the mid 1660s for the edification of his heir, and partly drafted by Colbert, was hard put to justify his retention of Fouquet; he insisted that at the time of Mazarin's death, "I already knew of his thefts." Louis's explanation was that he recognized Fouquet's talent and imagined that "if he confessed his past faults and promised me to reform, he could render me some great services." As a precaution, he noted, he assigned Colbert to the ministry with the rank of intendant of finances, to keep an eye on Fouquet.[47] When Colbert was appointed to this post in March 1661, he was also given control of the superintendant's register of activities, a function hitherto exercised by Hervart. This gave Colbert the window he needed onto Fouquet's day-to-day dealings.[48]

There may be some truthfulness in Louis's account. Fouquet later asserted that several days after the cardinal's death, he revealed to the king in a private audience that under Mazarin, there had been financial transactions that violated both in form and substance the edicts governing royal borrowings. He explained that much of this was due to the stress of warfare in the previous decade, and everything had been done at the cardinal's direction and with his consent. Louis is supposed to have replied that any offenses committed under those circumstances were forgiven and to have encouraged Fouquet to continue his services, presumably without future abuses. This discussion and Louis's alleged pardon for past derelictions was to be raised as a defense in Fouquet's trial.[49] Louis XIV's memoirs imply that some such conversation did take place, since he accused Fouquet of disregarding his kindness and continuing to find "new subterfuges to steal from me."[50]

In these same months, however, Colbert used his access to the records of the superintendant's financial activities to convince Louis that Fouquet was embezzling vast sums of money and had built his ostentatious lifestyle with funds destined for the royal coffers.[51] Sometime during the month of May, Louis made the decision to dismiss Fouquet and perhaps put him on trial.[52] With Colbert's help, Louis had concluded that Fouquet's faults went far beyond embezzlement and "bad faith" but also included an unlimited ambition, "continuing his extravagant expenses, fortifying strongholds, decorating palaces, forming conspiracies, and purchasing important offices for his friends at my expense, in hope of soon becoming the sovereign arbiter of the state." Louis added that he originally intended only to dismiss Fouquet but eventually concluded, again no doubt with Colbert's help, that Fouquet, with his "restless disposition," would try "something new" and that he would have to be arrested after all.[53]

The king's comments about "fortifying strongholds" suggest that Colbert made good use of information about Fouquet's activities on Belle-Isle. In 1657, before Fouquet had purchased the island, Colbert had presented Mazarin with reports from his cousin, André Colbert du Terron, the intendant at Brouage in Brittany, about Fouquet's privateering activities and his construction of fortifications at Yeu. Mazarin did not see in such activities the subversion Colbert tried to suggest, but, as noted in chapter 2, simply a loss of revenues for his own holdings in Brittany. Not only did Mazarin see nothing alarming about this, but he almost simultaneously authorized Fouquet to purchase Belle-Isle and transfer his commercial and privateering activities there.

Three years later, Colbert du Terron returned to the charge, this time reporting on Fouquet's activities on Belle-Isle. There, Fouquet had undertaken works on a grand scale, deepening the harbor and reconstructing the citadel on the island. More than 2,000 workmen were engaged in the project. At the time of Fouquet's downfall, royal agents found that hundreds of cannon, as well as ample stores of other firearms and miscellaneous weaponry, were stockpiled there and guarded by a garrison of 200 men. Fouquet was later to insist that the cardinal was well aware of his activities, which were intended to strengthen the island's defenses against any future assault in wartime, and that much of the artillery and other weapons were for his fleet of privateers and armed merchant ships or for use in the colonies. But Mazarin left no record that he knew of these activities (we only have Fouquet's word for it), and no such motives were suggested by Colbert, who presented Louis XIV with another set of reports by Colbert du Terron in the spring of 1661. These detailed the ongoing work on Belle-Isle and the vast quantity of armaments in plain sight, many of which originated with the Dutch, with whom Louis was now on bad terms.[54]

Colbert du Terron was dismissive of the explanation that all of the munitions and supplies he observed on the island were intended for use in the trade between Belle-Isle and Martinique. "It is a fine pretext and an excellent cover for having both a war fleet and a store of munitions in abundance."[55] Louis XIV, who remained scarred all his life by the experience of the Fronde, took these allegations seriously.[56] These reports may well have convinced Louis not simply to dismiss Fouquet but to treat him as an incipient rebel, planning insurrection and armed defiance: in short, as a Frondeur. Some months later, speaking to Guillaume de Lamoignon, the presiding judge of the Parlement of Paris, Louis insisted that Fouquet "wanted to make himself king of Brittany and the adjacent islands; he got everyone on his side with his lavish gifts [*profusions*]; there is no one I can trust anymore."[57]

Timing, however, was an issue. Rather than alarm the financial community in the middle of negotiating new tax farming arrangements over the summer months, and wanting Fouquet's help in securing a "free gift" of 3 or 4 million livres from the Estates of Brittany, scheduled to meet in early September, Louis decided to postpone the superintendant's disgrace until the fall.[58]

Le Tellier, who had formed an alliance of convenience with Colbert against Fouquet, was let in on the secret, and he and Colbert worked out a plan in excruciating detail: where Fouquet would be conducted after his arrest; the route his escort would take back to Paris; the amount of money allocated for the mission and the upkeep of the prisoner; and arrangements for the seizure of Fouquet's papers, the arrest of his key subordinates, and measures to be taken against his family and other associates.[59] Anne of Austria, long on friendly terms with Fouquet, was persuaded by her old friend the duchess de Chevreuse, a newly recruited ally of Colbert's, to agree to Fouquet's disgrace.[60]

If Fouquet were to be charged with crimes and put on trial, the plotters would have to deal with his retention of the post of procureur général, an office he continued to exercise at least nominally after assuming the position of superintendence of finance. By longstanding tradition, the holder of this high legal office could only be tried by the Parlement of Paris. Such a trial would afford Fouquet the protections of the normal judicial process, as well as the likely sympathy of the magistrates, among whom he had many friends and relations. In addition, it would be an invitation to parlement, always hostile to the royal financial administration, to open up many lines of inquiry that neither the king nor Colbert wanted to see explored.

To overcome this obstacle, Louis lured Fouquet into a trap with fair words and suggestions that a contingency fund of about a million livres would be a welcome addition to the royal coffers. To help his king, Fouquet offered to sell one of his possessions, Vaux, for example, or his office of procureur général. The king graciously agreed that Fouquet might sell the office. After all, he intended to reform the judiciary, and, he hinted, the post might be an encumbrance to Fouquet's future advancement, perhaps to chancellor after Séguier, or even beyond. A hasty sale was arranged to a friendly parlementaire, Achille de Harlay, for 1.4 million livres. The transaction closed in mid-August. Of the proceeds, 400,000 livres were reserved for Basile Fouquet per an earlier family arrangement; the balance, a million in cash, was conveyed to Vincennes as a gift for the king's use. Having sold this office, Fouquet was no longer a member of the parlement or automatically entitled to a trial before that body.[61]

To cover his tracks, and to lull Fouquet, Louis accepted the invitation to the famous fête at Vaux on August 17 that so dazzled the court. The fête was beyond magnificent. For this occasion, Fouquet brought together all of the resources and talents at his command. The king, accompanied by his mother and the entire court, arrived from Fontainebleau in a glittering cortège of carriages escorted by troops of the royal bodyguard. When they alighted, the spectacle astonished them: a giant jewel box surrounded by water on three sides, with acres of gardens stretching beyond, fountains playing and statues beckoning. Within the château, guests passed through room after room filled with paintings and portraits, designed or commissioned by Le Brun, and elaborate tapestries, for which Fouquet shared a taste with the late cardinal Mazarin. At the center of the building, under the immense cupola of the oval grand salon—an unusual shape for the period—the courtiers could admire the views of the garden. Two antique statues, Augustus and Tiberius, kept watch in this vast room. Farther along, in the Chamber of the Muses, Le Brun painted *The Triumph of Fidelity*, in which Apollo, accompanied by Clio, the muse of history, protected that virtue. In the king's chamber, Le Brun introduced a style that Louis was later to copy for the royal bedroom at Versailles, with sculpted and gilt paneling and ceiling, allegorical paintings, and the royal bed safely nestled beyond a golden balustrade.[62]

Passing outdoors, courtiers could admire the vast gardens, the eleven hundred jets of water climbing toward the heavens, the grand canal and pool glittering in the distance, and the formal parterres laid out with geometric flower beds. After the tour of the grounds, the royal party was called to supper. Vatel, of course, was in charge of the meals. Thirty buffet tables held the delicacies prepared under his watchful eye, and eighty tables had been set up to seat the court. All of the serving plates and bowls and all of the individual place settings were of silver or gold.

Once the repast was finished, the guests made their way to a temporary open air theater at the end of one of the long walkways (*allées*) lit up with a hundred great torch lights. A popular playwright, Molière, took to the stage to recite a long series of compliments for the king, written by Paul Pellisson. There followed a first performance of Molière's latest work, *Les Fâcheux* (*The Bores*), in a new style, a comedy-ballet (of which Molière's later *Le Bourgeois gentilhomme* is the most famous example), with music by Jean-Baptiste Lully and Pierre Beauchamp.

The play was followed by a spectacular display of fireworks, one that supposedly rivaled the display put on for the formal entry of Queen Maria Theresa into Paris a year earlier. At the end of the evening, there was a final collation, mostly fruits, accompanied by music from twenty-four violins, before Louis and the court climbed back into their carriages and left, as they had come, to the sound of drums and trumpets.[63]

Years later, the abbé Choisy and the comte de Brienne, in their respective memoirs, provided the story that a furious Louis could barely contain his rage at the evidence of wholesale embezzlement such a display suggested and that he was only dissuaded from arresting Fouquet on the spot by the intervention of the queen mother. This tale was picked up by Voltaire, and is still found in many popular accounts, but the detailed arrangements for the arrest at Nantes only illustrate how elaborate and thought-out the exercise was to be.[64] Perhaps a more insightful comment was offered by Madame de La Fayette, who remarked that the king "could not hide his astonishment" at Vaux, nor Fouquet his surprise at the king's reaction.[65]

Choisy, seconded again by Voltaire, provided yet another reason for Louis's smoldering anger. According to him, in the spring of 1661, Fouquet had attempted to seduce Louise de La Vallière, one of the maids of honor in the service of Louis's sister-in-law, the duchess d'Orléans. His courtship was not successful: the young lady had already become the king's latest conquest. Fouquet compounded his mistake by sending Madame du Plessis-Bellière to offer Louise a "present" of 20,000 écus in return for joining the large network of informers that Fouquet maintained at court. An indignant Louise rejected the bribe and reported Fouquet's unwanted attentions to the king. Louis would thus have had yet another offense, both personal and political, to add to his grievances against Fouquet. The story has also found its way into many accounts of Fouquet's fall, from Choisy's time to the present. It rests not only on Choisy's account (repeating contemporary gossip) but also on a supposed letter of Madame du Plessis-Bellière to Fouquet detailing her approach to Louise. The letter, which was widely publicized at the time of Fouquet's trial, is considered to be a forgery by modern scholars, and Choisy, a protégé of Colbert's, must be approached with caution. Given his access to informants within the royal households, it is hard to believe Fouquet was not aware of the king's infatuation; such knowledge would obviously make a romantic overture unlikely, unless Fouquet had a suicide wish. Nevertheless, it is possible that he approached La Vallière with the hope of ingratiating himself with a monetary gift, and inadvertently created yet another point of friction with the king.[66]

Even without this added irritation, Louis's correct but cold behavior at Vaux may have given Fouquet some inkling that his standing with the king was tenuous. Court politics was always a treacherous business, and the rivalries with his competitors, notably Le Tellier and Colbert, to say nothing of Séguier, would have kept a man in Fouquet's position always on guard. Although the secret of Fouquet's impending arrest was closely guarded, some inklings of danger seem to have leaked. Fouquet received warnings from Madame du Plessis-Bellière, from another well-placed lady, Madame d'Huxelles, and also from Gourville.[67] Shortly before leaving Paris for Nantes, Fouquet confided his fears of disgrace to a friend, Louis-Henri de Loménie de Brienne, but saw no way out for himself.[68]

At the end of August, the king left Fontainebleau for Nantes, accompanied by his ministers and most of his courtiers. The royal caravan of coaches, wagons, and horsemen made its way to the Loire and took the classic route along the banks of the river. At Orléans, Fouquet and Madame Fouquet, accompanied by Hugues de Lionne, embarked on a river barge to continue the journey by water. The gaily decorated barge stopped en route at Angers, cradle of the Fouquet family, where a crowd of dignitaries welcomed the Fouquets at dockside.[69] As they continued their voyage, they were passed at one point by a second barge, this one conveying

Le Tellier and Colbert, also bound for Nantes.[70] Both vessels arrived in time to allow the ministers to greet the king on his arrival on September 1.

Fouquet had been suffering from a recurring fever since leaving Fontainebleau and was not present at the welcoming ceremonies for the king. The next morning he did attend a routine council meeting at the former ducal château at Nantes, where the king was staying, but he did not linger. He returned to his own lodgings at the hôtel de Rougé, where he was not well enough to receive a welcoming delegation of local peasants, leaving the honors to Madame Fouquet and his staff.[71] In a show of consideration, Louis sent Brienne to ask after him. Brienne had passed much of the day at the château, where he had been surprised by the unusual precautions taken there to bar even officials from the king's rooms: it was rumored that the king was working on secret matters with Le Tellier and others. Fouquet was not concerned about this.[72]

On that same day, September 2, Louis had summoned the lieutenant of his musketeers, Charles d'Artagnan (immortalized in fiction by Alexandre Dumas). D'Artagnan was famous for his devotion to duty, and had served Mazarin on confidential missions both during and after the Fronde. He was also indebted to Colbert for some financial assistance.[73] D'Artagnan had initially sent his excuses: like Fouquet, he too was suffering from fever. A second command brought him to the king's apartment, but Louis, recognizing that d'Artagnan was truly ill, told him to return when he was well.[74] The musketeer returned on September 4. Taking him into his private office (*cabinet*), Louis charged him with the mission of arresting Fouquet the next morning.[75]

As soon as the king received word from d'Artagnan that the arrest had been effected, the rest of the plan was put in motion. Royal officials seized all of Fouquet's papers at the hôtel de Rougé and arrested some of the subordinates who had accompanied him, most notably Paul Pellisson. At the same time, royal couriers set out for Paris and Fontainebleau with orders for royal officials, in particular chancellor Séguier, who had remained behind. Leaving nothing to chance, troops were dispatched from Nantes to seize Belle-Isle.

Although patrols had been placed along the roads leading from Nantes to intercept any other bearers of the news of Fouquet's arrest, one of his valets managed to slip through the dragnet and brought word to Paris of the superintendant's detention. A hurried convocation of some of Fouquet's closest friends and family members, including Basile Fouquet, who rallied to the family in the hour of crisis, debated what steps, if any, to take. Basile Fouquet supposedly urged the burning of Saint-Mandé, which housed most of Fouquet's official papers. Madame du

Plessis-Bellière countered that such a step would be viewed as an admission of guilt and would doom Fouquet in advance.[76]

Paralyzed by indecision, Fouquet's intimates took no action before royal officials arrived to seal and inventory all of the superintendant's papers at Saint-Mandé, Vaux-le-Vicomte, Fontainebleau, and Fouquet's Paris residence. Other agents seized the papers of Pellisson, Louis Bruant, and Gourville. These measures were authorized by chancellor Séguier on the arrival of the king's courier at Fontainebleau two days after the superintendant's arrest.[77]

The thunderbolt also fell on Fouquet's family and close circle. The bewildered Madame Fouquet, marooned at the hôtel de Rougé, was ordered to leave and take up residence in Limoges. The well-connected Gourville helped her with arrangements and later secured royal permission to lend her some money for living expenses.[78] François, archbishop of Narbonne, was commanded to take up residence in Alençon; Louis, bishop of Agde, was instructed to return to his remote see; Gilles, the Benjamin of the family, was deprived of his court post as premier écuyer of the Royal Stables (Grand Écurie); Basile was exiled to Guyenne. After the intervention of Anne of Austria, Fouquet's mother, the elderly Marie de Maupeou, was allowed to remain in Paris and take custody of the Fouquets' two small sons.[79] Madame du Plessis-Bellière was exiled to Montbrison and her papers seized; her son-in-law, the marquis de Créqui, recently created general of the galley fleet (*galères*), was divested of his office.[80] After "lending" the treasury 500,000 livres at Colbert's "suggestion," Gourville slipped out to live quietly near Angoulême as a houseguest of the duc de La Rochefoucauld.[81] Others of Fouquet's subordinates also scattered in the hopes of avoiding arrest.

A gleeful Louis, who had already written to his mother, made the announcement of Fouquet's arrest to the court himself, shortly after he had received confirmation via d'Artagnan that the superintendant was in custody. He had waited, he told his courtiers, to strike Fouquet when the superintendant believed himself at the high point of fortune and was in his ancestral district, where he enjoyed so much esteem. The king further announced that he would abolish Fouquet's post and oversee his own finances. Echoing his comments on the death of Mazarin, he added, "It's time I ran my own affairs."[82]

CHAPTER 4

Setting the Stage and Writing the Script

Now that the superintendant had been caged, a decision had to be made about the best way to proceed. Initially, Louis XIV gave orders to try Fouquet before a small panel of *maîtres des requêtes*, presided over by the chancellor, Pierre Séguier.[1] This would have been a relatively quick process and was not an uncommon procedure. It was also consistent with advice from the dying Mazarin, who had cautioned against any widespread inquiries into the financial affairs of the kingdom during his tenure, telling the king it would not be in the best interest of the state and would alienate many important families within and without the kingdom.[2] But Colbert preferred a more spectacular forum for the charges against Fouquet and saw the occasion as one that could be used for reforming the financial system by bringing to light the "abuses" to which it had been subjected in earlier decades. So he returned to his proposal of 1659 to Mazarin and persuaded the young king that Fouquet's spectacular arrest should be accompanied by an equally spectacular trial of the superintendant and his accomplices in malfeasance before a special court, known as a *chambre de justice*.[3]

There were certainly many precedents for such panels. Special courts set up to investigate corruption in public finance and to try those who had committed crimes of a financial nature against the state are traceable to the time of François I.[4] Such courts served several royal purposes simultaneously. They deflected public anger and resentment at the tax system from the crown to the financiers, conveniently blamed for the "bloodsucking" (of which the crown was the ultimate beneficiary). At the same time, the appointment of a special tribunal constituted a denial of the claims of jurisdiction and supervisory authority by the *parlements* and tax courts over the financial apparatus of the state. This repudiation was softened, and perhaps masked, by the appointment of prominent magistrates from the established court system to sit as individuals on these panels, thus flattering the individuals and their professional pretensions while bypassing the institutions to which they belonged. These chambers usually included not only members of the Paris-based courts but also others chosen from the provincial high courts, since the national jurisdiction of the chamber would supersede their jurisdictions as well.

J. F. Bosher has stressed the political purposes of such tribunals, while noting at the same time that a chamber was also "a royal business institution disguised as a court of law."[5] In economic terms, it provided the means for the state to force financiers to renegotiate the terms of transactions after the fact: the fines and amends paid by the financiers, usually in return for immunity from any further sanctions, were in effect a refunding of part of their profits. The crown's judicial power thus provided a means to redress the imbalance in the dynamics between the crown and its lenders, an imbalance that forced the state in time of crisis to agree to almost any terms proposed by the financiers in order to secure funding.[6]

The history of the chamber convened by Richelieu in 1624–1625 illustrates how these investigations usually turned out. In August 1624 Richelieu, newly come to power, had the superintendant of finance, Charles de La Vieuville, arrested for corruption and imprisoned in the château of Amboise. While La Vieuville languished in disgrace, the cardinal instituted a chambre de justice to investigate and try financiers accused of abuses in their financial dealings with the state. This prosecution, however, was a sop to public opinion; the reality, as Richelieu knew, was that the state depended on these financiers to fund its operations.[7] One hapless financier was executed; the rest paid a total of about 10.8 million livres in fines in return for a halting of further proceedings, a result that tracks very closely the outcome of the 1607 trial under Sully.[8] What were theoretically fines amounted to a forced renegotiation of the terms on which the financiers had lent to the crown, a partial refunding of their presumably ill-gotten gains. La Vieuville, sentenced to death by hanging, managed to escape, perhaps with official connivance. He repaid his tormentors with an apologia for his actions, published while in exile, which would serve as a model for Paul Pellisson's defense of Fouquet (see below).[9] In September 1651, more than a quarter of a century after his disgrace, a rehabilitated La Vieuville returned to office.[10] Fouquet would certainly have been familiar with this episode; La Vieuville, who died in early 1653, was his immediate predecessor, and his maternal uncle, René de Maupeou, was the royal *procureur général* of the chambre de justice that had condemned La Vieuville in 1625.[11]

In Fouquet's case, as in the earlier examples, the first step in the process was the selection of the judges and officers of the court. Colbert carefully reviewed possible candidates, doing his best to screen out those who might be favorable to Fouquet, or, worse yet, hostile to the crown.[12] All of this took some time, and the royal proclamation of the appointment of a chambre de justice to investigate and punish the individuals responsible for the financial "abuses and embezzlements, crimes and offenses" against the state as far back as 1635 only appeared in mid-November 1661.[13]

Pierre Séguier, the chancellor of France, was chosen to head the chamber. Guillaume de Lamoignon, the first president (i.e., presiding magistrate) of the Parlement of Paris, and François-Théodore de Nesmond, a second president (*président à mortier*), who was married to Lamoignon's sister Anne, were named to the court, as was Louis Phélypeaux de Pontchartrain, president of the Paris Chambre des comptes. The balance of the court consisted of a mixture of magistrates and royal officials drawn from both Paris-based entities and provincial counterparts. There were four ordinary magistrates (*conseillers*) from the Parlement of Paris, Jacques Renard (or Regnard), Pierre Catinat, Pierre de Brillac (or Brilhac), and Nicolas Fayet; and five maîtres des requêtes, Pierre Poncet, Olivier Lefèvre d'Ormesson, Louis Boucherat, Daniel Voysin, and Cyrien Besnard de Rézé. There were two magistrates from the Chambre des comptes in Paris, Moussy and Le Bossu; and two magistrates from the Cour des aides in Paris, Jérôme Le Féron and Baussan. From the provincial courts, the crown named Massenau, from the Parlement of Toulouse; Francon, from the Parlement of Grenoble; Pierre du Verdier, of the Parlement of Bordeaux; La Toison, from the Parlement of Dijon; Jacques Le Cormier de Sainte-Hélène, from the Parlement of Rouen; Pierre Raffélis de Rocquesante, from the Parlement of Aix; Hérault (or Ayrault), from the Parlement of Rennes; Noguès, from the Parlement of Pau; and François-Michel Le Tellier de Louvois (son of Michel Le Tellier and the future minister of war), from the Parlement of Metz. A second decree named two members of the Grand Conseil to the court, Chouart and Henri Pussort, who was also a judge in the Paris Chambre des comptes. Thus, of the 28 judges, 11 were drawn from the Paris courts, 8 (Séguier, Chouart, Pussort, and the 5 maîtres des requêtes) from the royal administration, and 9 from the various provincial parlements. Pussort, who was to play an important role in the proceedings, was none other than Colbert's maternal uncle.[14]

Denis Talon, the royal *avocat général* and Fouquet's former colleague on the king's bench in the Parlement of Paris, was named as procureur général, the royal prosecutor, for the chamber. Talon, son of the late and highly respected Omer Talon, also a royal avocat général and a fierce defender of parlementary prerogatives during the Fronde, had been overshadowed by Fouquet while the two served in parlement. In the 1650s, Denis Talon had been a highly vocal critic of the tax farmers and had clashed repeatedly with Fouquet during parlementary sessions, where, to Fouquet's astonishment, he often concurred in parlementary objections to financial measures proposed by the crown.[15] Talon was believed to resent his former colleague and had developed ties to Colbert. Colbert had seen to this appointment in the hopes that what he called Talon's "natural severity" would be of value to the crown's case.[16] A relative and business associate of Colbert's, Oudart Gomont, was added to Talon's team and charged with reviewing legal issues and drafting interrogations, briefs, and other documents. Another of Colbert's protégés, Louis Berryer, was to serve as Colbert's liaison with the chamber. A native of Le Mans, Berryer made a fortune as a foundry master (*maître des forges*) before entering Mazarin's service in 1655 to help manage the cardinal's newly acquired duchy of Mayenne. His duties were soon expanded to include arranging tax-farming syndications to exploit the crown's extensive forestry resources in Normandy. As a participant in those same transactions, Berryer grew even wealthier, making sure that Mazarin, Colbert, and even Fouquet benefited from them as well. Berryer, who had no legal training, was to take an active part in the proceedings, shaping the case against Fouquet and coming to be seen as Colbert's "eyes and ears," Finally, Joseph Foucault, also a client of Colbert's, was named the clerk of the court (*greffier*).[17]

The importance of the chambre de justice was underscored by the appointment of Pierre Séguier to be its nominal head. As chancellor of France, Séguier was the senior officer of state under the crown, heading both its judicial and administrative hierarchies. Séguier's family background was similar to that of Fouquet and of many other parlementary families. Although the Séguiers were to insist on a fictitious genealogical tie to a noble family of the same name in Languedoc, the first of the chancellor's known ancestors were apothecaries and spice merchants from the small town of Saint-Pourçain in the Bourbonnais. One of them, Etienne Séguier (d. 1465), became a royal *valet de chambre* in the time of Louis XI.[18] In succeeding generations, his numerous descendants established themselves in Paris, where some rose to positions of prominence in the world of the judiciary and the royal administration in the sixteenth century. The patronage of Catherine de' Medici helped members of the family rise still further in the hierarchy. At the same time, the family enriched itself by services to several aristocratic families and began to acquire landed properties to lay a firm foundation for the family fortune.[19]

The future chancellor, born in 1588, lost his father, Jean Séguier, a maître des requêtes, as a small boy but was raised in a large family of uncles and cousins who held important official posts, a clan that was already linked by marriage to other leading parlementary families.[20] Pierre Séguier became a magistrate in the Parlement of Paris at a young age and, in 1618, a maître des requêtes. Séguier found a patron in the powerful duc d'Épernon, and served as an intendant with Épernon's army in Aunois and Saintonge in 1621.[21] In 1624 he succeeded an uncle as a president in the Parlement of Paris.[22] In the next few years, Séguier managed to acquire a new and more powerful patron than Épernon, cardinal de Richelieu. Séguier was named keeper of the seals in February 1633, and in 1634 he married his eldest daughter, Marie, to Richelieu's nephew, the marquis de Coislin. Five years later he married his second daughter, Charlotte, to the heir of the duc de Sully, with an enormous dowry of 300,000 livres. In 1635, with Richelieu's sponsorship, Séguier became chancellor of France, traditionally the most prestigious of the great offices of state.[23]

Other honors continued to shower on him: knight of the royal order of the Holy Spirit in 1641, and, unusually for a magistrate, a dukedom *à brevet* (i.e., a title without parlementary ratification, which would not pass to heirs).[24] In 1634 Séguier bought the magnificent residence of the old duc de Bellegarde (a royal favorite of an earlier generation) on the rue de Grenelle Saint-Honoré, a suitable address to showcase his wealth and importance.[25]

At the beginning of the Fronde, Séguier was identified with the royal cause and seen as a fierce opponent of parlement. In August 1648, while en route to a meeting with the parlement, Séguier narrowly escaped death at the hands of an angry mob.[26] This almost fatal sacrifice did not save him from disgrace in 1650 when he was divested of the custodianship of the royal seals (a chief function of the chancellor). The seals were briefly returned to him but withdrawn once again in 1651. This may account for Séguier's errant behavior in 1652, at the very end of the Fronde, when he became entangled in the final maneuvers of Orléans and Condé and was accused of persuading his son-in-law, the duc de Sully, to allow Condé's army safe passage through Mantes. Although Séguier resumed some of his duties as chancellor shortly thereafter, he did not recover the seals until 1656, an indication of Mazarin's lingering mistrust.[27]

Like Fouquet, Séguier was a bibliophile. His library, which was known for its Greek manuscripts, was valued at 80,000 livres and eventually found its way to the collection of the abbey of Saint-Germain-des-Prés.[28] Like the Fouquets, the Séguier family was aligned with the "devouts" and had its own ties to the Order of the Visitation. The chancellor's brother was a bishop and his sister a nun; moreover, they were cousins of cardinal de Bérulle (d. 1629), one of the leaders of the Catholic revival in France in the previous generation.[29] The chancellor was known for his somewhat theatrical displays of piety, but not everyone was convinced of his good character. Madame de Sévigné reported gleefully that in some circles the chancellor was compared to Tartuffe.[30] Another contemporary, the gossipy Tallemant des Réaux, portrayed the chancellor as mean-spirited, vainglorious, avaricious, and married to an avaricious woman.[31]

Perhaps the most revealing insights into Séguier's character are found in the extraordinary painting by Charles Le Brun, now in the Louvre, depicting Séguier taking part in the great ceremonial entry of the newlywed Queen Maria Theresa into Paris in August 1660. The painting, commissioned by the chancellor himself, depicts Séguier on horseback, shaded by two great parasols and surrounded by young attendants. With his cloth-of-gold apparel and broad-brimmed hat, one is reminded of some Renaissance cardinal on parade. But it is the features that are most revealing. The set lips, arched eyebrows, and cold eyes staring down on the unseen onlookers speak volumes about his drive, ambition, and evident arrogance.

Throughout the trial, Séguier, who had also presided over the trial of Cinq-Mars in 1642, would distinguish himself for his hostility to Fouquet. The bad blood between them went back as far as the time of Fouquet's posting to Dauphiné in 1644, although the underlying reason for this earlier rupture is not clear. His attitude toward Fouquet after the superintendant's arrest is perhaps easier to explain. Fouquet had risen meteorically in the 1650s, eclipsing an older generation of high-ranking servants of state like the chancellor. While officially rehabilitated after 1656, Séguier may have felt some lingering coldness at court because of his activities at the end of the Fronde. His exclusion from the king's Conseil d'en haut in 1661, to which Fouquet was appointed, and thereafter the restriction of the chancellor's functions to legal and administrative ones, a great departure from the historic role of a chancellor of France, may have magnified his resentment toward Fouquet. For reasons unknown, Séguier ascribed his exclusion from the council to Fouquet's influence; in addition, he and Fouquet had fallen out in 1661 when Fouquet had refused to compensate him for his losses when the superintendant suppressed a tax farm in which Séguier had taken a share.[32] The fall of Fouquet and his appointment to preside over the chambre de justice offered Séguier the chance to prove his worth by delivering the verdict, and the sentence, that Colbert and Louis XIV expected.

Given his other duties, Séguier was rarely on hand for the early stages of the chamber's proceedings. In his place, the chamber was presided over by Guillaume de Lamoignon, the senior magistrate (*premier président*) of the Parlement of Paris. Scion of another distinguished "robe" family, Lamoignon had been a rising star in parlement in the 1650s and a champion of parlementary prerogatives against Mazarin. Nevertheless, when the office of first president became available in the fall of 1658, a post that was a royal appointment, Fouquet had prevailed on Mazarin to appoint Lamoignon instead of Nesmond, the candidate pushed by Le Tellier (Lamoignon would later dispute this version of the events).[33] Despite this tie, in subsequent years Fouquet had clashed with Lamoignon about parlementary objections to some of his financial measures, with Lamoignon, as senior magistrate, serving as spokesman for his colleagues. By the time of Fouquet's arrest, they were no longer deemed friends or political allies.[34] Lamoignon was considered by his contemporaries to be a man of great integrity. Like many of the Parisian high magistrates, he was also a man of letters, who counted Boileau and Racine among his friends. Pellisson, too, was a frequent guest at the Lamoignon literary salon.[35]

During the trial, Lamoignon was to fret aloud that his complicated relationship with Fouquet troubled him; their tie also disturbed Colbert.[36] The friction between Lamoignon and Colbert increased as Colbert infringed on standard judicial procedures, deeply offending Lamoignon's sense of "due process."[37] The impact of Lamoignon's reservations was magnified by his standing among the other magistrates: at least eight of the judges were known to be close to Lamoignon and in various votes during the proceedings often followed his lead.[38]

Despite Colbert's best efforts, it was difficult to find magistrates without some kind of connection, positive or negative, to Fouquet, which in modern times would require a judge to recuse him or herself. Colbert complained that Fouquet had given a pension to Renard, that Brillac had participated in a transaction of Fouquet's involving the *aides*, and Besnard de Rézé had received an intendancy in Normandy with Fouquet's help after ruling against the Colberts in a lawsuit with Le Tellier in 1657.[39] At the same time, six of the judges acknowledged at least some distant tie by blood or marriage to the Fouquets, although these ties were often offset by countervailing affiliations. Renard, for example, admitted that he and Fouquet called one another "cousin" (*cousinait*), but did not really know why—the exact relationship was too remote to recollect; Boucherat acknowledged a kinship but also an "enmity" with the superintendant. Poncet, who proved to be hostile to Fouquet throughout the proceedings, was a distant relative but was also related to Talon. So also was Voysin, who was married to Talon's sister, Marie Talon, while Pontchartrain was married to Talon's cousin Marie-Suzanne Talon.[40]

The chamber convened for the first time in a grand opening ceremony at the Palais de justice in Paris, seat of the high courts, on December 3, 1661. An audience of noble lords and ladies, magistrates of the high courts, and other dignitaries watched the members of the chamber, led by Séguier, process into the room, take their seats, and listen to the royal proclamation establishing the chamber and delineating its jurisdiction. Séguier gave a speech lauding the king for his decision to give his people not only external but also internal peace by putting an end to the stresses inflicted on them by the greed of the financiers. The chamber's work, he asserted, would foster the king's aims to be the restorer of the state. When it was his turn, Lamoignon spoke at length about the chamber's duty to fulfill the king's wish to ease the misery of his people and restore equilibrium to his state by confiscating the possessions of those who had accumulated great wealth by oppressing his subjects.[41]

Denis Talon, the chamber's newly appointed procureur général, reminded his audience that previous chambers had been inclined to settle with financiers accused of misbehavior, but he pledged this one would not do so. His explanation for leniency in times past was the power of the financial community, which had been based on the "protection of [unnamed] superior powers" and on its "alliances with the robe" (meaning the high judiciary)—a strangely undiplomatic assertion. The first of these protectors—presumably Fouquet—had been overthrown. With respect to the second, the king was exercising the plentitude of his authority in this current investigation, so no one could interfere with the course of justice. The present chamber would provide to posterity a "monument to severity."[42]

Long before the chamber convened, the machinery of state had been set in motion to facilitate that severity. Immediately after Fouquet's arrest, his papers at Saint-Mandé, Fontainebleau, Vaux, and his Paris residence had been sealed; after being inventoried, they were carried off to Vincennes for further examination. Colbert appeared at Saint-Mandé early in the process and put his hands on several supposedly incriminating documents, which were brought to the king for examination. If this were not enough, Paris was awash with rumors that Fouquet's papers contained not only evidence of financial misdeeds but also correspondence revealing amorous ties between him and high-ranking court ladies, letters the king ordered destroyed but which surfaced in apocryphal form in the Paris underground press.[43]

These efforts were not confined to Fouquet's papers. Pellisson's had also been seized and inventoried, and shortly afterward, in October 1661, the registers and papers of the royal treasurers (*trésoriers de l'Épargne*) were also impounded. Pussort, Colbert's uncle, and Louis Berryer, his confidential servant, were charged with examining them.[44] Once the chamber began its work, it cast a wide net: Fouquet's clerks and subordinates, various financial officials, and the royal treasurers were brought in for interrogation and detention. More than 60 people soon found themselves enduring the hospitality of the Bastille.[45]

The central figure in this drama, however, had not been seen or heard from in public since his arrest in early September. Immediately after his detention, Fouquet had been taken to Angers, where he was kept under close confinement in the ancient château that dominated the town. He was allowed no communication with the outside world and remained under the guard of the incorruptible d'Artagnan. At the beginning of December, he was transferred to Amboise. A fallen superintendant of finance was a convenient scapegoat for all the miseries of the kingdom, and as Fouquet was transported from one prison to another, angry crowds surrounded the cortège, mocking and threatening the prisoner. At the end of December, again to the cheers and jeers of mobs en route, Fouquet was moved to Vincennes, close enough for interrogations by the chamber or its officers.[46] He was imprisoned there on the first floor of the gloomy medieval donjon, a stone's throw from the handsome pavilions constructed there under Mazarin, the view of which was blocked by the donjon's surrounding walls and structures, and within walking distance of his own residence of Saint-Mandé. He was not permitted to have any books or papers, with the exception of several religious tracts, nor was he allowed any contact with the outside world except correspondence with his wife on family matters, with all letters passing through Le Tellier's hands to make sure of the contents.[47] Le Tellier, who oversaw these arrangements, did permit Fouquet's valet and a personal physician to share his captivity. The doctor, one Pecquet, who joined Fouquet several days after the superintendant's arrest, may have informed Fouquet of a few details: the arrest of Pellisson, the sealing of his papers, and the exile of Madame Fouquet.[48] But subsequent events, including the appointment of a chambre de justice, were apparently unknown to Fouquet.

In the first weeks of his captivity, Fouquet wrote a long letter that reflected his growing bewilderment and resentment at the harshness of his captivity. Although addressed pro forma to Le Tellier, Fouquet's remarks were clearly intended for the king. Fouquet recalled that during the Fronde, many high officers of state had committed treason but were now in the peaceful enjoyment of their offices; he, however, who had always stood by the crown, had been disgraced. He recounted his efforts during the crises of the 1650s to find the money to keep the state afloat. Now that peace had broken out, he had a right to expect a reward for his efforts, but instead he was being destroyed. He reminded his reader (or readers) of Mazarin's unorthodox and often contradictory conduct of state affairs. With that in mind, he had spoken to the king about these irregularities (after Mazarin's death), and the king had given him his word that all was forgiven. "However, I am imprisoned and pursued." Fouquet appealed to the king's goodness and mercy, "truly royal virtues," but also to his sense of justice, arguing that if justice served to punish faults, it also served to recompense services. He insisted again that the king had pardoned him and had done so in peacetime and not under duress, as in the case of Frondeurs. He confessed his bewilderment at his dismissal when matters were going well, but at the least royal word, he would have understood and accepted it. What he couldn't understand was why matters had been taken to extremes. Under the circumstances, he asked only that the king, in consideration of his past services and his ill health, allow him to live in some remote spot away from the world's affairs. He even proposed a "cottage" he owned in a remote district of Brittany where the royal governor, La Meilleraye, could keep an eye on him. Fouquet implored the king to spare a moment to read this long communication and others he hoped to write on important matters. He closed with a plea that the king accord him the same mercy that "he hoped God would someday grant him."[49] The response was curt: Fouquet's letters were too long; the king did not have time to read them. Fouquet was forbidden to write again without permission. In the meantime, Fouquet's keepers were told he was not to write or receive letters, nor was he to have writing materials.[50]

After a long winter, the silence engulfing Fouquet was finally broken in early March 1662 when two members of the chamber, Poncet and Renard, and the recorder or clerk of court, Foucault, entered his cell at Vincennes. A day earlier, Talon had announced to the chamber that the investigation of the activities of Fouquet's clerk Bruant (who had fled the country), and his review of the state's finances had revealed monumental disorders traceable to Fouquet. Talon requested that Fouquet be questioned on these matters. The chamber, after discussing the various personal ties between Fouquet and its members, assigned Poncet and Renard to this task.[51]

When the examining magistrates appeared at his doorstep, Fouquet received them cordially: Poncet was somehow a kinsman and Renard both a cousin and former colleague in the Parlement of Paris.[52] It was probably on that morning of March 4, 1662, that Fouquet first became aware that a chambre de justice had been created to investigate the state's financings. The two commissioners announced that they were there to obtain on the king's behalf certain "clarifications" concerning various financial transactions. At this pronouncement, Fouquet's legal skills immediately came to the fore. He was prepared to help with inquiries directed at those subject to the chamber's jurisdiction, but he asserted his own rights, meaning that he did not recognize the chamber's authority to judge his actions as superintendant. This reservation was repeated at his second interrogation on March 6, as was a request to speak with someone the king trusted, "even Colbert," about secret matters that could not be divulged to the chamber.[53] At his third interrogation, Fouquet demanded that he be provided counsel, and writing materials, protesting that it was unheard of that anyone was denied the right to petition the courts in the ordinary manner.[54]

Despite such often repeated protests, demands, and reservations of rights, the questioning continued through 34 sessions. Some of the questions were pro forma, asking Fouquet if he was acquainted with various financial officials, or even his own clerks and subordinates, and so forth. But others were more substantial, as the commissioners began to ask him about specific transactions. The length and breadth of the inquiries, even if sometimes unfocussed, gave Fouquet for the first time an understanding of the magnitude of the effort undertaken by the chamber, and they certainly made it evident that he was at the center of the investigation.

As a prisoner cut off from the outside world, without counsel or any knowledge of who else had been detained or questioned, Fouquet labored under terrible disadvantages. But he was not entirely without resources. As a former procureur général, he was familiar with both the methods and the objectives of the kind of questioning to which he was now subjected. He was careful therefore to avoid the common mistakes of those under interrogation, such as providing contradictory or inconsistent answers to questions repeated at different sessions or rephrased in misleading ways. In addition to the legal skills acquired as a member of the *parquet* in parlement, Fouquet also had a deep comprehension of the mentality of the high court judges who sat in the chamber. He had been born, raised, and practiced law in that milieu, and as a high-ranking official during the Fronde and its aftermath, he was aware of the lingering resentments and mistrust between the high courts and the royal administration. But the government had been forced to appoint a bench composed in part of magistrates drawn from those same courts—many of whom were well known to Fouquet—to investigate and adjudicate his activities and those of the financial community. Colbert and his collaborators counted on the deeply entrenched contempt of the magistracy for the financiers to drive the process and outweigh any lingering bad feelings between the courts and the crown. Fouquet, by contrast, was to gamble that this strategy could be overcome by rekindling those old resentments while appealing to the judicial traditions of autonomy, integrity, and adherence to process and precedent as essential elements of justice.[55]

If Fouquet's legal skills were more than a match for those sent to question him, his financial experience also proved to be a great advantage. The many complicated financial mechanisms used to raise funds for the crown were difficult for any outsider to understand. This was only too evident in some of the questions the commissioners put to Fouquet. It was not hard for Fouquet to lose them in the details, sowing doubt about any criminality in the transactions under review.

Fouquet also sensed very quickly another weakness in the crown's approach. The proclamation setting up the chamber and various pronouncements, including those at its opening session, had established a central theme: in the preceding decades, the country had been brought to the brink of ruin, and its people to unprecedented levels of misery, because of the greed of a few dishonest financiers. They had been aided and abetted in their activities by corrupt officials, among whom Fouquet was the chief culprit. Proof of this was to be deduced from Fouquet's participation in many illegal and illicit transactions and by evidence of his immense wealth, which could not be otherwise explained.

In his defense, Fouquet was to offer a counter- or alternative narrative: the country had indeed been pillaged for years by corrupt practices. But he was neither the author nor the beneficiary of such machinations. That distinction, he was to insist, belonged to Mazarin, who had left an immense fortune at his death, one dwarfing anything known in France to that point—Mazarin, whose memory was detested by most of the French judiciary, as well as by the common people, even more than they despised the financiers. Fouquet was to repeat endlessly that the cardinal stood at the center of all of the financing activities of the previous decade, that he had personally benefited from most of them, and that any financial irregularities or departures from standard procedures should be put to the cardinal's charge.

The elements of Fouquet's defense began to crystallize very early in his questioning. On March 9, for example, he quickly dismissed questions about the *marc d'or* and the alienation of *taille* revenues—the first had been arranged by Servien, the second had been canceled—and treated the commissioners to a disquisition on bridging the gap between the legal limit on interest rates (5.5%) and the rates at which the crown actually borrowed.[56] On March 10, he turned an accusation that he had pocketed about 578,000 livres in a transaction into an explanation: the sum in question was a rebate to Nicolas Jeannin de Castille to cover the difference between the legal interest rate and the rate agreed for the financing. In describing this transaction and many others, Fouquet insisted that Mazarin had approved these terms out of necessity, raison d'état, during those years of crisis.[57]

When asked if the cardinal gave written orders in such matters, the reply was simply, the cardinal "did not give written orders on any matters."[58]

On the next day, the commissioners confronted Fouquet with an order in blank (i.e., without the beneficiary named) for a pension of 120,000 livres drawn on the revenues from the salt tax (*gabelle*). They insisted that the document had been found in his office at Saint-Mandé. Taken off guard, Fouquet hesitated for a moment and then offered a startling explanation. He was familiar with the arrangement but was surprised that the order was found among his papers, since, in fact, the beneficiary was Mazarin. Mazarin, he continued, often helped himself to such sums without going through the official procedures and required that the proceeds be brought to his private office (*petit cabinet*) and handed over directly to his valet, Bernouin.[59] He recalled sometimes bringing specie to the cardinal concealed in his own carriage to safeguard the secrecy of the transactions.[60] Unwilling to pursue this dangerous line of questioning, the examiners confronted Fouquet with a laundry list of pensions and grants and asked if he or certain members of his circle, such as La Rochefoucauld, the duc de Beaufort, or Gourville, had benefited from them: the answer was negative in all cases.[61]

The most dramatic and damaging exchanges between Fouquet and the commissioners took place during sessions on March 14–17, when the two questioned Fouquet about his activities in Brittany. Many of these Fouquet characterized as commercial ventures, hardly a secret to anyone. As for Belle-Isle, he had bought it at the request of Mazarin and with the king's consent. The garrison there was no larger than it had been in the days before he owned it, and it consisted mostly of Swiss mercenaries formerly in royal service, and he had obtained written royal permission to maintain it. The session on March 14 closed with many detailed questions about Belle-Isle, to which the former superintendant replied that he simply did not remember.[62]

On March 16, the commissioners returned once more to the question of Belle-Isle. Fouquet noted that he had offered the property to the king on more than one occasion. At this point, the interrogators surprised Fouquet by producing the plan drawn up at Saint-Mandé concerning measures to take in the event of his arrest and asked him to confirm its authenticity. A stunned Fouquet admitted the handwriting was his, adding that he thought he had destroyed the document several years earlier. A break for a midday dinner allowed him to collect his thoughts. In the afternoon, he spoke for hours, denouncing Mazarin's capricious behavior toward the other ministers, his attempts to set one against another, and the atmosphere of uncertainty and mistrust this had created. The plan, he explained, had been drawn up in a moment of panic, a desperate scheme to save himself in the case of an arbitrary arrest by the cardinal. The moment had passed, and he thought he had burned it long ago.[63] He again asserted that after Mazarin's death, he had told the king that he had committed a number of improper actions during the cardinal's lifetime, and the king had pardoned him. Rhetorically, and obviously addressing an audience beyond the walls, he noted that former rebels and Frondeurs had been covered with a royal amnesty. He had been loyal during the times of trouble. Why was he treated less well? Clemency, he reminded his listeners, was a royal virtue.[64]

The commissioners continued this line of questioning the next day. Fouquet reiterated his claim that the plan reflected his unhappiness with his treatment at the hands of Mazarin at a particular moment. He was asked repeatedly if he had ever shown or discussed it with anyone. Fouquet insisted he had not. The commissioners pressed him hard. Not even those named in the plan? Did Madame du Plessis-Bellière have a copy? Had he never spoken of it with Gourville? Fouquet emphatically denied he had ever communicated with anyone on the plan. If Gourville is to be believed, this was not true, at least in his case.[65] But Fouquet was doing more than protecting his friends. He was also protecting himself: a conspiracy requires conspirators. If he had never communicated his plan to anyone, it could be dismissed as no more than a wicked fantasy.[66]

After this dramatic confrontation, the rest of the interrogations dragged on with questions and demands for specifics on transactions mentioned in the papers seized from Pellisson, Bruant, and others, sometimes returning to matters already covered, such as the transaction involving the marc d'or, which Fouquet had earlier insisted was entirely the work of Servien.[67] Fouquet used these sessions to restate his arguments. Insofar as transactions violated normal procedures or exceeded legal borrowing rates for the crown, Fouquet explained that such transgressions had been the result of wartime necessity. The crown, desperate for money, had been willing to borrow on almost any terms. All such transactions had been authorized by Mazarin and were known to the king. There was simply no time to worry about "the details of each loan" or whether the normal formalities had been observed.[68] As for himself, not only did he deny that he had enriched himself at the king's expense: he was in fact a poor man. His debts, largely incurred to support the state, amounted to 12 million livres, his assets were between 2 to 3 million livres: in theory, he was bankrupt.[69]

After more than six months in seclusion, the interrogations offered a way, however limited, for Fouquet to engage in the process set in motion against him. Knowing that as a matter of procedure, his interrogations would be read by the chamber, he made sure to include several critical demands and assertions. He denied the jurisdiction of the chamber over him, either as a minister of state whose commission made him answerable only to the king or as a former member of parlement entitled to trial before that body. He demanded the right to counsel and access to his papers and writing materials in order to prepare his defense. He also protested the harsh conditions of his captivity and the mistreatment of his wife and family.

Fouquet's voice was not the only one to be raised in his defense. His mother, the aged Marie de Maupeou, who had taken in his small children after his arrest, addressed a long letter to the king that soon became known all over Paris. Part of it was a plea for mercy, reminding the king of her son's many years of service to the crown. Part of it, possibly drafted by one of the many lawyers in the family circle, was a restatement of Fouquet's right as a minister of state to be judged directly by the king for his official actions, and, failing that, his right as a former magistrate of parlement to be tried by his "natural judges."[70]

No response was made to the legal issues raised by the letter, although the crown did grant a request in the same letter to permit Fouquet's wife to return to Paris to tend to his private affairs.[71] Within days of returning, the younger Madame Fouquet made her way to the Louvre, where she managed to intercept the king just after he had finished dining in public. Throwing herself at his feet, she began a long harangue begging the king for mercy. Embarrassed and annoyed, the king had no desire to prolong the scene. He helped the lady to her feet, murmured two or three unintelligible words, and moved on, leaving her in her distress. Touched by the plea, Anne of Austria remarked to her son that the "poor woman was so distraught [*troublée*] that she could hardly speak." The king replied by changing the subject. The author of this account, a well-connected law student, added that rumors were circulating that the interrogators had found proof that Fouquet had assigned himself a pension on the gabelle and that he was "lost."[72]

Such rumors were not surprising. Almost from the moment of Fouquet's arrest, Colbert and his agents had seen to "leaks" of compromising "discoveries." These insinuations and accusations were often spread by literary figures on good terms with Colbert. Colbert understood the power of the word and used royal patronage to create a stable of royalist authors and poets, including luminaries such as Chapelain, Contin, and Benserade to promulgate an anti-Fouquet point of view.[73] Chapelain, for example, wrote to Madame de Sévigné to accuse Fouquet of "ruining the state and making the king hateful to his people with the enormous burdens with which they are crushed." Fouquet, he insisted, had diverted royal funds to subvert the king's subjects and to make "insolent acquisitions," which would be fortified for use against the crown—meaning Belle-Isle.[74] Falsified versions of Fouquet's correspondence with ladies of the court circulated along with lists of the supposedly unauthorized pensions he had been providing to influential courtiers.[75] A satirical anonymous poem called "Confiteor de Fouquet" bracketed an imaginary personal confession between the words of the prayer of the same name used in the Mass. It offered gems such as "I had no other purpose than the ruin of France" and "I make my fortune from everyone, stealing from the merchant and the bourgeois."[76]

These attacks did not go unanswered. In the early spring of 1662 a long and anonymous "Address to the King by One of His Faithful Subjects on the Trial of M. Fouquet" made the rounds in Paris. The author, unknown at the time, was Fouquet's former secretary and protégé, the poet Paul Pellisson, who had been arrested at the same time as Fouquet and shut up in the Bastille. Pellisson had somehow managed to smuggle out of prison this lengthy appeal and admonition to the king. Speaking as a "faithful subject" with "nothing to fear and nothing to hope for," the author challenged the jurisdiction of the chamber of justice over Fouquet, based on his commission as superintendant of finance to answer only to the king.[77] Pellisson bundled this argument with an admonition about the wisdom of such extraordinary judicial bodies. They violated the royal coronation oath, and the king would be personally responsible before God (and perhaps his people?) for any miscarriage of justice that might result from using extraordinary means rather than ordinary court procedures. Indeed, the history of such chambers, so prevalent under Richelieu, was truly baleful in retrospect.[78]

If this was not enough, Pellisson asserted boldly that Fouquet's tenure as superintendant could not be investigated without examining the conduct of Mazarin, who had acquired so large a fortune in exactly the years Fouquet had served as superintendant.[79] And what had happened to all of Mazarin's communications with Fouquet, his orders and letters which, the author insisted, had been carefully saved and sorted by the superintendant and had been kept at Saint-Mandé?[80] As for Fouquet's own fortune, a simple comparison of his assets and liabilities would suggest that only the most foolhardy would want to assume the liabilities that had supported his extravagant lifestyle.[81] Turning to Vaux and Belle-Isle, he reminded the king that Fouquet had offered Vaux as a gift for the king's heir, the dauphin, and Belle-Isle, acquired at Mazarin's order, to the crown.[82] Citing precedents reaching back into the Middle Ages, Pellisson warned that several of the king's predecessors had tarnished their reputations by the prosecutions of faithful servants of state, as recently as that of La Vieuville.[83] If Pellisson was implicitly critical of this return by the crown to the methods of Richelieu and Louis XIII, he offered the king an alternative role model: Henri IV, whose clemency and generosity was celebrated. Louis on this occasion should look to his own generous heart.[84] Written in the highly rhetorical style popular in fashionable salons, at court, in legal circles, or at the French Academy, the address ran through three printings.[85]

Pellisson was not finished. Another anonymous letter, "Second Address to the King for M. Fouquet," appeared in June or July 1662.[86] The author again challenged the jurisdiction of the chamber over Fouquet as a minister of state who was answerable only to the king: it could investigate, but by right it was for the king to judge his superintendant's actions. He also pointed out that its inquiry into Fouquet's supposed treason—the plan found at Saint-Mandé—lay beyond the chamber's commission from the king to judge financial crimes. Other than the king, the only possible venue for a charge of treason was the Parlement of Paris.[87]

For good measure, Pellisson addressed some of the more sensational charges against Fouquet, including a supposed embezzlement of 6 million livres, and based his defenses on the practices of the state financial machinery, which were often in violation of the edicts governing those operations. He bundled examples with technical descriptions of the processes by which funds were borrowed and then accounted for. The endless issuing and reissuing of notes and assignations, the necessity of assigning repayments on future collections rather than in the year of borrowing, and the complicated bookkeeping entries required to conceal borrowings at rates in excess of the legal limit (5.5%) called into question the accuracy of all of the treasury's registers and records and illustrated the ease with which at any stage of the process embezzlements could occur.[88] It was impossible to lay the blame on Fouquet for the practices of prior decades that had come about because of necessity of state, and which had been approved by Mazarin and even occasionally by the king.[89] Mazarin, Pellisson claimed, handled more than 20 million livres per annum for use in the war against Spain and for other purposes of state, often disbursing funds with scant regard for legal formalities.[90] Once more, Pellisson ended with an appeal to Louis XIV for mercy. If the example of Henri IV were not enough for Louis XIV, Pellisson was happy to throw in Julius Caesar as well, who supposedly erected a temple to clemency, a better memorial than a "chamber of justice."[91]

A third anonymous letter by Pellisson, "Summary Considerations on the Trial of M. Fouquet" appeared in September 1662 and attacked in general terms the procedural irregularities in the trial.[92]

Underground poems and eulogies of Fouquet had already appeared before Pellisson's three appeals, most notably a poem in Latin, "Fucquetus in Vinculis," by one Nicolas Gervaise, an erudite physician and client of Fouquet's.[93] But it was Pellisson's work that inaugurated a slow but discernible shift in public opinion about Fouquet, at least among the literate classes able to appreciate what Voltaire many years later called Pellisson's "passages of touching eloquence."[94]

Pellisson had succeeded in publishing these three appeals with the help of a magistrate in the Paris parlement, Jacques Jannart. Jannart had served earlier under Fouquet as an adjunct procureur général and had also surreptitiously helped the Fouquet women draft their legal petitions.[95] He was a relative by marriage of one of Fouquet's literary clients, the poet Jean de La Fontaine, who picked up his pen that same spring to write appeals in verse to the king, "Elegy to the Nymphs of Vaux" and "Ode to the King."[96] In the first and most famous of these poems, La Fontaine attempts to comfort the weeping nymphs of Vaux, deserted by their former master, Oronte, who has fallen from his high station: "no one will fault your innocent tears." Now it is their task to soften the king: "he loves his subjects, he is wise, he is just." The nymphs must make the king eager for the title of "merciful" (*clément*), the virtue that makes kings like gods. Again the image of Henri IV looms large: once that great king had the power to avenge himself, he lost all desire to do so. "Inspire this same kindness in Louis: the greatest victory is over one's own heart."[97]

La Fontaine's two poems were originally published anonymously, although his authorship was widely suspected and was to cost him a lifetime of royal disgrace.[98] But his eloquent appeal was joined by many other clandestine works. The longest of these was a poem of 6,000 lines called "Innocence Persecuted," published anonymously in five parts between 1662 and 1664. It was to provide its readers with a running summary of Fouquet's defenses and objections to the chamber proceedings and roundly denounced the involvement of Colbert and his lieutenants in Fouquet's prosecution. It may be the "detestable book" (*livre abominable*) cited in Molière's *Le Misanthrope*.[99]

One modern scholar has called the works on Fouquet's behalf a "literary Fronde."[100] This civil war of letters between partisans of Fouquet and Colbert's *clientèle* was to keep Colbert's spies and the royal police busy rounding up authors and printers suspected of writing or printing pro-Fouquet tracts.[101] Notwithstanding their best efforts, the police were unable to eradicate these writings, nor could they contain the growing sympathy in the country at large for Fouquet's plight.

Nicolas Fouquet, superintendant of finance (1653–1661). Portrait by Charles Le Brun. The flamboyant minister is depicted in the modest robes of a royal magistrate.

Vaux-le-Vicomte. To many of his contemporaries, Fouquet's magnificent residence was visible evidence of his corruption and self-dealing with the king's finances.

Opening of the *chambre de justice* (chamber of justice), December 3, 1661. Gouache.
Collection Cinq Cents de Colbert, vol. 228. Courtesy Bibliothèque nationale de France.

Pierre Séguier, chancellor of France and nominal head of the chamber of justice. Portrait by Charles Le Brun. Commissioned by Séguier, the painting suggests the vanity and self-aggrandizement of its subject.
Musée du Louvre. Scala/Art Resource, NY.

Guillaume de Lamoignon, first president of the Parlement of Paris. His insistence on respecting established judicial procedures and precedents enabled Fouquet to mount a credible defense. Engraving.
Courtesy Bibliothèque nationale de France.

Denis Talon, *procureur du roi* at Fouquet's trial. A sworn enemy of Fouquet, Talon was to prove amenable to Colbert's directives during the trial. Engraving.
Courtesy Bibliothèque nationale de France.

Olivier d'Ormesson, *rapporteur* at Fouquet's trial. His findings and recommendations at Fouquet's trial earned him the king's displeasure and truncated his career. Engraving.
Courtesy Bibliothèque nationale de France.

Henri Pussort, Colbert's uncle and member of the chamber of justice. Throughout the trial, Pussort was to serve as the stalking horse for his nephew and Fouquet's most determined adversary. Engraving.
Courtesy Bibliothèque nationale de France.

CHAPTER 5

The Best-Laid Plans of Men and Ministers

Despite the pleas and petitions on behalf of Fouquet, the judicial machinery ground on inexorably. Pierre Poncet and Jacques Renard finished their interrogations on March 23, 1662. The results, however, were not entirely satisfactory to Colbert, and a decision was made to interrogate some of Fouquet's close collaborators, including Paul Pellisson and Nicolas Jeannin de Castille.[1] Once more the outcome was mixed. While Pellisson refused to recognize the authority of the chamber and demanded counsel, Jeannin de Castille's testimony seemed more promising. Among the malfeasances attributed to Fouquet was the retention of 6 million livres worth of treasury bills (*billets*) that had been prepared as part of an aborted financing. These bills should have been destroyed but instead had supposedly been kept for presentation to the royal treasury at some future date by Fouquet and company. This sensational charge had been deliberately leaked and widely publicized. Now Jeannin de Castille was prepared to admit to participating in this scheme with Fouquet.[2]

All of this took time, and it was not until mid-June 1662 that the March interrogations of Fouquet were read to the chamber. At least some of the judges were impressed by Fouquet's "presence of mind" and the quality of his responses. Nevertheless, on June 17, the chamber ordered Fouquet's arrest and detention.[3] Until that moment, Fouquet had been held simply by an order of the king: now the chamber was formally assuming control of the prisoner and his case, roughly the equivalent in modern terms of a finding of "probable cause."

This development triggered a long summer of judicial theater. During his interrogations, Fouquet had been careful to include protests and demands in his responses: he had challenged the right of the chamber to judge his actions; he had requested writing materials so that he could prepare his case; he had demanded counsel; and he had asked for access to his papers and documents, seized by royal officials, to help with his defense. Thus far, the chamber had dodged most of these issues, but as the process moved beyond the preliminary stage, they had to be addressed.

Fouquet's testimony showed him taking an active part in forcing the hand of the chamber. When Poncet and Renard confronted him with Jeannin's testimony, Fouquet responded by asking if the chamber had ruled on his petitions. When the answer was negative, Fouquet announced that until his demands were met, he would not answer any more questions. This defiance caused tempers to flare, and at one point the chamber voted to treat Fouquet as a "voluntary mute," meaning that the chamber would accept as proven all the charges for which he had undergone interrogation and which he refused by his silence to answer. The effect would be to foreclose any effort by Fouquet to defend himself against the accusations.[4] Perhaps anticipating this move, Fouquet had argued that the king had long ago pardoned him for any offenses of which he might be guilty. If this pardon was to be disregarded, then parlement, not the chamber, should sit in judgment on him.[5] While royal decrees in early July reaffirmed the jurisdiction of the chamber, the crown did concede to Fouquet having supervised access to writing materials to prepare his motions and defenses.[6]

The Fouquet women added to this unfolding melodrama. On July 19, Fouquet's mother, wife, and eldest daughter (Madame de Charost) appeared before the Parlement of Paris. Kneeling on the parquet, they demanded justice for the former superintendant. Their written petition, read aloud in court, challenged the chamber's jurisdiction over Fouquet and asked the parlement to nullify the chamber's actions and to take charge of the process brought against him. On July 27, the parlement took up the jurisdictional question, as well as Fouquet's requests for counsel and for access to his papers.

Ironically, Fouquet's demand that he be tried before the Parlement of Paris by virtue of his former membership in that body as *procureur général* reopened another point of contention between the crown and the magistrates. Although Fouquet asserted this right by virtue of his long tenure in parlement, the accusations against him stemmed from his duties as superintendant of finance. So the parlement would have been judging him in that capacity, which would have contradicted a longstanding insistence by the crown that the court's jurisdiction did not extend to the high administrative and financial activities of the state. This quarrel, which stretched back at least to the time of Sully and Henri IV, was part and parcel of the claims by parlement and its sister courts to hold the financial agents of the crown accountable for their activities, a power the crown had vehemently rejected and opposed on many occasions. In effect, Fouquet was inviting the magistrates to reopen the debate. The judges were clearly embarrassed. Acting on these petitions would be a direct affront to the king. Yet they were not prepared, as a matter of institutional standing, to concede or legitimize the exceptional jurisdiction of the chamber. So the decision was made to refer the entire matter to the king, to determine if he wished them to deliberate on Fouquet's motions.[7]

While the judges were waiting on the king's pleasure, Madame Fouquet the Younger struck again. At the end of July, she wrote a long open letter to King Louis. In it, she repeated the usual arguments about the chamber's lack of jurisdiction, but she also made a sensational charge of her own. She accused Colbert of misleading the king, of distorting the evidence against her husband, of having publicly advocated his execution, and having improperly involved himself in the proceedings when everyone knew that for the past six years he had been the "declared enemy" of her husband. For good measure, she urged the king to investigate how Colbert had amassed his own fortune, which she estimated at 12 million livres, and implied that Colbert had seized her husband's papers to conceal his own wrongdoing.[8]

All of these actions forced Louis XIV to intervene directly. On August 2, a parlementary delegation including Guillaume de Lamoignon and François-Théodore de Nesmond was summoned to an audience at the palace of Saint-Germain-en-Laye. The king received them in his own office (*cabinet*) in the company of Séguier, maréchal Turenne, and other high-ranking officials. Speaking first, Séguier reiterated that the king had already issued several orders in council confirming the powers of the chamber and denying to Fouquet any claims of exemption from its jurisdiction. In the future, parlement was not to accept any petition concerning those proceedings under pain of incurring the royal wrath (*indignation*). The king then added a few sentences to confirm Séguier's warning. Perhaps betraying some unease with one of the key assertions of Fouquet and his supporters, he also felt obliged to reply to the charge that Colbert had rifled through Fouquet's papers. It was on his direct orders, the king insisted, that Colbert had examined Fouquet's files immediately after his arrest, removing only those documents involving secrets of state. The delegation raised no objections to any of this. To Lamoignon's assurances that the court would act according to his wishes in the future, the king answered that he had made known his will and had no doubt that it would be obeyed.[9]

Whatever gratification the chamber may have felt about the reaffirmation of its authority, it now had to deal with Fouquet's demands as it moved the process along. Although it spent much of the summer on other cases and investigations, it also devoted some time to debating Fouquet's pending requests. In early September the chamber agreed that Fouquet was entitled to have counsel to help in his defense. Fouquet responded by asking once more for access to his papers: of what use was counsel if he was denied use of the documents that would provide the basis for a defense? It was a strong argument, but for the moment the chamber would only rule that that Fouquet could review the various inventories of his papers and files drawn up at the time of his arrest.[10]

Shortly after this last decision, the chamber met and agreed to Fouquet's nomination of two senior councilors in parlement, Barthélemy Auzanet and Jean-Marie Lhoste, as his legal advisers. What was more contentious was whether they would be permitted to confer with their client without auditors or court officers present. The question caused a deep divide in the chamber. Poncet argued against such access: if Fouquet were accused only of financial crimes, such would be the normal procedure. But he was also accused of high treason, a crime of state, and in such instances, the right of consultation was limited, based on a precedent some years before whereby the accused in that earlier case could only communicate with counsel in the presence of the clerk of the court. Henri Pussort, while agreeing with Poncet's recommendation, could not refrain from noting that under Roman law, no counsel was permitted in cases of treason. Eight other judges, including Nesmond, quickly aligned themselves with Poncet and Pussort.[11]

Surprisingly, Renard, Poncet's fellow interrogator, broke with his colleague, arguing that Fouquet could only have full confidence in his attorneys if they were both freely chosen and accessible without constraints. Seven other judges agreed with Renard, so the division stood at ten against free access to counsel, eight for such access.

Lamoignon now rose to speak. He was surprisingly dismissive of the "crime of state" about which Poncet and Pussort had waxed eloquent. He argued that Fouquet was charged primarily with financial offenses and that the "crime of state" arose out of those other charges, and was part of the mix, simply an ancillary matter (*incident*). Because the chief elements of Fouquet's offenses were financial, he should be allowed unfettered communication with his legal advisers (as would be the case in an ordinary criminal trial). Lamoignon's arguments swayed the remaining judges, and the final vote was twelve for such access, ten against.[12]

The whole issue must have been difficult for Lamoignon in a personal sense, as he had had been among those Fouquet named as potential allies in the Saint-

Mandé plan.[13] Lamoignon's stance certainly troubled Colbert; shortly afterward, he asked Lamoignon how he thought the case was developing against Fouquet. Lamoignon answered coldly that a judge only offered his opinion once, and that was from the bench.[14]

The provision of counsel meant that Fouquet now had his own channel of communication with the chamber, as well as a source of information about its proceedings. Some days afterward, the chamber made another equally important decision. Thus far, the investigation had included three stages: the examination of papers and documents; the interrogation of Fouquet; and his confrontation with "witnesses"—29 financiers under arrest—which had taken place, with very little to show for it, from mid-July to early September.[15] Now the question arose about procedures to be used for the balance of the trial. Once again, Lamoignon took the lead. There were a large number of charges involved, and, he pointed out, the crown was seeking both to punish Fouquet for his crimes and to obtain restitution of the funds misappropriated or diverted by the superintendant, a civil matter in law. The complexity of such a "mixed" case, as Lamoignon put it, was best managed by using a procedure normally reserved for civil cases: the principal vehicle for the court's deliberations would be written accusations and written defenses making use of the evidence accumulated. The chamber decided to follow Lamoignon's advice, setting the stage for a long and drawn-out proceeding.[16]

The next step in the organization of the trial was the appointment of two judges to act as "reporters" (*rapporteurs*). The rapporteurs were responsible for reviewing all the evidence gathered by the investigating magistrates, for interviewing the accused and other witnesses for additional clarification or verification of the matters at hand, and for advising the chamber on motions or requests made by either the royal procureur or the defendant. At the completion of the trial they were to provide their colleagues with an evaluation of the prosecution's case and, in the event of a guilty verdict, recommendations for sentencing. Given the size and scale of the *affaire Fouquet*, the role of the rapporteurs would be critical in guiding their fellow magistrates through the maze of charges and the mass of evidence accumulated to sustain them.

Normally, the presiding judge would recommend the rapporteurs for appointment by the court, and traditionally a defendant could request the disqualification of the designees for cause, such as bias or ties to the prosecution. In this case, however, the royal council intervened and provided Lamoignon with its choices for this role: Jacques Le Cormier de Sainte-Hélène, a magistrate seconded to the chamber from the Parlement of Rouen, and Olivier Lefèvre d'Ormesson, one of the *maîtres des requêtes* sitting on the court. The Fouquet women immediately objected to these candidates: Sainte-Hélène had ties to Colbert, while Ormesson had spent several months earlier in the year working with Louis Berryer, Colbert's lieutenant, on the examination of the treasury records and on the proceedings against Jeannin de Castille and against Bruant in absentia. It could be assumed that he might be biased against the superintendant as a result.[17]

Lamoignon, conscious of the image of the chamber and respectful of normal usages, tried to persuade the king to withdraw the nominations: the appearance of impartiality was important, especially in a criminal proceeding. But Louis and his advisers, notably Colbert and Michel Le Tellier, were not to be swayed: the objections by the Fouquets were proof positive that the crown had made the right choice. The Fouquets feared, said the king, "the well-known integrity of these magistrates, and that fear is one more reason to name them."[18] Lamoignon tried to reason with the king: ordinarily, he pointed out, an accused had to show cause to remove a judge, but not a rapporteur, since everyone understood that a rapporteur's findings would carry great weight with his fellow judges. Again, the answer was simple. This was the royal will. "Say I commanded you to do this."[19] Before leaving the Louvre, Lamoignon confronted Colbert and Le Tellier once more with his objections to this unorthodox procedure, and the bad light it would cast on the chamber. The ministers would give him no satisfaction.[20] After resisting for more than a week, and unable to find his way around the royal fiat, Lamoignon reluctantly presented the crown's nominations to the court on October 22.[21]

As the Fouquet ladies had anticipated, Sainte-Hélène was to show little independence of thought and throughout the many months of the trial often seemed aligned with the royal prosecutors. But Olivier d'Ormesson was to behave quite differently, so much so that in retrospect the failure of the Fouquet ladies to secure his recusal was an unintended victory for the superintendant, perhaps the crucial one.

Olivier Lefèvre d'Ormesson's background was similar to Fouquet's. The Lefèvre d'Ormesson clan sprang from non-noble stock, in origin tenant farmers of the noble house of Montmorency in the hamlet of Ormesson in the Île de France. Under the patronage of the Montmorencys, members of the family in the course of the sixteenth and early seventeenth centuries had climbed slowly through the ranks of the judiciary and royal administration to positions of prominence.

André d'Ormesson (1577–1665), the father of Olivier, had followed the usual *cursus honorum* for a *robin* aspiring to royal service. At the age of 23 he became a member of the Parlement of Paris, and in 1604 a maître des requêtes; by 1615 he had become a councilor of state and was entrusted with important tasks including service on the *chambre de justice* of 1624–1625 investigating financial irregularities allegedly committed by the financier François de Castille de Villemareuil (Madame Fouquet's grandfather). André d'Ormesson had remained as faithful as he could to the crown during the Fronde. By the time of the Fouquet trial, André was the dean (i.e., senior serving councilor) on the conseil d'État and a man much admired by his contemporaries for his integrity.[22]

The Ormessons, like the Fouquets and the Séguiers, were also known for their piety and their participation in the Catholic reform movement in France, and through a marriage several generations earlier, they could even claim a tie to Saint Francis de Paule (d. 1507), founder of the Minime fathers. Three of André's daughters entered religious life, while his second son Nicolas, the elder brother of Olivier, became a Minime monk.[23]

Olivier d'Ormesson, born in December 1616, the third of André's four sons, was nearly two years Fouquet's junior. The death of his oldest brother in 1636 and the decision of Nicolas d'Ormesson to enter the Church made Olivier the candidate to head the family in the next generation—a remarkable parallel to Fouquet's early career. After finishing his studies, Olivier became a member of parlement at the age of 20; by 1643, he had joined the ranks of maîtres des requêtes. Olivier was under the normal age for this post, but his father's influence, and the help of chancellor Séguier, took care of this obstacle.[24]

The world of the judicial and royal administrative hierarchy in Paris was a small and closed one, as was the world of the aristocratic "devouts" in which both families circulated. The Fouquet and Ormesson families would certainly have mingled both professionally and socially. Olivier and Fouquet had probably been acquainted since their early years, although there is nothing to suggest that they had ever been friends.

One important link between the two would have been their ties to Madame de Sévigné. Olivier's late sister Marie (1606–1659) had been married to Philippe de Coulanges (1595–1659). That couple had helped raise Philippe's orphaned niece, Marie de Rabutin-Chantal, the future Madame de Sévigné, who would become one of Fouquet's most devoted friends, as well as a close friend to Olivier. One can well imagine that Fouquet and Olivier encountered one another from time to time in the company of Madame de Sévigné. André and Olivier d'Ormesson, like the Fouquets, were bibliophiles and cultivated men. Olivier in particular enjoyed salon culture and was a habitué of the salon of Guillaume de Lamoignon. As Fouquet was also a frequenter of the fashionable salons of Paris, he and Olivier d'Ormesson may have had mutual acquaintances in such circles.[25]

As noted above, Fouquet and Ormesson crossed paths in January 1650, when

Olivier was made Fouquet's deputy as intendant for the *généralité* of Paris.[26] Unfortunately, no records of Olivier's activities in that post survive, or of the interaction between the two men. One scholar has noted, however, that Fouquet was away from Paris in the field during much of this period, leaving Olivier to function on his own in this post.[27] In any case, their official tie would have been sundered when Fouquet took up his new position as procureur général in November 1650.

In 1656 Olivier was appointed as an intendant in Picardy, this time working with the royal armies in the field under maréchal Turenne, a nomination that might have been supported by Séguier, although Le Tellier would have had the last word. Turenne, never an easy master, paid tribute to Ormesson's diligence in securing him the necessary money and supplies to pursue the campaign that ended with the Battle of the Dunes outside Dunkirk in June 1658—an effort in which Fouquet, as noted above, was also a participant. Ormesson's performance earned him the praise of Anne of Austria and the lifelong friendship of Turenne.[28]

Given his record, his father's service, and Séguier's patronage, Ormesson's appointment to the chambre de justice was a logical one. He was also on good terms with Fouquet's rival, Le Tellier, and actually learned of his designation as rapporteur from his friend Claude Le Pelletier, at that time a president in the Parlement of Paris and a protégé (and cousin) of Le Tellier.[29] In light of these ties, the Fouquets' objection to Ormesson's serving as a rapporteur is not hard to understand and probably went beyond the stated reasons. Ironically, Colbert had originally had some reservations about Ormesson, whom he characterized as a man of limited intelligence (*esprit borné*) and a creature of Lamoignon's. Nevertheless, Colbert had satisfied himself that Ormesson's initial exposure to the irregularities evidenced in the registers of the royal treasurers had brought him around to the crown's point of view.[30] As for Ormesson, he was honest enough to note that the king's selection of rapporteurs was controversial, with some faulting the king for interfering and others approving his action.[31]

No sooner had Ormesson assumed his new post than he became embroiled in a procedural debate instigated by Talon, the royal procureur général. Since Fouquet had not produced his defenses or any evidence in his favor within the time stipulated by the court, Talon moved that Fouquet be foreclosed and that the chamber proceed to the judgment phase of the trial. But when the writ to this effect was served on Fouquet, the defendant objected that he had never received a copy of the October 5 order that had set the process in motion: the order of foreclosure should therefore be rescinded. For good measure, Fouquet added that he could hardly be expected to reply to charges not yet submitted by the prosecution or to provide evidence when he was denied access to his papers. Weeks of wrangling in the chamber produced little in the way of agreement among the judges. For his part, Lamoignon heaped much of the blame on Talon for this procedural imbroglio, which, it was widely held, stemmed from Talon's neglect of his duties while in the throes of a passionate love affair, one that had made him the laughingstock of the Palais de justice. In the end, the court accepted Fouquet's arguments and granted him an extension.[32]

Once more Lamoignon had signaled a respect for process and an evident resistance to the crown's attempts to circumvent judicial procedures. Lamoignon may have had other motives as well: one scholar has suggested that Lamoignon may have wished to signal his distaste for certain measures taken by the royal government, such as recent, arbitrary changes in the return on annuities (*rentes*) and a reduction of judicial salaries (*gages*).[33] In any case, Lamoignon's approach did not augur well for the crown's hopes of a quick trial and a foreordained verdict. So once more, the king intervened. In early December, Lamoignon was again summoned to the royal presence. Lamoignon, the king observed, was attempting to do two jobs at once, presiding over the chamber as well as tending to his normal duties in the Parlement of Paris. This was too much for one man, the king opined. To relieve Lamoignon, the king declared, Séguier would preside over its sessions.[34]

On December 11 Séguier took his seat on the chamber for the first time in months. For the sake of the outside world, appearances were preserved: Lamoignon made a flowery speech of welcome. But Séguier announced shortly thereafter that the chamber, which had been meeting in the afternoon, would meet henceforth at nine every morning. Everyone understood that this arrangement would exclude Lamoignon from further participation, since he could not leave parlement at that hour to meet with the chamber.[35]

This outcome was not well received by many of Lamoignon's colleagues in the chamber. Ormesson noted in his diary that the entire maneuver was put down to the instigators (*premiers mobiles*) behind the chamber who now hoped, with Lamoignon gone, to steer it in the direction they wanted.[36] At the same time, the rapporteur observed, many felt that Lamoignon had been spared a heavy burden by showing himself to be a magistrate who was "firm and independent."[37] Somewhat later, when he realized the bad impression made by Lamoignon's exclusion, Colbert suggested that Lamoignon return to the chamber, perhaps as co-president with Séguier. Lamoignon refused, saying, "I have washed my hands of it."[38] He feared, wrote a biographer, that the chamber had lost the most important characteristic of a court, impartiality, and had become instead a vehicle "in the hand of the ministers of state for destroying their enemies."[39]

Although the substitution of Séguier for Lamoignon was to prove a major setback for Fouquet's defenders, Lamoignon's legacy was to prove invaluable for the former superintendant. Under his leadership, the chamber had already provided Fouquet with access to writing materials; had authorized the provision of counsel; and had agreed that Fouquet was at least entitled to examine the inventories of his papers and documents.

Fouquet was to make good use of those decisions in organizing his defense. He later explained to Ormesson that he wrote all of his own motions and pleadings. His faithful doctor, Pecquet, who shared his captivity, would recopy them and correct any grammatical or spelling errors. His two outside counselors would sometimes read the drafts and make occasional small editorial suggestions before the documents were put in final form. The counselors' chief responsibility, however, was to interact with the outside world, conveying Fouquet's writings to the court. Somewhat later, when Fouquet was finally permitted access to his papers, his lawyers reviewed the documents he required and briefed him on their contents—throughout the trial the superintendant's papers were held at the Louvre and had to be consulted there.[40]

Even with these limitations, Fouquet quickly demonstrated that he was a formidable adversary and one who intended to wrest control of the narrative away from his opponents. He did so by making his defenses public even before the chamber saw them. In late November 1662, he produced a pamphlet, "Extracts from the Reports on the Inventories of the Documents [found] at the Houses of M. Fouquet and His Clerks." In it, he attacked the many internal inconsistencies in the reports, flagged the irregularities in the chain of custody of his papers, and charged that his files had been tampered with. Because of the custodial questions, Fouquet argued, it was not possible to determine which documents had actually been found in his residences (or those of his clerks), which ones had been removed (thereby impeding his defense), and which ones had been planted to implicate him. In this last category Fouquet placed the notorious pension on the gabelle, which had been "found" by Colbert but missed in the first search of Fouquet's office at Saint-Mandé.

The specifics ran on for hundreds of pages, including comments on some of the well-publicized charges against him, but the central theme of the presentation was an attack on Colbert's integrity. Colbert, he insisted, was his true adversary (*partie*) in the proceeding; Colbert had attempted to undermine him with Mazarin and had poisoned the king's mind against him. And Colbert, of course, had taken charge of the papers and evidence being used against him.[41] Fouquet's accusations against Colbert may have received an unintended boost from another blunder on the part of his adversaries. The intercepted copy of Colbert's 1659 memorandum to Mazarin attacking Fouquet had been found among Fouquet's papers, and an indignant Colbert had had Gourville questioned about it. The exposure of this memorandum lent credibility to Fouquet's attempt to portray Colbert as someone who had been scheming against him for a long time.[42]

Fouquet's first lengthy production was followed within weeks by a second one, "Memoirs and Comments on [events] from September 5, 1661, to December 9, 1662," which provided a narrative from Fouquet's arrest to the moment that Séguier resumed the presidency of the chamber. Here, too, the stars were Colbert and Talon, with accounts of Fouquet's various requests to the chamber and the refusal to allow him to have writing materials to prepare his defense, the attempt to try him as a "mute," and other indications of their presumed malice. All of this was intended to show that Fouquet from the beginning had been denied the normal protections accorded a suspect or defendant in criminal proceedings.[43]

The Fouquets took these accusations a step further in January 1663, when Fouquet's wife and mother appeared before the doors of the chamber and asked to be heard. Fearing that the women were about to request that he be excused from further participation in Fouquet's trial, Séguier forbade the ushers to admit them. Talon rose to the occasion by delivering a learned disquisition on the precedents establishing that the chancellor could not be removed. Thwarted in their attempt to offer their petition to the assembled court, the Fouquet women presented themselves at Ormesson's residence that evening to hand it to him.

Séguier's alarm had been premature: the petition did not concern him. Instead, it demanded that Fouquet have access to all of the papers listed in the inventories he had been provided; it also called for the recusal of Joseph Foucault, the clerk of the court. Several days later, the Fouquet ladies followed up with a second petition, repeating the earlier request for access to Fouquet's papers and asking for the recusal of Daniel Voysin and Henri Pussort and the dismissal of Foucault. In the commotion that followed, Le Tellier spoke with Ormesson, Foucault spoke with Colbert, Colbert spoke with the king, and the king ordered Talon to bring any future request to recuse Séguier directly to him.[44]

These petitions were accompanied by a memorandum from Fouquet claiming Colbert had pillaged his papers to hide the record of the enormous sums that had passed through the cardinal's hands via Colbert's. He also accused Colbert once again of removing from his records all the letters and orders from Mazarin that would exonerate him, adding that the same papers would show that either Colbert or Berryer were collaborators of the cardinal on most of his financial transactions. Once more, Fouquet denied the competence of the chamber and asserted his right to be judged either by the king directly, in accordance with his commission as superintendant of finances, or alternatively by parlement as a former member of the court. Fouquet bundled these demands with a request that Talon, Voysin, and Pussort be removed from his case. Talon, he argued, was notoriously his enemy and had allowed himself to be manipulated by Colbert; Voysin was Talon's brother-in-law; Pussort was Colbert's uncle. These were sufficient reasons for the three to be excused from the chamber.[45]

Fouquet's requests gave rise to several days of earnest debate among the judges of the chamber at the end of January. Ormesson initially maintained that since Fouquet refused to recognize the chamber's jurisdiction, he had no right to petition the court to remove any of the judges. Séguier used the occasion to criticize the chamber for allowing Fouquet counsel and access to inventories without insisting on his recognition of its authority. Other judges argued that the court's competence did not depend on Fouquet's recognition; the king had affirmed their mandate, and they should exercise it by pronouncing on Fouquet's requests, a point of view that finally carried the day.

Talon was then summoned to argue against the motion to dismiss him. Talon insisted that he and Fouquet were not enemies, and there was a question in law about whether a royal procureur could be recused by a defendant. Ormesson opined that in a civil matter, recusal might be possible, but bad will between a defendant and a prosecutor, hardly unusual in a criminal trial, should not be grounds for removal. In the end, the judges split down the middle, and by one vote Talon kept his appointment. Then it was Foucault's turn to defend himself against the accusation that he had tampered with or removed pieces of evidence. Despite the unease of several of the other judges, Ormesson was not convinced and argued that dismissing Foucault on such grounds at this stage was tantamount to deciding the outcome of the trial. So Foucault was allowed to stay.[46]

The arguments against Pussort's participation were much stronger. He was Colbert's uncle and close collaborator, and Colbert's involvement could hardly be overstated. Searching for a diplomatic way out, Ormesson noted that Colbert's interest in the case was at the king's direct orders and thus could not be considered improper. At the same time, to maintain the appearance of judicial impartiality, Pussort should consider stepping down voluntarily. Only four other judges agreed with Ormesson, and Pussort certainly had no intention of leaving on his own. So he remained. The motion against Voysin was dismissed without debate, perhaps because in a judicial system with so many interconnected participants, a simple kinship tie to the prosecutor or other judges was hardly unusual.[47]

Fouquet's demand to have access to all of his papers and files and to the other documents available to the prosecution, such as the treasury registers, was debated in early February. The judges now found themselves dealing with the implications and inconveniences of the overly broad investigation put into motion by Colbert. The mass of material involved was enormous. Ormesson pointed out that there were an estimated 60,000 documents or papers impounded by the crown, of which, in his estimate, 50,000 were irrelevant to the charges against Fouquet. Allowing Fouquet and his counsel to pore through all of this meant the trial would never come to judgment. The ensuing debate was contentious. Some judges suggested that Fouquet only be allowed to see those documents entered into evidence in support of charges (which, as Ormesson pointed out, had not yet been finalized). That Fouquet was entitled to review such documentation was beyond question, but, as some judges noted, a defendant would traditionally have the right to examine any available files to identify those that might be of use in a defense. Sainte-Hélène argued that Fouquet's access should be restricted to specific materials he could identify. Pussort, still smarting from the attempt to recuse him, seconded this position with such vehemence that several of his colleagues were visibly startled. A surprisingly large bloc of judges, six or seven, favored allowing Fouquet unconditional access to all of the seized files. In the end, the court decided, at Ormesson's recommendation, to allow Fouquet to review all the materials used against him and confirmed his right to see any other papers which were listed in the various inventories and registers.[48]

What this judgment of Solomon might involve in practice became apparent some weeks later, in early April, when Fouquet submitted a request for the registers kept by three of his "clerks," Barthélemy Hervart, Colbert, and Guillaume de Bordeaux, another of Mazarin's confidants.[49] Talon immediately objected; this meant turning over 10,000 to 12,000 documents and would delay the process indefinitely. Once more the debate in the court was vociferous, and the final decision was that Fouquet had to specify the materials he wanted. At the same time, the chamber judges admitted this was difficult, because the papers in question were bundled up and only identified in general terms in the inventories. If this was in some sense a loss for Fouquet, at the very least it made the judges acknowledge the cavalier organization of much of the potential evidence, as Fouquet had argued earlier.[50]

At the same time, the chamber imposed yet another handicap on Fouquet. Despite his protests, he was still not allowed direct access to the documents he required. Instead, his counselors were obliged to examine them at the Louvre and then report to Fouquet on their contents. Fouquet had pointed out the inadequacies of this arrangement: his counselors were not familiar with the content of these papers, nor would they recognize the handwriting of various participants, including Mazarin. But his pleadings were overruled. He would have to make do with the concessions the court had already granted.[51]

While these motions were under consideration, yet another broadside by Fouquet was offered to the public. After the first of Fouquet's publications in late November 1662, Colbert's police had seized many of the copies and arrested the printers.[52] Refusing to be intimidated, the Fouquet women looked for alternative printing sites and set up a clandestine press on a family estate at Montreuil-sous-Bois, just outside Paris. Eventually, this would be supplemented with four other sites for printing and distribution, two in Paris, one at Rouen, and another in Champagne.[53]

This latest fruit of these efforts, "Defenses on All the Points of My Trial," which appeared in late January or early February 1663, addressed the substance of the accusations against Fouquet. The various interrogations, confrontations with "witnesses," and preliminary motions filed by Talon had given Fouquet a thorough picture of the prosecution's case. The potential charges could be divided into separate areas including embezzlement, unauthorized transactions, accepting bribes to arrange transactions, improper participation in transactions, trafficking in treasury obligations, engaging in transactions at illegal rates of interest, overall corruption and mismanagement in the exercise of his office, and high treason. Fouquet picked these accusations apart, one by one, instance by instance, in a document that ran for hundreds of pages. He insisted that some of the transactions cited were not his but Servien's; others were due to wartime necessity in the late 1650s when the state would accept almost any terms to stay solvent. In some instances, his participation was nothing more than an authorized means of reimbursing himself for money he had lent to the crown under those selfsame wartime conditions. Other matters that appeared corrupt or questionable seemed so to the uninitiated because of the complexities of the financial system. The argument of necessity of state was used to ridicule the charge that it was illegal for him as superintendant (and therefore as a director of payments) to make advances of his own funds to the crown. Mazarin had often requested such loans, as had Colbert, who had spoken to him about such a transaction on the evening before his arrest.[54] With respect to other accusations, Fouquet insisted that he required direct access to his own papers, still denied him, to justify himself.[55]

The star of Fouquet's recital, however, was still Mazarin. Rather than challenge the prosecution's portrayal of state finances in preceding decades as inherently corrupt and mismanaged, Fouquet simply reformulated the narrative. Indeed, those years of civil war and desperate struggle against a tenacious Spanish foe had encompassed all of the irregularities described by the prosecution. But he himself was neither responsible for the disorders in question nor was he their chief beneficiary. That, notoriously, was Mazarin's role, and Mazarin stands at the center of Fouquet's lengthy apologia. He reminded his readers that Mazarin was all powerful during those years and that he and the other accused wrongdoers were operating under Mazarin's "direct and absolute authority."[56] Wartime necessity certainly lay behind many of the questionable transactions at issue. Always, however, they had been sanctioned by the cardinal, who, he stressed, was often careless about the formalities. This could be proven from the letters and orders from the cardinal among his own papers, which he had not yet been allowed to access. In all cases, "I repeat it again: I have done nothing except by the order, agreement, and approval of the cardinal."[57]

If this entire machinery of corruption and inefficiency was not operating for Fouquet's benefit, then for whose benefit was it? Once more, Mazarin takes center stage. It was well known, Fouquet asserted early in his presentation, that Mazarin had come back from exile in 1653 a virtual pauper, but somehow he had died in 1661 extremely rich, and with no public accounting of the scale of that fortune—an omission he credited to Colbert's machinations.[58] The explanation for this incredible turn of the wheel in Mazarin's favor lay precisely in the matters before the chamber. During the years of war, Mazarin under assumed names had participated in consortiums selling food and munitions to the state; he had also approved the various financial arrangements used to pay for some of this.[59] It was Mazarin, not Fouquet, who had benefited from bribes in the form of unauthorized pensions from financing contracts, such as the now notorious pension for 120,000 livres on the gabelle.[60] For good measure, Fouquet added the accusation that Colbert and Foucault had inserted that document into his papers to falsely implicate him.[61] It was Mazarin, not Fouquet, who dabbled in the re-presentation of old treasury bills (*billets*); sometimes Fouquet had followed Mazarin's orders in such affairs, and at other times Hervart or Servien had acted at the cardinal's behest. But an examination of these transactions had to be done individually to determine the exact circumstances giving rise to them, and to answer accusations directed against him, he needed full access to his papers.[62]

Why was he really on trial? Because, Fouquet explained, he had been sacrificed to the ambitions of the "servant" (*domestique*) who had been Mazarin's bookkeeper, namely Colbert, who hoped to take the superintendant's place and who was using Talon, his sworn enemy, to bring him down.[63] Colbert had prevented any probating of Mazarin's vast estate, thus concealing from the public the obvious questions.[64] With the help of Berryer and Foucault, Colbert had rifled Fouquet's papers, planted others, and falsified accounts.[65] Fouquet knew this would be a difficult accusation to rebut as the lack of detailed inventories made it impossible to determine what had really been found among his papers, what might have been added later (e.g., the pension on the gabelle), and what might have been removed (Mazarin's written orders and letters).

In making these assertions about Mazarin, Fouquet may have counted on the familiarity of many of his judges with two earlier inquiries into Mazarin's fortune. In January 1649, during the first phase of the Fronde, the Parlement of Paris had opened an inquiry into Mazarin's finances and had ordered an examination of the books of several prominent bankers who were close to the cardinal. This inquiry was dropped in March 1649, after the Peace of Rueil. A second parlementary inquiry was opened in March 1651, once more focusing on the activities of bankers close to Mazarin, and also came to naught with the winding down of the Fronde of the Princes. Both inquiries, however, revealed widespread corruption and questionable financial dealings by Mazarin, acting through his collaborators and usually disguising his participation by the use of false names and proxies. The types of transactions uncovered for this earlier period were virtually identical in form to the ones Fouquet described for the period after Mazarin's return to power at the end of the Fronde. In some cases, notably that of Hervart, the same partners were involved. Ironically, during the 1651 inquiry, Fouquet, as procureur général, had worked surreptitiously with Colbert to delay and derail the investigation.[66] The judges on the chamber panel, at least those drawn from the Paris courts and the central administration, would certainly have been familiar with the findings of those earlier inquiries. As described by Fouquet, Mazarin's activities in the later 1650s followed the same patterns and often involved the same supporting cast. Those earlier findings would thus lend plausibility to Fouquet's narrative.

To drive home the contrast between his actions and those of Mazarin, Fouquet insisted that his papers would also show that he was not really rich. In fact, he was heavily in debt, to the tune of about 14 million livres, much of it borrowed for use by the crown. His personal expenditures had been financed by his income, about 350,000 livres annually, and by the use of his wife's fortune, including the sale of some landed properties.[67]

For good measure, Fouquet added somewhat piously that he, too, had been troubled by many of Mazarin's deeds and after the cardinal's death had reviewed all of these irregularities with the king. He and the king had agreed that in the future the state's finances had to be managed in an orderly fashion. Repeating yet again his earlier claim, he insisted that the king had pardoned him any part he might have had in Mazarin's misdeeds.[68] His accusers knew very well what the truth was, but they preferred to act like "Scribes and Pharisees."[69]

As a counterpoint to this fierce attack on Fouquet's adversaries, Fouquet's wife made another impassioned public plea to Louis XIV, this time asking the king for mercy in the name of "the holy Virgin Mary, Mother of God." As the king had received God's blessings through her intercession, so too he should accord his mercy to her fallen husband. Louis was not moved.[70]

All of these pleas, protests, and attacks had begun to rattle the prosecutors, who sensed that public opinion was moving against them. Looking for scapegoats, Colbert's police searched far and wide to pick up the printers working on behalf of the Fouquets. During the debates on allowing Fouquet access to his papers, Talon had moved to deprive Fouquet of counsel. The reasoning behind Talon's request was simple: Fouquet's counselors, well-respected and prominent members of the bar, had convinced themselves, and in the process, many others, of three things: that Fouquet's prosecution was simply a plot on the part of his enemies; that those same enemies had spared no pains to destroy him, even tampering with evidence; and that Fouquet had become a virtual saint in response to his misfortunes. Indeed, Fouquet's lawyers were insisting that by defending so illustrious a person unfairly accused, they were acting in the best interest of the state.[71] Talon, however, was not convincing. His motion was denied after Ormesson pronounced it unjust.[72]

Having failed to remove Fouquet's counsel, the crown looked elsewhere to strike at Fouquet's defenders. By midsummer, Pellisson had fallen under suspicion as the possible author of the pro-Fouquet tracts circulating in Paris (see chapter 4). The royal response was to revoke the visiting privileges of Pellisson's mother and to forbid any other communication between the two, on suspicion that the elderly lady was smuggling these writings out of the Bastille.[73]

Such frantic measures did not halt the drift of opinion. From far-off Autun, a royal official advised Colbert that spring that "the only thing people talk about here is the injustice done to M. Fouquet."[74]

CHAPTER 6

To Do Justice without Consideration of Fortune or Self-Interest

During the early months of 1663, while the chamber debated Fouquet's many motions, Talon and his associates were scrambling to put the charges against him and supporting documentation in final form. Part of the delay was due to a need to prepare the evidence derived from the registers of the royal treasurers, which had been seized some months earlier. Berryer and Foucault often went off on tangents, and Talon was sometimes caught in the middle, trying to reconcile the irreconcilable. As Ormesson commented caustically, it was a case of too many cooks in the kitchen.[1]

Finally, on April 10, Ormesson, as *rapporteur*, began reading aloud to the chamber Talon's charges against Fouquet and the supporting documentation. The chamber was to devote 42 sessions to this task, a chore that was not finished until mid-July. Once again, the prosecution went beyond criminal charges to attempt a broad narrative of the previous decade of French history. Talon's brief opened by recalling the heavy burdens of a long and difficult war imposed on French taxpayers and the failure of a final peace to achieve its hoped-for territorial compensations (i.e., the Franche-Comté and the Spanish Netherlands). All of this was blamed on Fouquet, who used his twin offices of superintendant of finance and *procureur général* first to deprive the king of essential resources at a critical moment and then to protect his collaborators from the long arm of the law. Accusations of embezzlement, self-dealing, and falsification of accounts and records were embellished with the specific examples already widely publicized: the pension on the salt tax (*gabelle*), the participation in the *marc d'or* transaction, the infamous diversion of 6 million livres worth of bills from the treasury, and so forth.

Talon also addressed two of the difficulties in proving his charges. The first was that the questioning of the contractors, who, along with the royal treasurers, were presumably Fouquet's accomplices, had yielded little that directly tied Fouquet to these crimes. That was, Talon argued, because the contractors could not implicate Fouquet without incriminating themselves. The second was the ability of Fouquet to find alternative narratives to explain the transactions imputed to him as crimes. The real proof of his guilt was by deduction from his extravagant lifestyle. The defendant's vast expenditures (although not quantified) could not be explained unless he had been embezzling state funds. All of this rhetoric was a prelude to the great "crime of state," his fortification of Belle-Isle and intention to use it as a base for a rebellion against the crown, as set out in the "Plan of Saint-Mandé." Indeed, Talon argued, the clandestine printing of Fouquet's defense was itself part of the plot, an attempt to stir up sedition.[2]

Fouquet's initial response to Talon had been surreptitiously printed and circulated in June 1663, before the formal reading of the charges was even finished. It so stung Talon that he felt obliged to issue a rejoinder, which in turn was followed by yet another rebuttal by Fouquet. Taken together, these exchanges in the summer of 1663 encompassed all the charges leveled at Fouquet and his standard responses.[3] In his presentations, Talon ridiculed Fouquet's narrative of himself as a man who virtually saved the state in the previous decade and answered some of Fouquet's criticisms of the prosecution. He denounced as slanderous Fouquet's accusation that his papers had been tampered with and accused the Fouquet family and their close associates of destroying incriminating documents at Saint-Mandé and elsewhere before royal officers could take custody of them. He also challenged Fouquet on one glaring inconsistency in his version of events: Fouquet had insisted that Mazarin rarely put his orders in writing, but he also maintained that many hundreds of letters and orders from Mazarin approving or authorizing his actions had been removed from his files. How could both of these statements be true? As for Fouquet's claims that he had gone into debt to serve the crown, Talon asserted that the debts were fictitious and Fouquet's assets had been hidden to conceal the fruits of his crimes.[4]

In his very lengthy replies, Fouquet restated many of his positions, often adding details that put his accusers in an unflattering light. The infamous 120,000 livres pension on the salt tax, he insisted, had been worked out between Mazarin and Claude Girardin, one of the cardinal's trusted financial associates, for the cardinal's benefit. Why had Girardin, who arranged the syndicate, not been questioned about this?[5] In the matter of the supposed scheme to embezzle 6 million livres, the testimonies of Nicolas Jeannin de Castille and Martin Tabouret (another financier) were highly suspect. Jeannin de Castille, a good man but easily intimidated, had only confessed to this crime on his third interrogation, after rounds of threats from Berryer. Tabouret had been promised immunity from all other crimes he might have committed in return for his testimony. Their statements were therefore unreliable. Another accusation of misappropriation of funds rested on documents dated 1662 and 1663, but he had been in custody since 1661. His sarcastic advice to the prosecution: before you charge a person with murder, be sure someone has been killed.[6]

The charge that fictitious transactions were created to mask the true costs of borrowing by the crown brought yet another history lesson: in 1657, the crown was desperate to raise funds, and what was done was a necessity of state.[7] Fouquet was particularly scornful of the charge that he had violated the law by borrowing personally and then on-lending the funds to the crown. The cardinal, he pointed out, had known of those borrowings and grateful for them. After the cardinal's death, the king on several occasions had authorized similar transactions, as Colbert was well aware. Was the prosecutor arguing that an order "from the king's own mouth" was illegal, that it was "criminal to have obeyed the king and helped him in his time of need?" If so, Fouquet suggested mockingly, then the judges of the chamber had an obligation to inform the king that obeying his orders could be a crime.[8]

Once again, Mazarin was at the center of Fouquet's defense. As long as the cardinal lived, Fouquet insisted, "all financial matters were determined by his orders, and I only acted under his authority."[9] Mazarin, he repeated, was the source of all the irregularities in the kingdom's finances in those years, as Louis had acknowledged at the time of his "confession" and pardon after Mazarin's death.[10] Fouquet could not refrain from taunting Talon that his charges were in fact accusations against the cardinal because that was where the "force of truth" was leading him.[11]

With respect to written orders from the cardinal, Talon seemed to catch Fouquet contradicting himself, but Fouquet had a response. Mazarin ordinarily gave his orders verbally and in person. But Fouquet would follow up with a letter advising the cardinal that he had executed his command, and there would usually be an acknowledgment of this from Mazarin, sometimes with a simple notation (*apostille*) on the original communication. Fouquet had preserved all of this correspondence among his papers, to which he did not yet have full access.[12] This explanation was bundled with a complaint about the custody of his papers. They were essentially in the keeping of Foucault, who, everyone knew, was a client of Colbert's and in a position to tamper with them at will.[13]

Fouquet spilled a great deal of ink defending himself against the charge of treason (*lèse-majesté*), for which the evidence was the plan of Saint-Mandé and his projects at Belle-Isle, which the prosecution had portrayed as the preparation for an insurrection. Fouquet began by separating his activities at Belle-Isle from the plan. His activities at Belle-Isle were hardly a secret. The cardinal had asked him to purchase the island and had further authorized his attempts to fortify it in defiance of the enemies of France. The work there had written royal authorization.[14] In later presentations, Fouquet was to embellish his answers. Belle-Isle had become the center of his overseas interests, which he traced back to the time of Richelieu, when that great cardinal had encouraged his father's involvement in France's maritime expansion. Fouquet had continued his father's work, although the Fronde had slowed or halted it temporarily. After the Fronde, with Mazarin's approval, Fouquet had resumed these enterprises. This accounted for the bustling activities observed by Colbert's spies.[15] Talon had charged that testimony from sailors in Fouquet's employ would prove that barrels full of silver were conveyed to Belle-Isle—a backhand way of accounting for Fouquet's "hidden assets." Fouquet had a ready answer. Of course money had been conveyed to Belle-Isle, to pay the wages of workers, the construction costs of fortifications, and other project expenses. All such sums had been borrowed and recorded in his ledgers.[16] Most of the barrels shipped to Belle-Isle contained steel, lead, gunpowder, and other materials intended for construction or shipbuilding. How could sailors tell what was in sealed barrels?[17] For good measure, Fouquet repeated that on more than one occasion he had offered to turn Belle-Isle over to the king, hardly an action compatible with a plan to use it against the crown.[18] Mazarin had signed the royal warrants authorizing the superintendant's activities and was in constant contact with La Meilleraye, the lieutenant-governor of Brittany. If Mazarin was not aware of Fouquet's projects, then he was "the stupidest minister who ever got involved in affairs of state."[19]

If the activities at Belle-Isle could be explained away, what about the plan of Saint-Mandé? Here Fouquet knew he was on thin ice, and once again he put Mazarin at the center of the stage. The cardinal was portrayed as a suspicious and capricious master, one who encouraged rivalries among his chief subordinates. The plan had been created in a moment of panic, when he feared that Mazarin would find a pretext to move against him, and was intended only as a means of ensuring his own safety.[20] Fouquet pointed out that it contained no mention of actions to be taken against the king or the state, only against Mazarin. This distinction might be barely comprehensible to later generations, but it was one familiar to a generation of Frondeurs who had insisted they were rebelling to save the state from a wicked minister. Fouquet also stressed that he had never taken any steps to implement the plan, nor had he ever spoken to those named in it.[21] It was only a fantasy, he insisted, and one in which he lost all interest after the cardinal's death.[22] That the plan was simply a fantasy, not conveyed or discussed with anyone, was central to more formal legal arguments that Fouquet inserted here. Earlier, in his reply to Talon's rejoinder, he had argued that Talon's position equated the thought of a crime with a crime, a temptation with a sin, something without legal precedent.[23] Now he elaborated on that argument. Neither in French customary law nor Roman law was a thought or wish, or fantasy, however malicious, a crime. Moreover, if there was an offense here, it was against Mazarin, and a crime against a non-sovereign could not as a matter of law be construed as a crime of treason.[24] Finally, even if one could establish that somehow a crime was involved, he had received the king's pardon after Mazarin's death: "out of his own mouth the king gave me a formal pardon and amnesty for everything that had happened during the cardinal's lifetime."[25]

These exchanges took months to unfold. The reading of Talon's charges and the supporting documents took from April to mid-July 1663, and from then until the fall to finish with Fouquet's first round of defenses. The long duration was due partly to the volume of the pleadings, but some of it came from Ormesson's respect for process. In early August, Talon requested permission to submit an additional brief in response to Fouquet's defense on the question of unauthorized pensions. Ormesson insisted that in fairness, for this instance and in any other matter Talon wished to revisit in the future, it would be necessary to reread Talon's original charge and his evidence, as well as Fouquet's response. The magistrates, Ormesson reasoned, could not be expected to remember the earlier presentations in any detail. Sainte-Hélène did not agree, and Pussort accused Ormesson of wishing to prolong the trial unnecessarily. After a sharp exchange between the two, most of the magistrates sided with Ormesson, so that the reading of this round of Fouquet's defense was not finished until mid-October.[26]

The harsh words between Pussort and Ormesson alarmed Colbert's party, who did not wish to alienate the rapporteur. Another judge, Ferriol, remarked to Foucault that Pussort's behavior had offended some of their colleagues in the chamber. Foucault called on Ormesson later that same day at his home. His tone was solicitous. Perhaps M. Colbert should have a word with Pussort, who, he added, had a great deal of esteem for Ormesson. His outbursts were not personal but simply a matter of temperament. Ormesson's reply was frigid. He really did not care what Pussort thought of him. He would do what he considered appropriate in the exercise of his function as rapporteur.[27]

At the end of August, Pussort and Ormesson again tangled. Some weeks earlier, in an extraneous matter, Ormesson had attempted to obtain a payment of a large sum of money owed him by the duc de Vendôme from funds seized by the chamber as part of another investigation. Pussort had opposed this, seeking to have the money paid instead to another creditor of Vendôme's who was a relative of his. As the assets in question came under the chamber's jurisdiction, the question was referred to it. Both Sainte-Hélène and Foucault attempted to mediate this quarrel, telling Ormesson that Pussort for some reason thought Ormesson would not oppose this strange intervention. Pussort, they assured Ormesson, was prepared to withdraw his petition as a mark of his esteem and friendship for Ormesson. Ormesson's reply was again cold. He didn't care about Pussort's friendship or his enmity. He would simply do his duty, determined, he wrote in his diary, not to be swayed by the offer of this supposed "favor."[28]

If Ormesson seemed indifferent to pressure, perhaps the chamber as a whole could be induced to move more quickly. Before leaving on campaign in Lorraine, Louis XIV summoned its members to his presence. He received Nesmond and the other members of the Parlement of Paris serving on the chamber, as well as most of the *maîtres des requêtes*, on August 22. After commending them for their zeal, he stressed that he was only interested in seeing justice done but urged them to speed up the process. He also reiterated his command that any request by Fouquet to recuse Séguier be immediately referred to him. The next day he met with the rest of the chamber, delivering the same message and singling out Pussort for special attention. Pussort was encouraged to wait on the king more often: he would be most welcome.[29]

Ormesson was not included in either group but was invited to the palace separately. The king repeated the same assurances about his intention to see justice done while encouraging Ormesson to expedite matters. Ormesson's answer was that the speed of the proceedings was not up to him as rapporteur, meaning that it was inherent in the complexity of the case. Louis affected to understand this, emphasized that he had spoken to those responsible already, but simply wanted Ormesson to do whatever was within his power to help.[30]

Louis was as good as his word. When the chamber reconvened several days later, Séguier opened it with a statement that the king was displeased with the slowness of Fouquet's trial, which, he suggested, would last another two years at its present rate. If this were not enough, he drove home the point by berating Talon for wasting time on some minor matter.[31] In the search for scapegoats, Berryer had turned on Talon, and that was enough for Colbert. Talon's mistress, the maréchale de l'Hôpital, the source of so much laughter in judicial circles, had been one of Colbert's agents, and he had tried to use her to urge Talon to make haste, but, as Colbert now informed Louis, to no avail.[32]

Talon, scrambling to redeem himself, advised Colbert of his attempts to print replies to Fouquet's many broadsides and assured the minister of his devotion to the task at hand.[33] Talon had already caused Louis a serious embarrassment. Among his many examples of corrupt practice he had cited an order from Fouquet to his clerks approving in advance any requests for funds from two courtiers, Messrs. de Graves and Gaboury. This, Talon thundered, was surely a misuse of the king's resources. Fouquet had pounced: the gentlemen in question had been delegated by the queen mother to ask Fouquet for money for her many private charities. Of course, Fouquet had complied, adding slyly that her majesty was "a good enough witness" to prove it. Anne of Austria felt obliged to confirm this with a letter to the chamber in July. This was precisely the kind of distortion of fact, Fouquet maintained, that underlay the entire set of charges against him. A furious Louis exchanged a few sharp words with his mother and then ordered Graves to leave court.[34]

While these debates raged, both Fouquet and his judges were getting used to new quarters. In late June 1663, the decision was made to transfer Fouquet from his cell at Vincennes to the Bastille. Fouquet, his doctor, and his valet were duly moved to the great royal fortress that guarded the approaches to the capital from the east. Fouquet was lodged in the Chapel Tower, so called because it also housed the prison chapel, with d'Artagnan and a detachment of musketeers mounting guard over him.[35] At the same time, the chamber relocated from its quarters in the Palais de justice to the Arsenal, a vast and gloomy building from which one could access the nearby Bastille by means of an adjacent park. Although no reason was stated for the changes, most likely it was tied to security issues. At some point, Fouquet would have to appear in person before his judges, and it would be easier and safer to transport him the short distance from the Bastille to the Arsenal rather than from Vincennes into central Paris.

The move did not disrupt Fouquet's rapid-fire production of his defense, nor did it help in any way to speed up the process. Indeed, the chamber, meeting in its new quarters, shut down from September 9 to September 26 because two of the judges were ill. The king, newly returned from campaigning and frustrated by another delay, decreed that the chamber would only recess in the future if the chancellor or one of the two rapporteurs were indisposed. Otherwise, it should carry on.[36]

The fall brought two other changes. Given Séguier's advanced age and fragile health, the king authorized the chamber to meet at Séguier's residence, although all judgments and sentences had to be pronounced in the formal setting of the Arsenal.[37] At the same time, in late November, Talon was dismissed, on the pretext that his services were required in *parlement*. His duties in the chamber were split: Fouquet's trial and matters related to the investigation of the royal treasurers were entrusted to another maître des requêtes, Guy Chamillart, a protégé of Colbert's who was also related by marriage to Le Tellier. All other matters under the chamber's jurisdiction were handed over to another prosecutor, Vincent Hotman de Fontenay.[38]

What had probably been the last straw for Talon was his failure to derail a motion filed by Fouquet in mid-October. Some months earlier, in June 1663, Fouquet noticed that Talon, supposedly to simplify matters, had dropped 24 of 33 reports on the treasury registers from his presentation of evidence. Fouquet had flagged this as suspicious in his July response to Talon's charges.[39] Fouquet had long insisted that the accusations against him misrepresented many transactions. He now demanded access to a wide range of documents, including the registers of the treasurers, in order to verify the contents of the reports or summaries drawn up as part of the prosecution's case. His judges were faced once more with the consequences of an overly broad prosecution. As a matter of standard judicial practice, Fouquet would ordinarily have had access to any materials that would support his defense, but this request risked yet another open-ended delay. After nearly a week of discussion, the judges rejected Talon's motion to dismiss Fouquet's request. Instead, they agreed that he could have any specific documents that he identified, and further, that the summaries of the treasury registers would have to be verified in his presence by comparison to the original registers.[40]

This decision was followed by another written charge by Fouquet asserting that the summaries contained false statements or misrepresentations.[41] This in turn triggered back-stair communications involving Foucault, speaking for Colbert, and Claude Le Pelletier, speaking for Le Tellier, who warned Ormesson that Colbert had complained to the king about those "well-intentioned" but misguided judges inclined to grant Fouquet's motions to examine the registers. Ormesson stood by his opinion: Fouquet's request to examine the registers of the treasurers would be difficult to refuse.[42]

Early in the new year 1664, Guy Chamillart called on Ormesson. There were rumors that Fouquet intended to petition the chamber to recuse Séguier. Chamillart reminded Ormesson that the king's orders were explicit: if Ormesson received any such demand he was not to present it to the chamber but give it to Chamillart to bring to the king. Passing from this to Fouquet's pending request to review the treasury registers, Chamillart suggested that it might be useful if he and Ormesson could coordinate their views on the subject beforehand. Ormesson was not receptive to this proposal. He would simply give his recommendations to the chamber and let his colleagues decide for themselves.[43]

On January 7, Fouquet's wife and mother appeared on Ormesson's doorstep to hand him the long-expected motion to recuse Séguier. It argued that the rivalry and dislike between the chancellor and Fouquet was common knowledge; it was also well known that during the trial Séguier had frequently conferred with Colbert, Berryer, and the other "instigators" of the trial. In addition, the chancellor had signed off on many of the transactions entered into evidence. For all these reasons, he should not continue to participate in the trial.[44]

In obedience to the king's directive, Ormesson forwarded the motion to the king. At a council convened to discuss it, the king's advisers split. As a matter of law, there was a question as to whether a chancellor of France, who embodied the king's judicial authority, could be recused. Two of the four senior officials present (Sève and Villeroy) argued that a recusal was possible in principle but that in this case it should be left to Séguier's judgment. Le Tellier countered that as a matter of policy, the chancellor should not be recusable, that the crown required a representative (*officier*) who could not be removed, and that Séguier was essential as the presiding officer of the chamber. The remaining royal councilor, d'Aligre, agreed with Le Tellier, so that the council was evenly divided. The king made the decision: Séguier would stay.[45] In the chamber, this was not universally well received. Many of the magistrates believed that a chancellor could be recused for cause. In the case of Fouquet, it was "unjust" that Séguier should sit in judgment on him. In guarded terms, Ormesson added that the outcome was really not to the king's advantage, as it would fuel comments by "malcontents" that the king wanted to "regulate and decide everything" by himself.[46]

Louis XIV did not interfere, however, in the other important motions concerning the verification of the reports on the treasury registers. Most of these reports had been prepared by Berryer over several months in 1662 but had been signed by judges acting on behalf of the chamber, notably Poncet, Voysin, and Ormesson.[47] In his demands for a reexamination of these reports, Fouquet had singled out two in particular, certified by Poncet and Voysin, as containing falsehoods. To Ormesson's surprise, Pussort and Voysin spoke out on the issue, with Pussort arguing for dismissal of Fouquet's motions for verification. But only a handful of judges agreed. Most accepted Ormesson's recommendation that Fouquet's challenge to all of the reports be allowed, and that the ones he cited specifically would have to be verified. That meant the treasury registers would be reviewed in Fouquet's presence to confirm the statements and summaries made in the official reports prepared by Berryer and signed by the two judges.[48]

In the last week of January, the doors of Fouquet's cell opened to admit three visitors, Ormesson, Chamillart, and Foucault, charged with the task of certifying those treasury reports in Fouquet's presence. Foucault was well-known to Fouquet from his duties as the recorder or clerk of the chamber, but Chamillart and Fouquet were scarcely acquainted. Ormesson made the introductions, and the two men took an instant dislike to one another.[49]

With Ormesson, however, Fouquet was more than civil. In a quiet hour, waiting for a clerical task to be completed, the two chatted cordially. Ormesson found the former superintendant little changed in the years since they had last met: Fouquet had put on some weight, and his eyes looked tired. This last was not surprising: most of his day, he explained to Ormesson, consisted of conferring with his counselors and drafting his briefs and motions, often working until 11:00 in the evening. He did attend daily Mass and was allowed a few religious books. His chief pastime was translating some of the psalms from Latin into French; he also had a few caged birds to cheer him up.

Sensing a receptive audience in Ormesson, Fouquet became philosophical. He was not surprised that he had been removed from office; perhaps he was not temperamentally suited for it. Still, he could have been useful elsewhere, as, say, an ambassador. If not, the king could have sent him back into private life. What he could not understand was why his enemies were persecuting him without mercy. Perhaps this was God's chastisement for his own sins. He was ready to pardon his persecutors—Berryer was mentioned by name—although he was sure God would punish them someday. He professed himself surprised that Colbert had refused his many requests to speak with him. An hour's conversation would put to rest the "misunderstandings" between them. All in all, it was a remarkable performance. Somewhat earlier, Ormesson had marveled at Fouquet's legal skills; now he admired in a more general way his "presence of mind, free-spiritedness [*liberté*], and calm" in the face of adversity.[50]

In the days that followed, Fouquet and Chamillart clashed repeatedly. This was not surprising, but it was to Fouquet's advantage that the new prosecutor and Ormesson also crossed swords frequently. Chamillart, a decade younger than Ormesson and proud of his new post, often disputed the rapporteur's authority. At one point, on a trivial matter concerning overnight custody of the treasury registers, Chamillart tried to countermand an order of Ormesson's to d'Artagnan. When Chamillart insisted that he represented the king and that neither d'Artagnan nor Besmaux, the governor of the Bastille, would obey a command from Ormesson contrary to the king's (presumably conveyed through Chamillart), Ormesson was not moved. "It is for you to request and for me to order; make your request and I'll decide." At the end of the exchange, Ormesson noticed Fouquet's amusement at Chamillart's evident inexperience and his apparent approval of the rapporteur's assertion of authority.[51] Not too long afterward, as Ormesson was dictating to the recorder Fouquet's answer on a point, Chamillart impatiently interrupted and accused him of trying to be both "judge and advocate" by speaking for Fouquet. Fouquet asked that the exchange be documented as an example of Chamillart's prejudice against him. Ormesson, however, simply dismissed Chamillart's comment as an "impertinence" and continued his dictation.[52]

Ormesson began to come under pressure from Séguier, who remarked frequently on the slowness of the proceedings, which he blamed on Ormesson's willingness to let Fouquet make lengthy observations on the records and reports under review. At the rate things were going, he complained on several occasions, the trial would go on for another two years and outlast him.[53] Pussort, echoing Séguier, suggested angrily that the chamber recommend its own suppression, since it seemed unable to conclude the trial, a "shameful matter." Nesmond rose to defend his colleagues: the slowness was the fault of those who set the trial in motion, meaning the prosecution, not the judges. If the solution was to fix those initial errors by dispensing with the usual procedures, then they should find other judges to do it. Séguier had to intervene with platitudes to quiet the flaring tempers.[54] But Séguier kept up a constant scolding of Ormesson for bringing Fouquet's observations and requests before the chamber. Ormesson complained to colleagues in the chamber that he was treated like an abused schoolboy. "I don't like being whipped every morning."[55]

Exchanges of this type continued throughout February and March, as the chamber digested Fouquet's responses on Belle-Isle and on his extravagant spending. After these sessions, Ormesson and Chamillart would make their way to the Bastille to continue the verification process with the prisoner. From time to time, Ormesson would provide interim reports to the chamber on that exercise, and the findings were not good for the prosecution. In early March, Ormesson called the chamber's attention to a seemingly modest discrepancy. A report had omitted Servien's name from a series of measures signed off by Fouquet, Servien, and Séguier, listing them as signed by Séguier, Fouquet, "*etc.*" Chamillart was dismissive: the *etc.* clearly referred to Servien. Fouquet was sarcastic in his reply: when and where did *etc.* ever mean "Servien"? The point would not be lost on the judges: Fouquet had insisted throughout his defenses that financial measures taken in the 1650s always were agreed on jointly by the co-superintendants. Omitting Servien's name under these circumstances suggested—incorrectly—that Fouquet had been acting alone and illicitly.[56]

More was to follow. Several weeks later, Ormesson was astonished to discover that a report contained seven or eight lines that were "entirely false," describing transactions for which there were no corresponding entries in the registers of the treasury. "I could not understand," wrote Ormesson, "how one could invent things that didn't exist and report them as if they did."[57] Some weeks later, there was yet another important find: things that did exist were omitted or altered. In a report dealing with the proof that Fouquet and his partners intended to embezzle 6 million livres, certain notes (*billets*) presented to the treasury and not routinely destroyed, but found in Fouquet's papers, were cited as evidence of this intended crime. One of these, for 181,500 livres, turned out to have been liquidated by Berryer. In another place, an entry that Berryer had received 120,000 livres had been altered by inserting next to it the letters S.E. ("His Eminence"), implying that Mazarin was the ultimate beneficiary. The report in question had been drafted by Berryer and signed off by Poncet and Voysin.[58]

Such findings tended to undermine the credibility of the evidence gathered against Fouquet and increased tensions between Fouquet and Chamillart. On one occasion, when Chamillart took exception to one of Fouquet's denunciations of Berryer, Voysin, and Pussort, the defendant expressed surprise. Chamillart had not had a hand in these matters, since when they occurred "you were not *yet* part of the plot against me."[59] When Chamillart insisted that the "proofs" drawn from the registers were as "true as the gospels," Fouquet shot back that they could not be so, since Chamillart was mistreating the "evangelists," meaning the treasurers who were also under arrest: a bon mot that made the rounds of polite society.[60] Not surprisingly, Fouquet used these discrepancies to impeach every one of the reports in question and to demand that additional reports be compared to the underlying registers.[61]

All of these matters were brought before the chamber in the spring of 1664 and did little to improve Ormesson's standing with Pussort, Voysin, Séguier, or the judges aligned with them. In one exchange, Ormesson conveyed to the chamber Fouquet's petitions to examine the registers of the treasury on the charges involving the *octrois* (internal customs duties or tolls) and the scheme to embezzle 6 million livres. Ormesson recommended that these requests be granted, and carried a vote easily, despite the violent opposition of Pussort and Séguier.[62] The vote reinforced Ormesson's belief that the public and many of his colleagues approved his method of dealing with Fouquet.[63] At the same time, street songs mocking the king as being in the pocket of Colbert and Séguier as a biased judge hoping to condemn Fouquet had reached and offended the royal ears.[64]

Whatever the general public believed about the case, within the circles of power there were some who bet that its uncertain trajectory might damage Colbert's standing, and they were prepared to encourage whatever might bring about this result. In early March, Ormesson visited maréchal Turenne on another matter. The great soldier brought the conversation around to the chamber, told Ormesson that all honest people approved of his behavior, and added a denunciation of Séguier as a man "without honor" who had "prostituted" himself before power.[65] Some weeks later, a mutual friend conveyed Turenne's compliments to Ormesson on his exchanges with Pussort.[66] Shortly afterward, Ormesson saw Turenne again, who repeated his congratulations in person. The maréchal opined that it would be very difficult now to put Fouquet to death and passed on a joke of Le Tellier's: that at the beginning all they would have needed was a string to strangle Fouquet, but they had made the noose so wide that now it was impossible to close it tight, a pleasantry Le Tellier later repeated directly to Ormesson.[67]

These words of encouragement were paired with warnings from the same sources that Colbert, looking to blame someone for the disarray in the trial, had criticized Ormesson's behavior to the king, accusing him of openly siding with Fouquet. The king had reportedly replied that Ormesson had been treated too gently to date.[68] At a dinner attended by Ormesson's brother, Friar Nicolas d'Ormesson, as well as by Berryer and Foucault, the gossip at table held that Ormesson, disregarding advice from his father, was being encouraged by Madame de Sévigné to favor Fouquet, an insinuation that Ormesson found "stupid."[69] Some days later, Colbert suggested to the king that several intendants busy with other duties be removed from their posts. The list included Ormesson, who was still the intendant for Soissons. In his case, Le Tellier had tried to dissuade the king from taking action, arguing it would play badly in public. But Louis liked the suggestion, and Ormesson found himself deprived of a significant source of income.[70]

As Ormesson was trying to digest the implications of this action, Colbert struck again. One of Ormesson's fellow judges, Louis Boucherat, received a visit from Colbert, who told him that the king was dismissing him from the chamber, on the pretext that he had once served as a legal adviser to one of the arrested royal treasurers. Colbert made it clear to the startled jurist that the real reason for his removal was his well-known skepticism about the treason charges against Fouquet. To save face, a story circulated that Boucherat had disqualified himself on grounds of kinship with Fouquet, but it does not seem to have been believed, at least not by Ormesson.[71]

A day or two later, while Ormesson, his octogenarian father, and his brother, Friar Nicolas, were discussing these events, they were startled by the announcement that Colbert himself had appeared on the doorstep. The stern-faced minister announced that he wished to speak to André alone. Once the two brothers had left the room, Colbert began his oration. He had come on the king's behalf to complain that Olivier was not using his authority as rapporteur to move the trial along but seemed instead to be dragging it out. The king understood Olivier's good intentions and his desire to do justice, but it was important to finish the trial.

Then the mask dropped. The trial, snarled Colbert, was ruining the crown's image. It was extraordinary that the king, the most powerful and feared monarch in Europe, could not bring the trial of a subject like Fouquet to a conclusion. The elderly royal councilor expressed his regret that the king was not satisfied with Olivier's services, insisting on his son's good faith and desire to serve God, the king, and justice "without exception." The length of the trial was not Olivier's fault but the result of an overly complicated indictment. There were thirty or forty separate charges to consider, when two or three would have been enough. As for favoring Fouquet, his son would be mad to favor a disgraced minister over a king with the power to offer him anything. His son only sought justice, and, he pointed out, very often the chamber followed his advice, implying that Olivier's opinions were well founded, at least in the eyes of his fellow jurists. He added that many people had commented on his impartiality.

Colbert rejoined that many others felt that Olivier seemed to champion Fouquet's arguments more forcefully than the positions of the royal procureur. André countered that a rapporteur had to evaluate all the arguments in an evenhanded way. Before Colbert could find something else to say, André went on the offensive. Depriving his son of his post at Soissons would not keep him from doing justice. Neither he nor Olivier had much, but what they did have came from their forebears, and that was enough to sustain them. He had always told his son to do justice "without exception for anyone and without consideration of fortune or self-interest." Colbert, taken aback by the outburst, replied that he understood Olivier only wanted to render justice; the question was how to expedite the process. The elder Ormesson insisted once more that his son was doing everything in his power to do so, working night and day on the trial and nothing else. After a few more inconclusive exchanges, a frustrated Colbert took his leave.[72]

Olivier d'Ormesson was thrilled by his father's brave defiance of Colbert and by the reaction to it beyond the family circle. Word of the confrontation between the minister and the royal councilor of state made the rounds of high society in Paris. Ormesson and his father were showered with congratulations and words of encouragement from all sides, even from Le Tellier.[73]

But Colbert was not finished with Ormesson and the chamber. When Ormesson called on Lamoignon to tell him of the incident, he learned that Colbert also knew how to reward his friends. The king had named Berryer a councilor of state—to a post confiscated from Gourville, now safely in exile—and awarded him a pension of 6,000 livres. The king had also directed the royal prosecutors in the chamber to include Berryer in their deliberations and make use of his advice, a somewhat belated authorization of what Berryer had been doing since the creation of the chamber.[74]

All of this inspired a rare outburst of indignation from Ormesson. Everyone, he said, disapproved of Colbert's behavior, especially his adding insult to injury with his dismissal of Boucherat and his visit to Ormesson senior. To deprive him of his intendancy of Soissons because as rapporteur he refused to countenance unjust acts was to cover Colbert with shame and Ormesson with honor. The overall result would simply be to "spoil the trial." If he were to recommend anything in favor of the prosecution in the future, one would assume he had done so out of fear or self-interest, not a sense of justice. To top it all off, promoting Berryer and putting him in a place of prominence in the chamber meant "glorifying infamy and shame, because Berryer is the most disreputable of men." Ormesson also saw in these actions a cunning ploy on the part of Colbert. Colbert, he reasoned, now feared that the trial of Fouquet would drag on forever or end disastrously, and he was looking for someone to blame. Hanging it all on a rapporteur was not enough; he had now positioned Berryer, too, to take the fall if necessary.[75]

If there was any doubt about what was expected from the chamber, it would have been put to rest by the fate of another victim of Colbert's dragnet. In mid-June, the chamber sat in judgment on a minor provincial tax collector named Dumont, accused of embezzlement. The judges had no doubt of his guilt but divided bitterly on the penalty. The rapporteur Ferriol recommended the death penalty and was seconded by Pussort, Voysin, and Séguier. The precedent was the death sentence imposed in absentia a year earlier, in April 1663, on Gourville. But others argued for a lighter sentence: the royal decrees still on the books did not treat simple embezzlement as a capital offense. Some felt that the Gourville precedent was not controlling, arguing there was a difference between stealing a hundred crowns (*écus*) and embezzling a hundred thousand. Pierre Catinat, seconded by Ormesson, cited deficiencies in the trial as another reason for leniency.

His recommendation was a fine, banishment, and disqualification from holding office in the future. The final vote, however, was 13 for the death penalty and 8 for a lesser sentence.[76] That same day, Dumont was taken out and hanged in the square in front of the Bastille. This visible severity frightened many of those still awaiting interrogation and judgment, as one official put it, "giving sleepless nights to many."[77]

The next episodes in this long-running morality play took place in the idyllic setting of Fontainebleau. Fresh from the triumph of the great outdoor festival at Versailles, still remembered as the *plaisirs de l'île enchantée*—about which Ormesson received a full report from his friend Madame de Sévigné—the king decided to spend the summer months at Fontainebleau.[78] He decreed as well that the chamber and its most prominent detainees—Fouquet, three royal treasurers also under arrest, and Jacques Delorme—would accompany him. The rationale for this move may have stemmed from developments in Paris, where some of Colbert's financial reforms had been greeted with dismay. Among the most unpopular was the forced redemption of annuities secured on the tax revenues of the city of Paris (*rentes sur l'hôtel de ville*). These instruments had been a staple, secure, and lucrative investment for generations of the elite strata of society, including nobles, magistrates, and wealthy tradespeople. There had been demonstrations against the recall at the hôtel de ville and elsewhere. The issue was discussed in parlement and even in the chamber, where Séguier lauded the king's actions and Pussort compared the disorders to the riotous days of the Fronde.[79] Colbert used the occasion to attribute much of the protest to "agents" of Fouquet and to insinuate to the king that Fouquet hoped to make use of this unrest, perhaps to secure his freedom.[80]

Against this background, the chamber was transferred to Fontainebleau, where lodgings and meeting rooms were set aside for the magistrates. It fell to Ormesson to see to the packing of all the documents and files assembled in the case and to turn them over to d'Artagnan. Some days later, in late June, the lieutenant set out at the head of a convoy of carriages and carts carrying prisoners, documents, and baggage. Each of the five prisoners rode in a separate, heavily guarded carriage. The captives were kept apart at all times and even took their meals separately under the watchful eyes of their musketeer escorts. Their destination was not the great royal residence but the nearby estate of Moret, where they were housed in a gloomy medieval keep or donjon that had been semi-abandoned for years.[81]

When the chamber reassembled for the first time at Fontainebleau, Séguier advised his colleagues that one of their members, Le Bossu, would not be joining them. Le Bossu, it seemed, did not hold the law degrees required to sit as a judge in criminal cases (although this deficiency would not have disqualified him from civil cases). This explanation was widely viewed as a pretext. Ormesson was convinced that Le Bossu was excluded simply because he was one of those "outcasts determined to do justice."[82]

The judges also were told of another change in procedure. By the king's order, Fouquet was henceforth restricted to seeing his legal counselors twice a week, on Wednesdays and Fridays, and in the presence of both d'Artagnan and the recorder, Foucault. Fouquet immediately filed a motion with the chamber to reaffirm its earlier ruling of 1662 giving him unlimited and confidential access to counsel. An embarrassed chamber forwarded the petition to the king for decision. Several days later, Ormesson and Sainte-Hélène were summoned to the king's presence. With Colbert and Hugues de Lionne listening, the king gave vent to his impatience. When he had given Fouquet unlimited access to counsel, he thought the trial would not last long. But two years had gone by, and he was anxious that the trial should finish. It was a question of his reputation, especially abroad, where he wished to be respected. People would not think he was powerful if he could not even bring to a close the trial of "a wretch." He did not want the access to counsel to be "eternal." He was convinced that Fouquet's lawyers had exceeded their mandate, accusing them of ferrying documents in and out of the prison and of conferring with outsiders (probably meaning the Fouquet ladies). He alluded also to the dangers arising from the plot to "overthrow the state." Nevertheless, he insisted, he only wanted justice done, and he did not want to say a word too much when "the life of a man" was at stake. Now that he had explained his reasons for acting as he had, he returned the matter to the chamber. Let them make the decision.[83]

The chamber found itself in the difficult position of having to agree or disagree with the king's wishes. As Ormesson noted, Fouquet had against him the king's order and many precedents but had in his favor the previous order of the chamber, its practice to date, and the leeway usually accorded to an accused. The debate provided Pussort with a chance to deny any conflict between the king's orders and his justice, which, he insisted, were the same thing. In the end, by an overwhelming majority, the chamber voted to follow a recommendation of Ormesson's. The king's order limiting counsel to twice a week would be honored, with two important modifications. The restriction would be waived when an important issue was scheduled for debate in the chamber; in those circumstances, Fouquet could confer with counsel at will. In addition, any and all future consultations would take place in the presence of d'Artagnan but not of the recorder.[84] Fouquet responded to this by objecting pro forma to d'Artagnan's presence, although he and the lieutenant had reached a gentleman's agreement. Fouquet accepted the musketeer's word that he would not reveal any of Fouquet's conversations with his lawyers concerning the trial but would report exchanges on any other subject.[85]

Fouquet continued to produce motions designed to create tension between the crown and the chamber. Once the issue of access to counsel was settled, the chamber had to deal with a demand of Fouquet's that Le Bossu be reinstated on the panel. The judges found themselves divided again. Some asserted that a defendant had the right to request the recusal of a judge but not the appointment of one. Others claimed that since Fouquet had never recognized the authority of the panel, he had no standing to argue anything. Still others insisted that because the king had appointed the chamber members, he could revoke those appointments at will and had done just that in Le Bossu's case. In this particular instance, tradition and usage were clearly on the side of the king, holding that in criminal matters judges had to hold a bachelor's degree or higher in the law to sit in judgment. Nevertheless, as Le Bossu had pointed out some weeks earlier, there were a few precedents to the contrary. Ironically, most involved royal appointments of magistrates to earlier chambers of justice.[86] In the end, Fouquet's motion was dismissed, but not before Ormesson wondered aloud if the real issue was that the king "wanted to decide all the details of the trial" (*incidens du procès*).[87]

As the judges finished their deliberations on Le Bossu, Ormesson presented them with another petition from Fouquet. This time, Fouquet took direct aim at Colbert, insisting that the court open an investigation into Colbert's tampering with his papers at the time of his arrest. He supplemented this demand with a request that the chamber investigate the actions of Berryer and Foucault as well. The reaction was swift and fierce. Before the next session, Chamillart intercepted Ormesson to say that he intended to ask that the motion be dismissed and that Fouquet be forbidden to file additional pleadings on the subject. To accuse Colbert, who sat on the royal council and enjoyed the king's confidence, was to dishonor the king.

When the chamber convened, Séguier asked Ormesson if he was going to waste time with Fouquet's request, and the rapporteur replied that he would not. The request was premature. It should not, however, be dismissed out of hand. The chamber could decide later whether such alleged activities were of importance. He recommended that in the meantime the matter be taken under advisement for later consideration.

Once more the chamber was divided. Voysin denounced the motion as nothing but a maneuver on Fouquet's part (*finesses*), which should be dismissed forthwith, while Séguier also thundered away. The chancellor insisted that there was no reason to believe Colbert had tampered with Fouquet's papers. This was insulting to a man who served the king in so many important affairs and who was doing a much better job than Fouquet in bringing order to the king's finances. Echoing Chamillart, he warned that the accusation alone was an affront to the king's honor. The motion should be dismissed, although, he conceded, Fouquet could not be precluded from bringing similar ones: he had that right. In the end, most of the judges agreed with Ormesson to take the matter under advisement. The chamber thus postponed to another day a determination on the underlying issue, Colbert's involvement with the handling of Fouquet's papers. Their decision, however, not to dismiss the motion summarily could only be seen as a victory for Fouquet.[88]

Fouquet had not yet finished. In mid-August, his wife and mother again appeared on Ormesson's doorstep with additional petitions, including one demanding the recusal of Pussort and Voysin, the two judges most closely aligned with Colbert. They had, Fouquet charged, conspired with Berryer to falsify the reports on the treasury registers and signed off on those falsified reports; consequently, they should be removed from the chamber.[89]

The resulting uproar lasted for weeks. Colbert flew into a rage, not against Fouquet but against Ormesson, who had recently exposed another falsification by Pussort during a chamber session.[90] Ormesson, he told the king, was attacking his honor, and that of his uncle, Pussort, who had served the state with distinction for 30 years and was being treated as a "forger" (*faussetaire*) by the rapporteur. For this insult he vowed revenge on the entire Ormesson clan. Voysin, not to be outdone, asked the king's permission to "defend himself" against Ormesson (i.e., permission to challenge him to a duel), a request presumably not granted.[91]

Ormesson spent the next two days reviewing the drafts ("minutes") of the reports in question, which he ordered Foucault to bring to him. He compared them to assertions made in a follow-up brief by Fouquet alleging specific falsifications and to the registers. He uncovered several suspicious alterations or variations and reconfirmed some of the errors he had noted in his earlier investigations in the spring. On August 28, he presented his findings to the chamber. He had discovered several alterations that disguised the payment of large sums to Berryer. A report supposedly confirmed as accurate by Macé Bertrand de La Bazinière, one of the treasury secretaries, had not been initialed by him and may never have been seen by him. Worst of all, a note identified as among those supposedly kept by Fouquet for the planned 6 million livres embezzlement was one that had been presented routinely to pay the salary (*gages*) of a maître des requêtes, whose name had been partially eradicated on the notation, none other than Ormesson himself. These discoveries were more than an embarrassment for the prosecution. This last transaction had been widely publicized by Talon and his allies. Not only was the physical evidence now discredited but the testimony of the witnesses against Fouquet in this matter—Jeannin de Castille and Tabouret—was obviously suspect, as was the behavior of the investigating magistrates who had certified the reports.[92]

The presentation of his findings and the reading of Fouquet's accusations and requests took nearly two days. On the evening of the first day, Ormesson received yet another visit from Le Pelletier. Having to choose between his uncle Pussort and his protégé Berryer, Colbert had opted to protect Pussort. He told Le Tellier that he had been shocked at these revelations and blamed everything on that "rogue" Berryer; all of this misconduct had been reported to the king. Le Tellier, sensing which way the wind was blowing, had joined in the chorus blaming Berryer and faulty procedures for the mess but agreed there was no reason that the two judges should be recused. Le Pelletier's next remarks revealed that there was more at stake here than Colbert's family pride. Colbert was convinced that a majority of the judges would not support the removal of Pussort and Voysin. Nevertheless, the king had authorized Le Tellier to speak with three of the judges about the matter: Nesmond, Catinat, and Ormesson. Le Pelletier was there on Le Tellier's behalf, but he added an oblique warning. If Ormesson intended to vote for recusal, it was best that he not meet with Le Tellier. If he did so and then voted for recusal, he would be acting after speaking with a minister of state conveying the king's wishes to the contrary. Forced to show his hand, Ormesson told Le Pelletier that under the circumstances, he had already concluded that the two should not continue as judges in Fouquet's case.[93]

In what was perhaps the most bizarre twist yet, on a Saturday morning, August 30, Pussort and Voysin appeared before their colleagues. Instead of taking their usual places, they were forced to stand "before the bar" and account for their actions. For the moment, they were the accused and Fouquet, through the intermediation of Ormesson, the accuser. Their defense followed Colbert's lead: it was all the fault of Berryer. The treasury registers were virtually indecipherable, and neither judge knew anything about finance or routine treasury procedures. They had relied on Berryer, who had been vouched for by Talon, the then royal prosecutor. They had signed the reports without reading them, and no doubt there were still more errors and omissions in them. As for La Bazinière, they could not remember whether he was present as indicated in the report. In short, what was not Berryer's fault was Talon's, and what was not Talon's fault was Berryer's;

their only fault was incompetence. It was an astonishing performance by magistrates charged with verifying evidence in a capital case. By the time they had finished, the day was fading, and Séguier, perhaps fearing the initial reaction of his colleagues, cut short deliberations and put the matter over to the following Monday.[94]

Once more the machinery of state swung into motion to protect the crown's position. Chamillart spent Sunday visiting all of the judges and pressing them hard, using the king's name and not bothering in any way to disguise his mission or his orders.[95] When visiting Ormesson, his own discomfort at defending the indefensible slipped out. After repeating a questionable explanation for the tampering with the evidence in the 6 million livres transaction, he conceded, "I see that you don't find my explanation convincing, and neither do I, but I don't have a better one to offer."[96]

On Monday, Ormesson rose before his colleagues to give his recommendation. Le Tellier's warnings and Chamillart's lobbying, both in the king's name, may have had some effect on his presentation. He was willing to exculpate the two judges from the accusation of malice. They had behaved imprudently but innocently. Berryer was the true villain here, having falsified at least three of the reports before the chamber and probably others as well. Having said that Berryer bore the ultimate responsibility, Ormesson nevertheless believed that under the circumstances the two judges should be recused. Sainte-Hélène, seconded by Séguier, took a different position, defending not only the judges but also Berryer as a representative of the king, and called for the dismissal of Fouquet's request. He further asked that Fouquet be precluded from filing any similar motions unless they were countersigned by his two counselors.

The vote was surprisingly lopsided. Only four judges agreed with Ormesson that their two colleagues should be excused. Fifteen voted that Pussort and Voysin should remain.[97]

For once, Ormesson seemed to please everyone. Fouquet's supporters congratulated him for exposing Berryer's misdeeds. Lamoignon, whom Ormesson saw frequently, assured him that his actions were widely approved of, while Turenne sent his compliments. Chamillart, Foucault, and their allies conveyed word that his decision to blame Berryer was much appreciated, even if his advice to recuse the judges was regrettable.[98]

Fouquet's demand that Colbert, Foucault, and Berryer be investigated for tampering with his files was still pending. The matter was not settled until mid-September, and by the crown's intervention. A royal order dismissed Fouquet's motion and forbade the chamber to discuss the matter further. Séguier felt obliged to explain the king's reasoning to his fellow magistrates. The king reaffirmed that whatever Colbert removed from Fouquet's papers was by his command and concerned secrets of state. There was ample precedent for such actions. For all practical purposes, the king was thus personally denying Fouquet's accusations. Furthermore, Séguier warned, the king did not want Colbert, a man to whom he confided the most important matters of state, to be hauled before a chamber of justice. As Ormesson said to Chamillart, since the king had decided the matter, there was nothing to do but obey.[99] The king's order was duly registered without debate by the chamber.[100]

By the time these arguments were put to rest, the king had returned to Paris, the chamber to the Arsenal, and the prisoners to the Bastille. In mid-August d'Artagnan put his charges, the files, and the baggage into carriages and wagons, and headed back to the capital. At Charenton, a large crowd of well-dressed people, families and friends of the prisoners, had gathered to watch the convoy pass. D'Artagnan, usually so inflexible in the execution of his orders, was softened by the sight. Without stopping, he ordered the cortège to proceed as slowly as possible. This enabled Madame Fouquet to lean into her husband's carriage and embrace him. It was the first time since the day of his arrest in September 1661 that Fouquet had seen his wife and children, including the four-year old Louis, who would have had no memory of his father. Fouquet's fellow captives, in their separate coaches, were accorded similar liberties to greet their waiting families.[101]

It was a rare act of grace and one not offered by a crowned head, who had dismissed so many appeals for mercy with disdain, but by a gruff old soldier moved by the poignancy of the moment.

CHAPTER 7

A Performance beyond Comparison

By the fall of 1664, the *chambre de justice* was approaching its third anniversary and, at long last, the conclusion of Fouquet's trial. Dramatic episodes such as Fouquet's demands that Colbert be investigated or that Pussort and Voysin be recused did not halt its more routine elements, including the seemingly endless readings to the chamber of Fouquet's defenses. Much of the summer was devoted to his responses on Belle-Isle, while the chamber passed the fall months looking again at several arcane financial transactions, at the "crime of state" in the plan of Saint-Mandé, and at Fouquet's additional questioning of the inventories of his papers and the reports on the treasurers' registers.

The scale of Fouquet's writing was simply astounding: a first complete collection, published several years after the trial, ran to 13 volumes of excessively small print. (It was reprinted a generation later in 16 volumes.) Underneath the endless detail and arguments repeated from one pleading to the next, a few basic themes stood out. Any irregularities or illegalities in the raising of funds during the 1650s were attributed to wartime necessity and had been approved by Mazarin. If there was any self-dealing and enrichment at the expense of the crown, the chief beneficiaries were Mazarin and his close associates, not Fouquet. Fouquet's own wealth, which his accusers saw as proof of his looting, was an illusion. It rested on heavy borrowing, much of which he on-lent to the crown and which accounted for any sums he subsequently collected from the treasury—they were simply the repayment of money he had advanced to support the operations of state. The accusations against him were fabricated by his political enemies, who, as he had demonstrated, had falsified records, tampered with evidence, and misrepresented innocent transactions, such as funding the queen mother's charitable causes. To reinforce his self-image as a devoted servant of state during years of crisis, Fouquet submitted to the chamber the letters of gratitude for his efforts at Valenciennes written to him by Mazarin in 1656. Somehow, these had not been removed from his seized papers, and they were read in the chamber in late October 1664; some of the judges were visibly moved.[1]

Thanks to the clandestine publication of his defenses, yet another departure from normal judicial procedures, much of the literate public had been exposed to these arguments, and it was widely conceded that Fouquet was winning the war for public opinion. What really counted, though, was the battle for the judges' votes. Here, the crown still seemed to have the upper hand. Indeed, the vote in the chamber to recuse Pussort and Voysin was so lopsidedly against Fouquet's motion (15 to 5) that it suggested that the judges were inclined against him. Ormesson observed that many people saw that vote as a "predictor of the outcome of the trial."[2] If so, then Fouquet was still very much at risk.

At the same time, however, Fouquet's enemies were also uneasy at the turn events had taken. There were rumors once more that Colbert talked about winding down the chamber and that the charges against Fouquet would be reduced to the single charge of treason.[3] Séguier, anxious to bring the trial to a close, was openly hostile to Ormesson's presentations of Fouquet's briefs to the chamber (one of his duties as *rapporteur*), treating him as if he were "Fouquet's advocate."[4] On one occasion, he sarcastically suggested that Ormesson's views were inspired by the Holy Spirit (i.e., wiser than those of others). Ormesson snapped back that "up until now I had never had any communication with the Holy Spirit."[5] There was almost constant bickering among the judges, and the exchanges were sometimes unintentionally ironic. When Mazarin's letters commending Fouquet for his funding at Valenciennes were read in the chamber, one judge commented on Mazarin's warm words. Without hesitating, Pussort interjected that the king's exchange with Fouquet on the evening before his arrest was even warmer.[6]

On November 12 and 13, Ormesson read aloud Fouquet's last production, a final attack on the handling of his papers and the tampering with evidence by Colbert, Berryer, and company, seeking one more time to discredit all of the financial charges against him by impeaching the documentation used to support the charges.[7] As he put his pen down several days earlier, Fouquet was asked by d'Artagnan if he wanted him to advise the king that he had finished his written defenses. Fouquet replied proudly that d'Artagnan should tell the king that he was not trying to avoid judgment and that he was ready to answer any of the judges' questions. He supposedly added a request that the king specify in which manner he be heard, meaning standing or sitting, since as a former member of the king's council he did not wish to diminish its status when appearing before an inferior body like the chamber. The king sent no answer.[8]

On Friday morning November 14, d'Artagnan escorted Fouquet from his cell at the Bastille to a small waiting room at the Arsenal, while the king's musketeers took up positions in the nearby hallways. In the next room, where the chamber met, his judges went through formalities, including a reading by Ormesson of the demands of the prosecution that Fouquet be convicted of embezzlement and treason, for which crimes he should be hanged and his property forfeit to the crown. This task fell to Ormesson as rapporteur because under the rules of procedure of the time neither the prosecutors nor defense counsel was permitted to take part in the interrogation of an accused by his judges. Once the reading was complete, Séguier, as the presiding magistrate, ordered d'Artagnan to produce his prisoner.

When the former superintendant entered the hall, he saw that a small wooden stool (*sellette*) had been placed before the rapporteurs' table, facing the chancellor and the other members of the chamber. This was the standard accommodation for a criminal before a court, and in effect the answer to Fouquet's earlier question to the king.

To his audience Fouquet appeared composed. He was dressed simply, in a black suit with a white collar, like a respectable bourgeois. After bowing to his judges, he apologized that he was not properly dressed, as a magistrate in a long robe, which was his right as a former member of *parlement*. He had not been permitted to do so. This was by way of prelude to a substantive issue symbolized by that forced choice of costume: Fouquet refused to take the traditional oath before testifying because it meant recognizing the authority of the chamber. His years of service as a member of parlement entitled him to a trial before parlement, his "natural judges." In claiming this right, he maintained, he was preserving it for his listeners, all of whom as individuals were members of the various high courts and enjoyed the same privilege. He was not there to take an oath and recognize the chamber's jurisdiction over him but to provide clarifications to his written defenses.

These assertions provoked a strong exchange between Séguier and Fouquet. Séguier insisted that the king had ruled in the matter and that parlement had no jurisdiction. Fouquet answered that someday the king would recognize the "nullity" of his own order in council, that "a judgment rendered contrary to procedure (*les formes*) is not a judgment, and that the judges' hands had been tied."[9]

Frustrated by Fouquet's refusal to take the oath, Séguier ordered the prisoner to be removed while the judges deliberated on what to do.

The debate among the judges on how to proceed was lengthy and sharp. Some followed Séguier's lead and argued that if Fouquet would not be sworn, he should be precluded from testifying and treated as a "voluntary mute," and the court should proceed immediately to judgment and sentencing. Others, led by Ormesson, pointed out that the chamber had allowed Fouquet to respond to Poncet and Renard's interrogations without taking an oath. Many were uneasy that in a criminal trial a defendant should not be heard, with or without an oath. In the end, it was agreed that Fouquet would be asked again to take the traditional oath to testify truthfully, and if he refused, to continue the proceedings without it. Fouquet was summoned, asked once more to take the oath, and when he declined, Séguier cut the debate off by starting the questioning on the charges against the former superintendant.

Séguier began with the infamous 120,000 livres pension on the salt tax farm, evidenced by a document Colbert had found on his desk at Saint-Mandé. Additional documentation had supposedly been found in Fouquet's papers at Fontainebleau, and a member of the syndicate administrating the transaction, one Châtelain, had testified that he had dealt with Fouquet on the matter. Fouquet's answers in his interrogations and written defenses were inconsistent. How could he deny his involvement? What followed was a long and acrimonious exchange, as Fouquet used the chancellor's observations or objections to draw an increasingly detailed picture of the transaction. He had never been inconsistent in his earlier replies, he insisted, but had not initially had access to his papers or inventories to allow himself to refresh his memory. Once these were available to him, he was able to fill in details. And he had hesitated to implicate the true beneficiary of the transaction.

The pension did exist. It had been created in 1655 when the farming of the *gabelle* had been up for bid, and two competing groups had been merged under ministerial sponsorship and awarded the franchise. The combined group had been told at the time that the pension was a necessary condition of the transaction. The name of the beneficiary was left blank. That beneficiary, however, was none other than Mazarin. Fouquet had become aware of the transaction in 1658 when the cardinal had authorized Fouquet to collect arrearages of 180,000 livres on the pension and to use the money to repay a comparable sum the cardinal had borrowed from Fouquet. This was the occasion on which Fouquet had dealt with Châtelain, one of the syndicate leaders. Fouquet had then returned the document, which had many marginal notations indicating payment dates and sums, to Mazarin. Fouquet again disputed that the note had been found by Colbert at Saint-Mandé, reminding the judges that the first inventory of the papers in his office there by royal officials indicated that there were no documents of importance among them. So how did Colbert find it in the same place a day or two later? The documents found at Fontainebleau, he added, were not relevant to the transaction.

Séguier's questioning gave Fouquet the opening he needed to reaffirm his basic defense: putting Mazarin at the heart of the suspect transaction. Fouquet had earlier apologized jokingly to his judges for his defective memory, claiming that he could not even remember his children's birthdates. Now he provided a remarkably detailed account of the circumstances of the transaction. He reminded his listeners that Mazarin had wielded the royal authority, that "his orders had been obeyed as those of His Majesty; that the chancellor and the secretaries of state knew it . . . that he [Fouquet] had no right, much less the power, to defy his wishes."[10] Mazarin had used one of his bankers, Contarini, as a middleman in the transaction with the syndicate, and payments of the pension were usually handled by Contarini. Fouquet added slyly that if he himself had negotiated the terms of the tax farm with a personal interest in the transaction, "that would be a crime."[11] If anyone wondered whether a crime had been committed, Fouquet offered a calculation that over the life of the contract, the syndicate had paid out a total of 480,000 livres to the unnamed beneficiary, which could only be done by "diminishing the [contract] price for the farm" at the expense of the king.[12] He insisted that the transaction was concluded at Mazarin's "insistence" and "made with such authority" that "the pension was agreed and the merger of the syndicates resolved."[13] In short, "this pension was for the cardinal, who was all powerful, and who didn't answer to anyone for his actions, and who feared neither the censure nor reproach of anyone in the kingdom."[14]

By the end of the session, a badly outgunned Séguier was complimenting Fouquet on his powers of recollection and responded to Fouquet's bow by lifting his bonnet. Ormesson noted that many of his colleagues seemed impressed, while the "zealots" were dismayed at Séguier's performance.[15]

The interrogation resumed the following Monday, November 17, and opened with more skirmishing between Fouquet and Séguier about the chamber's competence. The king had ruled on the matter, said Séguier. Fouquet replied that the king could judge an issue either according to the laws or "above the law." If one applied the law, Fouquet's arguments should be heard. If the king were judging "above the law," from the plenitude of his powers, there was nothing to say. Séguier then snapped that Fouquet was accusing the king of abusing his authority. To which Fouquet replied that he had said no such thing, but Séguier had just done so.[16]

Séguier, however, was intent on returning to the substance of the previous session, the 120,000 livres pension. They tangled once more on the "proofs" that Fouquet was the true beneficiary of this bribe. How could Fouquet deny the evidence found in his papers? Where were the witnesses to Fouquet's claim that Colbert had planted the documents found at Saint-Mandé? What about the notations concerning the tax farm found on a document in his office at Fontainebleau? Fouquet stood his ground, helped by Séguier's ineptitude in mentioning once more the discrepancy between the original inventory at Saint-Mandé and Colbert's discovery of the pension papers. The answer, said Fouquet, was that the insertion had been made by someone in a position to lay hands on the document, either Colbert or Foucault, his "creature." As for the documents found at Fontainebleau, this was a misreading; the notations referred to other tax farming transactions he wished to discuss with colleagues. Before he finished, Fouquet added a few more damning details. Another proposal for the farming of the gabelle had been submitted earlier by an important tax farmer named Rambouillet. Rambouillet's offer had included a bribe in the form of a pension. Mazarin, in awarding the contract to the rival syndicate, had remarked that "since the Rambouillet group had offered a pension, the [other] farmers had to do the same." Fouquet continued, "What is absolutely true is that the pension was for the cardinal, although it was recorded under Contarini's name."[17]

Séguier then tried another approach: if Fouquet had used the pension document to reimburse himself for a debt owed by Mazarin, why were there no proofs of the loan or any record of it on the books of Fouquet's clerk, Charles Bernard? Here again, the answer was simple. The cardinal rarely bothered about formalities. Fouquet had lent the cardinal enormous sums without any documentation. The cardinal would use transactions like the one in question to repay the borrowings, in this case assuring him that "I will give you a document on which you can draw the money without any problem."[18] A complicated exchange on Bernard's bookkeeping brought no more light to the matter, and Séguier was simply unable to get past an obvious hurdle: there was nothing presented so far that tied Fouquet to the creation of this pension or that proved he was the unnamed beneficiary. Fouquet had offered a detailed alternative explanation of its origin, one that might appeal to his listeners. During the Fronde, Mazarin's critics in the high courts had accused the cardinal of exactly the kind of looting and mismanagement of state funds that Fouquet was now describing. As Fouquet reminded his audience, it was the prosecutor's responsibility to prove the charge against him, but the probabilities favored his explanations.[19]

By the end of the exchange, Séguier was visibly exhausted, while Fouquet, by contrast, seemed more than satisfied with himself.[20]

At the next session, November 18, Séguier examined Fouquet on other supposed pensions drawn on various tax farming arrangements. The evidence for these transactions consisted mostly of cryptic notes found in Fouquet's papers or in the accounts of his fugitive clerk, Louis Bruant. Séguier chose to lead off with the most dramatic, a pension of 140,000 livres drawn on a farming of the *aides*. The chief evidence here was a kind of memorandum of protest drawn up by the tax farmers awarded the transaction and deposited with a notary as a formal record of what had transpired. But Fouquet had already flagged the document in his written defenses to argue that Bruant's name had been inserted in the protest in a different ink and different handwriting from the rest of the document. This was clearly a fraud and was evidence tampered with to incriminate him. Citing this protest did nothing to buttress Séguier's assertions and provoked confusion in the chamber. For the other items, proof consisted largely of notations by Fouquet on different documents, which he insisted were intended to remind himself to investigate these transactions. Here again, there was nothing to tie Fouquet indisputably to their terms, no proof that he had ever received a distribution of funds from any of them. Much of the evidence seemed to point to wrongdoing by the absent Gourville, but Fouquet was not Gourville. The exchanges between Fouquet and Séguier that day provided some of Fouquet's best rejoinders thus far. Séguier was reduced to citing the assertions of Talon as proof of wrongdoing. The prosecutor could say whatever he wanted, Fouquet retorted, but his charges were not proofs. Judgments should not be based on "allegations and presumptions" but on "witnesses and evidence."[21] Dismissing Séguier's entire presentation, Fouquet insisted that all the things that could be proven against him were "not criminal, and all the things that could be criminal were not proven."[22]

As he finished, the look on Fouquet's face suggested that once more he believed he had held his own. Several judges lifted their bonnets as he left the room. This time, Séguier kept his firmly on his head.[23] Fouquet's spirits may also have been buoyed by an unexpected pleasure. As he waited in the small antechamber before the session, he was able to look out the window, where he saw familiar faces, including his younger brother Gilles, gathered to provide silent moral support for the prisoner.[24]

With each session, the exchanges between Fouquet and Séguier became more acerbic, as Séguier stepped into a role more appropriate for a prosecutor than an impartial magistrate weighing the evidence. Fouquet in turn began to treat Séguier as such, with replies designed to undermine Séguier's credibility. When the chamber reconvened on November 20, the charges before it concerned the *marc d'or* (see chapter 4). One of many expedients to raise money in 1657 was the doubling of the administrative posts for the royal Order of the Holy Spirit. These offices would be sold, to the crown's benefit, and the purchasers, before assuming their duties, would also have to pay an initiation fee known as the marc d'or. Both the offices themselves and the right to collect this fee would thus generate revenue and would be sold to bidders or syndicates that would pay the crown in advance and make their profit from the resale of the offices and the collection of the fees. Fouquet was accused of having arranged the winning bid, of participating under two assumed names, Duché and Montrésor, and of paying for his share with worthless treasury assignments. The crown would thus have received little or nothing from the financing.[25]

Fouquet professed himself amazed that the prosecution (and Séguier) could have advanced such a charge. He had been a participant in the transaction and did so to reimburse himself for the 900,000 livres he had lent the prior year at the siege of Valenciennes (1656), taking care to remind his listeners once more of the glowing letters sent to him by Mazarin at that time. Its terms had been set and approved not by Fouquet but by Abel Servien, who was also the administrator (*commissaire*) of the Order of the Holy Spirit. The use of "front men" was hardly unusual in such affairs. Addressing himself to Séguier, he asked, "What does that prove? . . . Haven't you acquired claims on the crown under assumed names? I have the proof of it; I can bring it here if necessary . . . Why is this a crime in my case?"[26]

In his written defenses, Fouquet had already made the same point, providing the aliases of several senior officials, including some high-ranking judges, as well as those of Mazarin, Séguier, Talon, and Colbert.[27] Fouquet also reminded his listeners that Duché was one of Servien's servants, one more indication that Servien had instigated the transaction. Whether it had been worthwhile for the crown was a question for Servien's heirs to answer, not him.

Séguier then made an amazing blunder. He disputed Fouquet's well-known services at Valenciennes, insisting that the money had been not been raised by Fouquet but had been provided by members of the king's council and that he had himself advanced 20,000 *écus*. Fouquet was all astonishment. This was not a claim made previously by the prosecution (and therefore Séguier should not have introduced it) and it was "shameful" to raise it now, without proofs from the treasurers' accounts.

He directly questioned Séguier: where and when had this happened? Séguier's answer made it clear that the "small sum" in question had nothing to do with the 900,000 livres raised by Fouquet. Séguier had also demanded Fouquet's written proofs that the money had been lent and that his reimbursement had been approved. Now Fouquet returned the question: was the chancellor's loan of 20,000 écus documented? Rather lamely, Séguier answered that he had given the money to Colbert without any receipt, and several years later Colbert returned it the same way, without any documentation.[28] Lest anyone miss the point, Fouquet provided a small lesson on usages under Mazarin. When dealing with financiers or contractors, the written formalities were always observed. But high officials often lent to the crown and were reimbursed without formalities. Séguier's own experience was proof of this.[29]

The session left Séguier seething. Several of the judges raised their hats to Fouquet as he withdrew, and Séguier rounded on one of them, Hérault, from the Parlement of Rennes. The chancellor observed sarcastically that tipping one's cap to a defendant must have been a custom of the Breton court, because such things were not done at the Tournelle (the criminal court in Paris).[30] The chancellor's mood was not improved by the distribution that same day of Fouquet's written defenses on an upcoming subject, the municipal customs duties (*octrois*). Copies were delivered, as in the past, to all of the judges, with three exceptions: Pussort, Voysin, and Séguier.[31]

The next two sessions, November 21 and November 22, were largely devoted to an accusation that Fouquet had secretly participated in the farming of a tax on sugar and beeswax imported through Rouen. Since Fouquet had negotiated the terms of the sale with the tax farmers, his participation constituted dealing for his own account at the expense of the crown. Once more, Fouquet lost Séguier in a complicated narrative, weaving together the essentials of the transaction and the formalities used to structure and document it. The proposal, he claimed, had originated with two leading tax farmers, Messrs. Giraudin and Agauri, and had been approved in the usual fashion. But it proved harder to find participants than assumed. Under these circumstances the tax farmers had suggested that Fouquet participate in what had become a "difficult matter," arguing that the superintendant's status in the marketplace would give it credibility. He allowed himself to be persuaded that this made sense.[32] At the same time, he was already owed 750,000 livres by the crown, and he was permitted to offset the crown's obligation to pay him against the cost of his share in the new transaction. In effect, he did not have to provide any funds for his participation. The arrangement was neither a bribe nor self-dealing, because the cardinal had approved it. If it seemed somewhat irregular, Fouquet again pleaded the necessity of the time. Raising his voice, he argued that in time of need, it was appropriate for a general to assume the duties of a private soldier.[33]

Pressed by the chancellor to prove this was done with Mazarin's approval, Fouquet shot back that he could find the documentation quite easily if allowed full access to his papers. But his persecutors had "suppressed and diverted everything, and after tying my hands, tell me to defend myself."[34] The late cardinal's secretaries could confirm his statements. Why not question them? If the cardinal was aware of all this, demanded Séguier, why did Fouquet hide his participation under an assumed name? Fouquet's answer was dismissive. There was nothing unusual about this, he repeated. He had discussed the transaction with the cardinal at Saint-Jean-de-Luz, and the cardinal had approved its terms and his involvement, as Messrs. Colbert and Berryer well knew.

Throughout this session, Fouquet had varied his tone, sometimes raising his voice or speaking sharply to Séguier when pressed, returning to a more civil tone when the crisis had passed. Some of the judges seemed offended by this, and Fouquet, although initially pleased with himself, asked Foucault at the end if he had gotten his points across to the chamber. Foucault was sure he had. On the other hand, Pussort seemed pained at Séguier's poor performance, and Séguier, it was said, spent the evening denouncing Berryer, perhaps for leading him into a procedural and factual quicksand.[35]

A second round on the same subject, on November 22, proved equally frustrating for Séguier. Fouquet would answer the chancellor's leading questions or overly broad accusations with a welter of detail, dispute procedure and formalities, and assert once more that the transaction had Mazarin's approval. He insisted that either his papers or testimony from Mazarin's secretaries would prove it, a challenge that was not taken up by Séguier or his associates.[36]

The balance of the session of November 22, as well as those of November 26 and November 27, was consumed with sparring about Fouquet's interest in the collection of municipal customs duties imposed on consumables (*octrois*), the subject of his most recently published defense. Séguier accused him of hiding his participation by using Madame du Plessis-Bellière's brother as a nominal party and of not paying for his share, thus depriving the crown of its rightful payment. Once more, while apologizing for his faulty memory, Fouquet took his listeners through an elaborate narrative that seemed to bewilder Séguier, but which rested on two points. First, Mazarin had approved the transaction and did not disapprove of Fouquet's acquiring rights that anyone could purchase, so to speak, in the marketplace. Second, Fouquet had bought his share from a contractor, not directly from the crown. How and under what circumstances he paid the contractor was irrelevant. If the crown had an issue about payment, it was with the contractor, the initial purchaser, not Fouquet as a secondary buyer (i.e., holder in due course).[37]

These sessions were probably most notable for the interaction among the judges. On November 26, before Fouquet was admitted to the chamber, Ormesson interrupted Séguier's remarks to correct several of the chancellor's calculations. The following day, in similar circumstances, Ormesson felt obliged to read Fouquet's earlier responses to Séguier's comments in an exchange that provoked laughter from their colleagues. At the close of one session, Séguier was observed to be quietly nodding off, a commentary on his own impaired health and on the tediousness of the arguments.[38]

The magistrates' theatrics were matched by those outside the courtroom. The trial had been interrupted for a day by news that Queen Maria Theresa was at death's door following a miscarriage. Prayers were ordered in all the churches, and saints' relics were carried in procession to the queen's bedside in the hope of a miraculous cure. The senior Madame Fouquet offered a country remedy, a salve or mustard plaster, to the queen mother, and shortly thereafter the young queen began to improve. The story made the rounds of Paris and with it the rumor that the king would reward this service with a pardon for Fouquet. Not everyone was convinced. Madame de Sévigné, who had heard "a bit about the tender-heartedness there," was skeptical of any such outcome.[39]

Several days later, the Fouquet ladies, strategically placed in a corridor at the Louvre by some unknown protector—perhaps the queen mother—threw themselves in front of the king imploring his mercy. Unlike the previous occasion when Louis had at least raised Madame Fouquet to her feet, this time he passed by without a glance or a word.[40] The king remarked several days later that the matter was with the chamber. He had no doubt that justice would be done, and he did not want to hear any more about it.[41]

Refusing to entertain a plea for clemency did not mean that Louis had no further interest in the progress of the trial. An increasingly impatient king summoned Séguier during the sessions on the octrois to urge him to expedite matters by not engaging in debates with Fouquet. The chancellor should simply read the charge and let Fouquet respond as he wished, advice the chancellor evidently did not follow.[42] At the same time, the crown attempted to put an end to the circulation of Fouquet's defenses. Royal officials raided the home of Fouquet's brother Gilles and seized all the copies found there. They also arrested some of Madame Fouquet's servants who were involved with the publications. Madame Fouquet petitioned the chamber for their release, and in the ensuing debate, Ormesson and Séguier again crossed swords when Ormesson observed that the royal presses were printing elements of the crown's case. The chancellor retorted that the king could print whatever he pleased; as for Madame Fouquet, she should apply to the royal officials involved, not to the chamber, for relief. One of the other judges, Massenau, added shrewdly that the seizure would not stop the circulation of Fouquet's defenses, since if the printed versions were seized, handwritten ones, perhaps a bit more expensive, would be peddled in the streets.[43]

Fouquet may have drawn some strength from the knowledge that his wife and mother had persisted in their courageous attempts to sway both royal and public opinion. He was certainly encouraged by an incident as he was leaving the chamber on November 27. A group of aristocratic ladies, including Madame de Sévigné, had stationed themselves at the windows of a house overlooking the walkway between the Arsenal and the Bastille. As Fouquet passed by, deep in thought, d'Artagnan called his attention to this audience. Immediately Fouquet donned his mask. He bowed and, said Sévigné, "put on that lighthearted expression" (*mine riant*) known to his friends.[44]

The next day's session, dedicated to a review of four loans that Fouquet had made directly to the crown, only demonstrated how much he had come to dominate the proceedings. Séguier's attempts to pin him down provided Fouquet with another opportunity to demonstrate his recall of detail and his grasp of the administrative formalities—whether observed or not—and to use that mastery in his own defense. Nor was Fouquet above taking aim directly at Séguier. For instance, when trying to find a simple example of the sequence of presentations and receipts required for disbursements, he used as his example the manner in which he had paid Séguier's various emoluments of office, leaving the chancellor at a loss for words.[45]

In a rare meeting of the minds, both Fouquet and the prosecution in the aftermath of that session expressed dissatisfaction with the pace of the presentations. Fouquet complained to d'Artagnan that the proceeding had begun at 11:30 and had only lasted three quarters of an hour. This was typical, and after all of these sessions to date, Fouquet had barely presented his defenses on a fraction of the charges. He wondered if the judges were interested in bringing the trial to conclusion.[46]

The prosecutors, too, were dissatisfied. On Sunday, November 30, Guy Chamillart, his colleague Vincent Hotman de Fontenay (who handled all the other prosecutions before the chamber), Berryer, Foucault, and their subordinates met at Chamillart's house to discuss the progress of the case. The king's request to Séguier to speed up the process had proved difficult to fulfill for several reasons. Séguier seemed determined to show he could hold his own with Fouquet. Given his advanced age and poor health, however, he could not sustain the exchange of arguments in the chamber for much longer than the forty-five minutes or so they routinely lasted, not counting the time devoted to procedures before Fouquet was admitted to the chamber. The chancellor had rejected the suggestion that he not engage in endless disputes with Fouquet, even though interrogation of the prisoner on the stool was "not intended to convince the accused."[47]

However, attempting to speed up or cut short the deliberations might result in protests from Fouquet that the prosecution was attempting to interfere with his right to defend himself on all the pending charges. This would not be in the crown's best interests, since it was not enough on the king's part to have "just and sincere intentions, but it was still necessary to save appearances." In an astonishing confession, the participants further agreed that appearances were more important than ever before because "not only is the public in favor of M. Fouquet, even the greater number of judges in the chamber are leaning strongly for him, such that the king's cause has been abandoned."[48]

Fouquet had given them an opening by stating that he, too, wanted the trial to move along. The prosecutors concluded that the best way to do this was to have the king make clear to Séguier that for reasons of state he wanted the whole trial over before Christmas. The sessions should start earlier, and rather than engaging Fouquet, Séguier should simply read the accusation and let Fouquet speak as long as he wanted without interruption. Colbert was enlisted to help with the plan, and Séguier was duly summoned by the king and so directed. Séguier resisted because he felt allowing Fouquet to present without comment or objection would give him too great an advantage. Louis, not willing to debate with Séguier, had Colbert reiterate the message. In a follow-up meeting later in the day with Chamillart and his team, Séguier was still not convinced, but he promised to obey "a command from his master's own mouth."[49] When the chamber reconvened on December 1, Séguier announced to his colleagues that beginning with the following session, Fouquet would be admitted at 9:00 a.m. to begin his presentation. This, said the chancellor, was to remedy Fouquet's complaints that the sessions were too short. The complaints of the king were not mentioned.[50]

True to his word, Séguier refrained from debating Fouquet on several transactions reviewed on that day, thus giving Fouquet the opportunity to present his version of events unchallenged. On major matters, as always, his first and last defense was Mazarin. Speaking of a loan of about 10.8 million livres raised in 1658, Fouquet noted that Servien had signed off on it, that it had been arranged at the time of the siege of Hesdin, when once more Mazarin was clamoring for money, and that the interest rate of 10 percent was far from excessive. Everyone knew that Mazarin had written him a letter thanking him for his efforts and promising that the superintendant, who had borrowed some of these funds under his own name, would not lose a "farthing" (*teston*) on the transaction. The king had thanked him in person, but nevertheless the cardinal's "successors have not scrupled to make a crime out of a most praiseworthy act."[51]

Fouquet made full use of Séguier's newfound latitude at the next session, where he addressed the mysterious case of the 6 million livres of treasury bills supposedly issued to cover an interest rate differential for a large royal borrowing that was never consummated. Rather than be destroyed, the notes had allegedly been kept thereafter by Fouquet and his associates to cover future embezzlements. Jeannin de Castille had testified to this effect. Fouquet now repeated arguments that had long been in print: Jeannin de Castille's testimony had only come about after several visits from Berryer and the threat of torture. Moreover, he had testified without the corroboration of his registers, and when the relevant register was made available, it had evidently been tampered with.[52]

A long disquisition on structures and bookkeeping to prove that no embezzlement took place eventually folded into Fouquet's standard defense, that when the cardinal was urgently demanding money for the necessities of state, one could either move matters expeditiously or stand on ceremony and let the royal treasury go barren. In this case, "one did not observe the formalities; but it is the reality which makes a crime, not the disregard of a formality."[53]

Fouquet spoke without pause for more than two hours, never, marveled Ormesson, "becoming agitated, embarrassing himself, or leaving out a justification to his advantage."[54] His colleague Renard called Fouquet's performance beyond comparison: "He never spoke as well as this in parlement."[55]

Fouquet also announced that he still had clarifications to offer on many of the charges before the chamber but that he was aware that the king wanted to see the trial concluded. He would therefore move along as fast as he could, "not being able to offer His Majesty any other service in the position to which he had been reduced."[56]

The next day, December 3, Fouquet again spoke for more than two hours, providing a few more "clarifications" on the infamous 6 million, before passing—at Séguier's instigation—to the charge that his extravagant lifestyle had been paid for by diverting funds from the crown's coffers to his own. Séguier introduced figures to show that vast sums of money passed through Fouquet's hands, and, he insisted, much of it had been embezzled. The figures Séguier offered were derived from several sets of registers and were often blatantly inconsistent. At one point, Séguier alleged that Bruant's records proved Fouquet had handled more than 100 million livres of funds per annum in the years 1658–1661. But later, taking his figures from another clerk's records, the figure he provided for borrowed funds in the years 1657–1661 was 16,680,000 livres, of which a mere 800,000 livres found their way to the king's coffers; the rest, Séguier insisted, had been spent on Belle-Isle, Vaux-le-Vicomte, lavish entertainments, and the like.[57]

Fouquet was dismissive. Séguier, he explained, simply did not understand bookkeeping. Vast sums received from Claude Girardin, for example, were loans directly to him, which Fouquet sometimes used personally and at other times used to support the crown by buying crown obligations. The gross amounts he borrowed, therefore, did not necessarily reflect sums intended for the king's coffers. It was for the prosecution to prove the contrary, and that could not be shown from the registers Séguier cited.[58]

Passing to Séguier's comments on his showy lifestyle, Fouquet admitted that he had spent extravagantly, but his position required it. He had entertained the royal court on several occasions, as well as foreign dignitaries, including the queens of Sweden and England. To do so required a vast establishment, with houses well-provided with fine furniture, tapestries, and silver plate. The cardinal and the king had approved of all this display. How was it paid for? His private revenues, the pensions and gratifications he received from his offices, his wife's income, and the amounts he had borrowed exceeded the amount he had spent in those years. If his expenses were "a folly, they were not a crime."[59] It was to his creditors that he had to answer, no one else. Whatever one wanted to make of this, "there was nothing out of which to make a crime."[60]

The final day of the oral presentations, December 4, was set aside for the "crime of state," the plan found in Fouquet's Saint-Mandé study. This document had been an unexpected gift to Fouquet's enemies, who had originally conceived of his prosecution for purely financial crimes. Treason, plotting an uprising against the crown, was far easier for the public to understand and harder for Fouquet to dismiss, as the relevant documents were entirely in his own handwriting. Even if Fouquet could explain away many of the questionable financial transactions at issue, conviction on the treason charge alone would be enough to send him to the scaffold.

Séguier took full advantage of this opportunity. Despite his protests, Fouquet was forced to listen not only to the prosecutor's charge but also to a reading aloud of the plan. Sitting on his low wooden stool, he listened impassively, with his eyes fixed on the large crucifix on the wall above Séguier's place. The reading rattled Fouquet. When Séguier asked if he had anything to say, Fouquet replied that he was embarrassed to have written something so foolish.[61]

Séguier cut him short. The prosecutor—speaking through Séguier—considered this the most important evidence in the entire trial. Fouquet had repeatedly insisted on his loyalty and zeal in the king's service, on the many sacrifices he had made to advance the king's interests, and on his deep devotion to the king's person. Now, one could see the truth. This document, containing his most private thoughts, "speaks in a very different tone." Here was a minister preparing to betray his oaths of office, plotting to subvert officials and foment rebellion, and one who had diverted royal funds to build a following and to pay for the places, vessels, and bribes to be used for this purpose. And, Séguier added sarcastically, the accused wanted them to believe that the plan was nothing but a fantasy, a will-o-the-wisp (*fumée*).[62]

Taken aback by Séguier's powerful assault, Fouquet at first tried to take refuge in the law. The chamber, he argued, had been commissioned to investigate and punish financial crimes; it had no authority to investigate a crime of state. It was a weak retort, and one to which Séguier had a quick response. Fouquet's conspiracy arose out of his hope to retain his office. Thus, the offense arose from precisely what the chamber was empowered to investigate, Fouquet's actions as superintendant. Fouquet's own conscience, he suggested, told him he was not innocent. Fouquet's claim (in his written defenses) that he only wanted to protect himself against Mazarin was absurd. His proposed actions would have damaged the state, and the king "would have suffered the most from the civil war with which the accused threatened the kingdom."[63]

Fouquet again offered objections on legal grounds to the chamber's jurisdiction over a "crime of state," but sensing that this was not effective, he switched his argument in mid-sentence. Keying off his earlier comments, he argued that what he had done was nothing more than a fantasy, an ill-digested composition that he had disavowed as soon as it had escaped him. Proof of this, he implied, was in his own behavior during the Fronde. He had remained loyal to the king and had performed important services at a time when "the chief officers of his state were at the head of his enemies and served in their councils."[64]

Raising his voice, Fouquet announced that he would give the chamber an example of a crime of state. One of those senior officers persuaded his son-in-law to open the gates of a city to the Spaniards, letting them penetrate into the heart of the realm, putting the kingdom and the crown at risk. That was a true "crime of state."[65] The allusion was to Séguier's behavior in March 1652, when the chancellor, aligned with the Fronde, had convinced his son-in-law, the duc de Sully, royal governor of Mantes, to allow Spanish troops to cross the Seine unopposed. Struck to the core, Séguier could think of no reply. If Madame de Sévigné is to be believed, "the chancellor didn't know where to hide, and the [other judges] had a great urge to laugh."[66]

Fouquet did not give Séguier a chance to recover but plunged ahead. The plan had been written at a moment when he feared the cardinal's intentions toward him, but in fact the two had managed to reach an accommodation. Thus, the scheme was a "fantasy," and he had never spoken to anyone about it, the implication being that without conspirators, there was no conspiracy. Others had sought to slander him by publishing what had been nothing more than a chimera. Its publication, however, did prove something very different, that there was a longstanding plan to discredit him, directed by Colbert. For this, another proof could also be found in the superintendant's papers, Colbert's letter of 1659 to the cardinal denouncing Fouquet and calling for a chamber of justice with Talon as prosecutor and Fouquet as its chief target. The copy of the letter in Fouquet's papers (intercepted by Fouquet's agents, as noted earlier) was partly in Gourville's handwriting. The letter had revealed to Fouquet the hatred of his enemies.[67]

Séguier, finally recovering from his own shock, tried to counter. The plan had been altered several times over two years (1657–1658), so how could it be construed as simply a stray bad thought? Fouquet replied by offering a history of his frequent strains with the cardinal over those years. Again, the writing was nothing more than a way of letting off steam, nothing more than "fantasies he had put on paper" as his resentment flared up over that period, only a "vapor and chimera."[68]

Séguier managed a rhetorical question: was it a "vapor" to subvert royal officers, to steal the king's money, to fortify places and construct ships to be used against the king, to set fire to the kingdom with a civil war? Fouquet repeated that all this was bad in theory but nothing compared to actually helping an invading enemy, once more alluding to Séguier's behavior during the Fronde.[69]

Séguier tried again: to criticize the government was to criticize the prince. No, said Fouquet. He had been afraid that a minister, Mazarin, would use the power of the crown to destroy him, and the writing simply reflected that fear. He offered a current analogy: from the way his trial was being conducted, it would seem that it was in the interest of state to abandon all standards of justice to destroy Colbert's enemy, meaning himself.[70]

With Séguier silenced, Fouquet was free to restate his arguments and to address some of the weaknesses in his earlier presentations. He reminded his hearers of his important services during the Fronde and of Mazarin's suspicious and sometimes capricious behavior that had created the resentment underlying the plan of Saint-Mandé. To the assertion that he had admitted under interrogation that he had shown the document to Gourville, his answer was that he had communicated his resentment to Gourville, not the written plan, adding that Gourville had sometimes alerted him to Mazarin's intentions and had helped him transcribe Colbert's 1659 memorandum to the cardinal.[71] This was an important distinction, since without collaborators there was no conspiracy, just foolish thoughts about which he was embarrassed in retrospect. But it was without precedent to prosecute someone for a thought alone; "such things had never been broached in any jurisdiction."[72]

The fate of Belle-Isle, he continued, was proof that he had harbored no treasonable designs. When arrested, Fouquet had offered immediately to sign an order to the local commander there to submit to the crown's authority and had done so, although this had been unnecessary. The commander, never having received any contrary instructions, fully obeyed the king's directives. Fouquet pointed out that the crown prosecutor had not even questioned most of the people named in the plan to test how much this reflected an operative scheme, arguing that preparations to execute it would constitute a "crime of state," but none existed. The real conspiracy, he maintained, was against him, with the establishment of a chamber of justice to hear charges that should be tried if at all before his "natural judges," meaning the Parlement of Paris. To guarantee the result, the conspirators had rigged his interrogation and tampered with his files. All of this was because of the great services he had rendered to the crown and the jealousy this had aroused. He would name those responsible whenever the king would hear him.[73]

Sensing he had taken his arguments as far as he could, Fouquet stopped and asked the chancellor whether he would be called again to testify. When Séguier answered in the negative, Fouquet asked the chamber's indulgence to clarify some of his earlier comments on his personal finances. Fouquet's arguments about the plan of Saint-Mandé were largely self-contained, whereas the many charges of financial irregularity had been presented as proofs of a broad-based effort by the superintendant and his financial collaborators to loot the state's coffers. Fouquet's vigorous defenses, both written and oral, had poked holes in many of the individual charges. Still, there remained one nagging consideration. If Fouquet had not been embezzling, could his extravagant lifestyle really have been supported by his own resources? In the absence of a convincing explanation, his entire defense might simply fail to convince his judges. It was worthwhile, therefore, to make one final effort to address the question.

Fouquet repeated that an examination of his books and registers would show that his expenditures did not exceed the funds available to him from his and his wife's private income and investments, his compensation for the high offices of state he held, and his accumulated debt, somewhere between 8 and 9 million livres. He offered to provide more exact and detailed calculations if the chamber wished him to, a reminder that the prosecutors, who had full access to his records, had not produced this key proof of embezzlement.[74]

Fouquet followed this last comment with a demand for justice against those who had persecuted him, who had seized and pillaged his papers, falsified inventories, and who "with all of that had not proved anything" against him.[75] Had his papers been left intact, they would have demonstrated conclusively the evidence of his great services to the state. Instead, in the months following his arrest, his enemies had systematically tampered with his files, removing some documents, substituting others, forging or falsifying still others. Once this was done, they had solicited perjured testimony from discredited witnesses, testimony contradicted by written evidence produced at the trial. Shamefully, the public prosecutor had protected rather than pursued these same tainted witnesses. Fouquet, however, had not hesitated to expose these slanders and abuses to a chamber composed of magistrates from the leading courts of France. Who was behind all this? Fouquet wanted to leave no doubt in his judges' minds: the culprit was Colbert, whose "slanders" had persuaded the king to act. He now asked that the chamber do its duty to punish these perversions of justice. His request to have the court investigate these abuses had been foreclosed by a high authority (the king's decree), but the chamber was still free to act against false witnesses, to make an example of them, since "nothing could be a greater scandal" than leaving them unpunished.[76]

On this final, defiant note, Fouquet fell silent. He had spoken forcefully, sometimes angrily, during this final appearance before the chamber. After his customary bows, he left the room, walking straight ahead, with a firm step and without stopping to speak to anyone.[77] It was now time for his judges to do their duty.

CHAPTER 8

The Honor and Conscience of Judges

In the waning days of the trial, the prevailing mood on both sides had been one of apprehension. The prosecutors fretted that Fouquet's passionate arguments and his widely disseminated defenses had turned not only the literate public but even the judges against the crown's case.[1] Séguier's exchanges with Fouquet did little to reassure those favorable to the crown that a conviction was inevitable. Angry that Fouquet had dominated the last two sessions, Poncet, Sainte-Hélène, and Pussort had upbraided Séguier in front of their colleagues for not introducing evidence that Fouquet had indeed taken steps to execute the plan of Saint-Mandé; even Ormesson expressed his surprise to the chancellor about this. Séguier was dismissive. The evidence was so weak that Fouquet would have made use of it to discredit the charge, "fine proofs" the chancellor pronounced "ridiculous." Such an admission by the chancellor must have dismayed those counting on a guilty verdict.[2]

Anxieties ran deep in the ranks of Fouquet's supporters as well. The Fouquet family were said to hope for banishment at best, but rumor had it that their earlier doubts about Ormesson had resurfaced. These fears were fed by the gossip in some circles that Ormesson had been punctilious about the formalities to underscore his impartiality as a judge but in the end would prove himself a king's man.[3] Madame de Sévigné spoke for Fouquet's friends when she wrote that "the days pass very slowly, and the uncertainty is frightful . . . it will be a real miracle if things come out as we hope."[4]

At least outwardly, the chief actor in the drama seemed surprisingly calm. On the morning after Fouquet's dramatic exit from the courtroom, a curious d'Artagnan found a pretext to enter his cell at an unexpected hour. He found the prisoner sitting by a fireplace reading a prayer book. To d'Artagnan's jest about finding him idle, Fouquet replied that there was nothing to do now except await his judgment, and he hoped to receive it calmly no matter what it was. In telling the story, d'Artagnan added that Fouquet was not certain that he had said enough to convince the judges. Knowing, however, that the king wanted to expedite the process, he had decided, against the advice of his lawyers, to take the initiative rather than be forced to cut short his defense.[5] What d'Artagnan did not know was that as an extra precaution, Fouquet had somehow arranged that an unnamed woman friend would provide him with a secret sign—perhaps some gesture visible from his windows at the Bastille—that would let him know the verdict before court officials would arrive to read it to him. With a half hour to steady himself, he was sure he could receive even the worst news without flinching.[6]

With Fouquet's testimony finished, the next steps in the trial fell to the *rapporteurs*, Ormesson and Sainte-Hélène. They were each required to prepare a recapitulation of the charges against Fouquet, and of the evidence presented by both sides to support or deny the accusations, and to provide their own opinions on each charge. If they found him guilty on any count, they were also to recommend the appropriate penalty. The other judges were free to comment or to question them during these presentations and were not bound by the rapporteurs' conclusions. Nevertheless, since the burden of work during the trial had fallen on the shoulders of the rapporteurs, who were deemed to be most familiar with the entirety of the evidence, their conclusions carried a special weight. The final decision on each count would be by vote of the entire bench of magistrates.

The membership of the court had changed considerably over the many months of the trial. Lamoignon had removed himself from the proceedings, and, as noted, Le Bossu had been forced off the court by royal fiat, as had Louis Boucherat on Colbert's initiative. Francon of Grenoble had died in 1662 and had been replaced by La Baume from the same court; Chouart had been replaced by his colleague on the Grand Conseil, Cuissotte de Gisaucourt; Le Tellier's son, Louvois, sitting as a representative of the Parlement of Metz, had been replaced in 1662 by Ferriol, also from that court. During the oral presentations in November 1664, Fayet, another judge aligned with Lamoignon and believed favorable to Fouquet, fell ill and was removed from the court by Séguier.[7] Lamoignon's brother-in-law, Nesmond, a very respected second president (*président à mortier*) of the Parlement of Paris, died in late November 1664 as the trial entered its last phase. It was said that on his deathbed, Nesmond expressed regret that he had voted against the recusal of Pussort and Voysin, a useful admission for Fouquet but one more than counterbalanced by the loss of his vote.[8]

It had been agreed that Ormesson would speak first, and he was only too aware of the expectations placed on him. He told his colleagues he required several days to prepare and several more days to present. In the meantime, not wishing to be unduly influenced by others, he asked to be left alone, a request that extended even to his close friends. "He is in conclave," wanting no contact with the outside world, wrote Madame de Sévigné, adding that she nevertheless let him know her opinion as he was taking his leave of her.[9]

In the days that followed, Ormesson, alone with his thoughts, could draw on centuries of legal tradition and jurisprudence to guide him as he wrestled with the evidence and formulated his conclusions. As one modern scholar, Antoine Astaing, has pointed out, two of the legal maxims held in high esteem at the time provided flatly contradictory principles. The first held that it was better to leave a guilty person unpunished than condemn an innocent party; the second held that no crime should go unpunished.[10] The judge's craft consisted of determining which principle was applicable in any given case. As a practical matter, judges were counseled to adhere strictly to the rules of procedure that had been developed over time.[11] Such rules applied in particular to the weighing of the kinds of proof acceptable in criminal cases: confessions (not applicable in Fouquet's trial); the testimony of witnesses, at least two of whom were required to sustain a charge; and physical evidence, including documents or other artifacts that could be tied to the alleged crimes.[12] Since the procedures of the time did not provide for any adversarial process to test the evidence and testimony gathered in the early stages of a case, the responsibility for such scrutiny fell largely on the shoulders of magistrates at the trial level. For this reason, appellate court judges were enjoined to examine closely the evidence offered in trials in the lower courts and to dismiss or disregard anything that was somehow tainted, testimony from witnesses whose credibility was suspect, and so forth. The chamber of justice was a special court of first instance but one composed entirely of magistrates from the higher courts who would have been familiar with these exhortations.[13]

In capital cases above all others, it was held, a conviction and condemnation required proof that was "clearer than the day."[14] In practice, however, the same legal theorists accepted that "judgment calls" or discretionary conclusions were inevitable, given the imperfections inherent in the system. Once again, a great deal fell to the judge, who was expected to be guided by a sense of justice and morality. If the crown and accepted customs were the proximate sources of the law,

zle millions that were spent on Saint-Mandé, Vaux-le-Vicomte, and Belle-Isle.[49] He accepted without reservation the prosecution's version of the affair of the 6 million livres, insisting that both Jeannin de Castille and Tabouret were credible witnesses to a planned embezzlement. That the suspect notes (*billets*) were found in Fouquet's papers proved intent to do so at some future time. He offered the analogy of a servant caught red-handed with his master's purse who explained that he was only guarding it to return to his master. How credible would such an excuse be?[50]

Sainte-Hélène expended the most energy on the even more sensational "crime of state," the plan of Saint-Mandé. Unlike Ormesson, he argued that such offenses were "so odious and so damaging" to the state that even the idea was a punishable offense. Like Ormesson, he reached into the past for an analogy from the time of François I, citing the (apocryphal) case of an unnamed nobleman executed for having admitted to dreaming in his sleep about harming the king. Implying that Fouquet intended to harm the king was deliberate: planning a regicide was the only recognized "crime of thought" in French law.[51] In this instance, the plan itself was in Fouquet's own handwriting. What would have happened if it had fallen into Madame du Plessis-Bellière's hands after Fouquet's arrest? The kingdom would have been ablaze with civil war. Luckily, "God, who watches over [*préserve*] France, did not permit the execution of these terrible schemes."[52] Sainte-Hélène concluded rather hypocritically that he hoped Fouquet would benefit from the king's mercy. But as a matter of law, Fouquet was guilty of embezzlement, malfeasance in office (*malversation*), and treason. In consideration of his high birth and the offices he had held, Fouquet should be spared hanging. Instead, he should be publicly beheaded at the Bastille and his assets forfeited to the crown.[53]

The two rapporteurs had spoken, offering diametrically opposed conclusions and recommendations for their colleagues to follow. There only remained the polling and voting by the assembled judges. This would hardly take place in a vacuum. "People speak of nothing else," wrote Madame de Sévigné, "they argue, draw conclusions, count with their fingers . . . one is overwhelmed."[54]

The pressures on the judges from every direction had mounted as the trial came to its climax. Just before Ormesson opined, Foucault called on the judges. He showed them a letter signed by the king that repeated that he had ordered the removal from Fouquet's files of certain documents bearing on affairs of state and that nothing in them was useful for Fouquet's defense. The king would therefore be displeased if any judge based his conclusions on that removal. If this were not enough, Louis made a point of remarking in public at about the same time that Fouquet was a dangerous man.[55]

Some of the judges were singled out for special attention. Hérault, who had inclined toward Ormesson's point of view, received a visit from one of Le Tellier's subordinates urging him to reconsider. Chamillart and Foucault called on La Baume with promises of offices and commissions in return for his vote, while the duc de Lesdiguières tried to persuade him to clemency, as did the marquis de Créqui, a son-in-law of Madame du Plessis-Bellière.[56] Colbert spoke with La Toison and offered to review any questions or doubts he might still have about the evidence. But Colbert's efforts were offset by those of the prince de Condé, governor of Burgundy, who made La Toison aware of his hopes that Fouquet would be treated leniently. In Burgundy, the memory of the rigged trial of the maréchal de Marillac in 1632 by a special court still weighed heavily. Those judges who had served on that court and voted to condemn him were still held in contempt, those who voted against the death penalty still esteemed. La Toison was urged not to disgrace his province. Catinat's children begged him not to shame them with a death sentence. Louis Phélypeaux de Pontchartrain, one of the most respected judges and one whose vote was uncertain, was heavily solicited. Spokesmen for the crown alternated promises and threats, and as the voting drew near, Séguier took him aside to tell him that the king expected him to do him a great service in the matter. Against these inducements, Pontchartrain had to weigh his son's pleas for mercy, which the son delivered on bended knee, begging him not to dishonor the family name and vowing to quit the law if his father did so. Rocquesante was lobbied by members of the family of Fouquet's son-in-law, the comte de Charost.[57]

Fouquet's connections in the *parti dévot* were also active. Like many parlementary families, the Fouquets and Ormessons were parishioners of Saint-Nicolas-des-Champs, whose pastor, Claude Joly, was a leading dévot. As Ormesson left Mass on the eve of his presentation, Joly spoke to him about Fouquet.[58] Even Séguier was approached on Fouquet's behalf. Séguier, also a well-known figure in dévot circles, visited the Convent of the Visitation on the rue Saint-Antoine in late November 1664 to give thanks to for a recent improvement in his health. The mother abbess had the relics of François de Sales brought out of storage for his veneration and used the occasion to intercede for Fouquet, whose sisters were associated with the order. Séguier promised to do justice to Fouquet in the sight of God, without any other considerations. Fouquet's friends were—with good reason—skeptical of what Madame de Sévigné called "a comedy."[59]

Rushing to finish before the holidays, Séguier convened the chamber at eight in the morning of December 17 to begin the voting. Pussort, the first to speak, went on for five hours, with a passion and a vehemence that startled some of his listeners, offering in effect a rejoinder to Ormesson's more nuanced conclusions and an endorsement of Sainte-Hélène's. Promising his audience that he would restrict himself to five or six of the major charges against Fouquet, he began with the murky affair of the 6 million livres. Citing the testimony of Jeannin de Castille and Martin Tabouret, Pussort insisted that this was undoubtedly a scheme to embezzle that sum from the treasury by use of the treasury notes handed over to Gourville, Fouquet's accomplice, in September 1658.[60] After reviewing and dismissing Fouquet's defense at length, he closed by answering one of Fouquet's strongest arguments. Fouquet had asked, rhetorically, why he had never presented the notes for payment, if that was his intent. The reason, Pussort replied, was that the king's appointment of Colbert to watch over the treasury records made it impossible to execute the plan. Pussort also pointed out that this was not a charge that Fouquet could refute by alleging the removal from his files of orders or instructions from Mazarin (since the cardinal would obviously not approve an embezzlement). In short, the charge was duly proven.[61]

Pussort then addressed Fouquet's argument that in many of his transactions with the crown he was only reimbursing himself for loans to the state. Contrary to the law, Fouquet's clerks had both received and paid out funds, mingling royal funds with the superintendant's own. So who could say if the large sums Fouquet supposedly lent to the crown, the 900,000 livres at the siege of Valenciennes, or the 3.8 million livres on another occasion, were really his? Perhaps he was only advancing the king the king's own money.[62] Where would the money have come from? Records indicated that in the years 1656–1659 at least 8 to 10 million livres per annum flowed into the treasury from "alienations" (i.e., sales) of the crown's rights. This, Pussort emphasized, would have provided the money that Fouquet "lent" to the crown.[63]

Pussort turned next to the pensions to which Fouquet had illicitly helped himself, beginning with the 140,000 livres drawn on the farming of the aides. Here, the evidence was circumstantial (*présomptions*) but strong enough to amount to proof: the involvement of one of Fouquet's clerks, Lespine, who handled his personal finances, was persuasive.[64] The 120,000 livres pension on the gabelle was one Fouquet had always insisted had been intended for Mazarin. But the order establishing it, with the beneficiary's name in blank, had been found at Saint-Mandé among Fouquet's papers, and he had admitted receiving payments drawn on it. What more was to be said? Dismissing all of Fouquet's arguments that the drawings represented reimbursement authorized by Mazarin, the true beneficiary, Pussort concluded that charge was proved.[65]

Reviewing the charges involving the pensions drawn on the convoi de Bordeaux, the tax-farming of the octrois, and several others, Pussort argued that the circumstantial evidence was strong enough to conclude that either Fouquet directly benefited from them or did so through the agency of his cronies like Gourville or Madame du Plessis-Bellière.[66]

Pussort saved his strongest remarks for the "crime of state," the plan of Saint-Mandé. He took his listeners over the elements of the plan and the roles Fouquet had assigned to his confidants and agents. Fouquet had always insisted it was simply a "wicked idea" directed against Mazarin. Pussort, like the prosecutors and Sainte-Hélène, treated it as an ongoing conspiracy only thwarted by the superintendant's arrest. He was dismissive of Fouquet's insistence that he had bought and fortified Belle-Isle with the consent of the cardinal. Mazarin might have known of the purchase, but could not do anything about it until peace with Spain had been achieved.[67] He stressed the extraordinary level of fortifications at Belle-Isle, the strongest in the kingdom.[68] Fouquet, in his double capacity as *procureur général* and superintendant of finance, had the king's confidence, and he abused his positions by using royal funds to foster his designs. The execution of the plot might well have led to the "overthrow of the state."[69] If Madame de Sévigné is to be believed, Pussort was inept enough to compare Fouquet's plot to that of constable de Bourbon against François I in the previous century, hardly a welcome subject to the reigning Bourbon dynasty.[70]

In conclusion, Pussort insisted that death by hanging was the proper death for such crimes, but, out of consideration for Fouquet's many distinguished relatives, he would agree to a nobleman's death by beheading. He also proposed confiscation of Fouquet's assets to recompense the crown for its losses at the former superintendant's hands.[71]

By the time Pussort finished speaking, the day was done, and the chamber was adjourned to the next morning, December 18, when once again it started early. Perhaps mindful of the king's desire to see the trial ended before the holidays, or perhaps because the earlier speakers had thoroughly reviewed the major points of contention, none of the remaining judges spoke as long as the two rapporteurs or Pussort. Gisaucourt, the first speaker of the day, dwelt on the pension on the gabelle, the marc d'or transaction, and the "crime of state." He found Fouquet guilty on all three and emphasized that the "crime of state" was no "chimera." At the time Fouquet was contemplating these actions, the authority of the state was weak and the crown had had to deal with uprisings and rebellions in Normandy and elsewhere. He accepted the recommendations of Sainte-Hélène, death and confiscation of assets.[72]

In a speech laden with Latin tags, Ferriol had no problem finding Fouquet guilty of various financial crimes, in which Gourville was his accomplice.[73] He was also guilty of the crime of state.[74] Ferriol drew a direct link between the crushing levels of taxation during the 1650s and Fouquet's extravagant spending. Although a member of the Parlement of Metz, Ferriol was a Dauphinois, and he chose to talk about his native province. In Dauphiné, tax collectors in 1658 had used the cruelest and most ruthless methods to extract more than 300,000 livres out of the people, about the cost of a bastion at Belle-Isle or a waterfall at Vaux.[75] Warming to the theme, Ferriol poured scorn on public opinion in Paris, which had turned from initial condemnation to a capricious demand for Fouquet's release. But in the provinces, popular sentiment was very different. The heavy taxation that people had endured had funded Fouquet's fortifications and "criminal pleasures." The amounts he wasted at his table would have been sufficient to feed millions.[76] For all these crimes, Ferriol agreed with Sainte-Hélène's recommendations.[77]

Noguès found that Fouquet was guilty of financial crimes.[78] He preferred, however, to dwell on the "crime of state." Fouquet was a dangerous man, as evidenced by the plot. Its conception alone was criminal, even without steps taken to execute it.[79] In fact, the plan of Saint-Mandé was comparable to the Catiline conspiracy against the Roman republic.[80] As superintendant of finance, Fouquet had violated the king's trust, and he had plotted against his sovereign. He deserved death.[81]

The Breton Hérault was brief. He was dismissive of Fouquet's insistence that his private means plus borrowings funded his extravagant spending. In itself this was proof of his embezzlement of state funds. He was also guilty of the "crime of state." He, too, agreed with Sainte-Helene's recommendations: death and confiscation of assets.[82]

The last speaker of the day, Pierre Raffélis de Rocquesante, offered a glimmer of hope to Fouquet's supporters. The *parlementaire* from Aix began by calling attention to the extraordinary public interest in the case, and then launched into his findings. The various pensions were not Fouquet's; the claims on the crown (the "sugar and beeswax," octrois, and so forth) were handled correctly.[83] Mazarin was aware of the marc d'or transaction, and the issue was the price paid—a civil matter, not a criminal one.[84] The affair of the 6 million livres was a question of poor housekeeping, not of embezzlement.[85] As an indication of the many irregularities common at the time, Rocquesante cited the revelation that Mazarin had received 20 million livres per annum without any proper accounting for its use.[86] The so-called crime of state was not a crime, even if it had been communicated to others, absent action on anyone's part.[87] Like Ormesson, Rocquesante saw Fouquet as filled with greed and ambition, guilty of negligence and maladministration in carrying out his duties. For this, the penalty should be banishment and confiscation of his assets.[88]

Thus far, only Rocquesante had sided with Ormesson, but observers believed that eight others would join him, for a total of ten votes against death: six judges had already voted for death, and there was no doubt that Voysin, Poncet, and Séguier would follow. The tally would then be ten for banishment, nine for death. The swing votes were La Baume, Catinat, and Pontchartrain, all three of whom, as noted above, had been heavily solicited by both sides. A single one of these agreeing with Ormesson would produce a tie vote, thus sparing Fouquet the axe, which would require a majority vote. If all three voted for death, the vote would be twelve to ten and, as Ormesson realized, would mean certain death for Fouquet, since to all appearances there was no hope of royal clemency.[89]

On his way into the Arsenal the next morning, Ormesson exchanged a few words with the Fouquet family, gathered there, as they had the previous day, in the hopes of influencing the judges. Within the chamber, Ormesson noticed Voysin lobbying furiously with La Baume. Pontchartrain approached Ormesson and whispered assurances from La Baume that he would not waver in his opinion, notwithstanding all of the pressure.[90]

La Toison, the first speaker of the day, voiced skepticism about the evidence on the financial charges and was dismissive of the crime of state. He sided with Ormesson.[91] La Baume, who spoke next, only offered a few sentences. He, too, agreed with Ormesson's findings and recommended that Fouquet be sentenced to perpetual banishment.[92]

Massenau, from Toulouse, was brief but sarcastic. Like Ormesson, he dismissed out of hand the plan of Saint-Mandé. Was it a "crime of state?" Massenau thought not, since Fouquet had never acted on it.[93] The discovery of the plan only proved that Fouquet was a fool and covered him with ridicule.[94]

With respect to financial crimes, Massenau was actually accusatory, but not toward Fouquet. He was astonished that other high-ranking persons had signed and sealed the financing arrangements in question, meaning, presumably, the late Servien and Séguier, sitting just a few feet away as he spoke.[95] If this were not enough, he reminded his listeners that the investigation phase of the trial (*instruction*) had been marred by many "extraordinary" things, meaning evidence tampering, and by the participation of Berryer, who was now accused in another proceeding of embezzling a million livres from the king. All of this was very troubling and made it difficult to arrive at firm conclusions about the charges against Fouquet.[96] Nevertheless, he agreed with Ormesson's findings and recommendations, adding only that the sentence should include the razing of Vaux-le-Vicomte.[97]

Du Verdier, from the Parlement of Bordeaux, now rose. After reviewing the major financial charges, he concluded that the prosecution had not proved any of them. As for the "crime of state," du Verdier, who had evoked the memory of Saint Louis earlier, did not believe that thinking about a sin was a sin, or that it rendered all one's other acts sinful.[98] He did agree that Fouquet, a blindly ambitious man, had neglected the responsibilities of his office, creating much confusion in the king's affairs.[99] For this, the proper precedent was the punishment suffered by Poyet under François I: loss of office, internal exile (i.e., house arrest at some remote location), and a fine of 100,000 livres.[100]

Catinat, another swing vote, was not sympathetic to Fouquet, whom he portrayed as a man of ambition, jealous of his position, and ungrateful to his patron the cardinal.[101] The plan of Saint-Mandé had arisen from those circumstances, but it was a "chimera," and not a "crime of state."[102] Fouquet's embarrassment (*confusion*) at its revelation was sufficient punishment for that offense. He did not believe the prosecution had proved Fouquet guilty of any of the financial crimes with which he was charged, adding that while he personally believed Fouquet was guilty of arranging the 120,000 livres pension on the gabelle, the evidence was not indisputable.[103] Fouquet was responsible for the maladministration of the king's financial affairs. For this malfeasance in office, Fouquet should be punished, although the chamber should take into consideration the times and circumstances in which these events had taken place. Like Ormesson, Catinat had thereby accepted one of Fouquet's strongest arguments. He accordingly agreed with Ormesson's recommendations.[104]

The tally thus far was six for death, seven for banishment, including two of the "swing votes," Catinat and La Baume. Fouquet's friends believed that his life was likely to be spared, but they could not be certain until the final votes were cast.[105]

On the next day, December 20, with some of Fouquet's family standing in the hall outside the chamber, the remaining judges were scheduled to speak.

Poncet, hoping to save the day for the crown, opened up by observing that clemency was the king's prerogative: his function was to dispense justice. He then offered a recapitulation of the crown's case. Circumstantial evidence proved that Fouquet was the beneficiary of the pension on the gabelle. The documentation had been found among his papers, and he had acknowledged receiving payments under it.[106] As superintendant, Fouquet had repeatedly abused his office and acted as if he was "more sovereign than the king," since the king "acknowledged the law" while Fouquet "refused to submit to it."[107] The plan of Saint-Mandé had been a real conspiracy against the crown, as evidenced by Fouquet's actions.[108] His conclusion was that Fouquet, guilty of embezzlement and sedition, deserved death. As for Belle-Isle, it was too important a fortification to leave in private hands and should be confiscated.[109] He did not, however, insist on forfeiture of the rest of Fouquet's assets, out of consideration for his creditors.[110]

Poncet was followed by Jérôme Le Féron, who took a very different approach. Fouquet was certainly responsible for confusion and maladministration in the king's affairs during his tenure of office.[111] There was no doubt that his sumptuous lifestyle gave rise to suspicions that he paid for it with crown funds.[112] But after reviewing the specific charges of embezzlement and self-dealing, the results were ambiguous.[113] The plan of Saint-Mandé was reprehensible but simply a bad thought, not a crime.[114] In the end, he agreed with Ormesson's findings and sentencing recommendations.[115]

It was the turn of Moussy, who was very brief. None of the specific charges against Fouquet had been proven, although there had been mismanagement of the king's business. His recommended sentence: 100,000 livres restitution to the crown, a fine of 50,000 livres, and internal exile to a place of the king's choosing.[116]

Brillac, too, wasted few words. The question of the 120,000 livres pension on the gabelle troubled him, but the accusation was not proved.[117] Fouquet had not administered the king's affairs well and had comingled his personal assets with the crown's money, adding to the confusion.[118] He was dismissive of the charge of high treason. If true, why had Gourville not been charged as well?[119] In what might have been a criticism of the entire trial, he reminded his colleagues that in the past, superintendants of finance had been condemned, and later it was said that "the envy directed [*conçue*] against them was their greatest crime."[120] As punishment Brillac recommended the public humiliation of an *amende honorable*, banishment for nine years, and a fine of 100,000 livres.[121]

Perhaps emboldened by Brillac's comments, the next speaker, Renard, was blunt. Renard, who had been involved in the initial phase of evidence gathering after Fouquet's arrest, spoke openly of the "irregularities" in the investigation and its many "astonishing" aspects.[122] Fouquet had been denied access to his papers in preparing his defenses, and even to the treasury registers, at the instigation of the royal *procureur*.[123] In October, Renard had openly mocked the analogy of a valet caught red-handed with his master's purse. Now, he accepted Fouquet's explanation of the 6 million livres transaction. The other financial charges, even if proven, were only civil matters, requiring restitution, not the death penalty.[124] The plan of Saint-Mandé was dismissed with a few sentences. Renard's sentencing recommendation was five years internal exile in a place to be determined by the king.[125]

The vote was now 12 for banishment or internal exile, 7 for death. The outcome was no longer in doubt: a majority of the 22 judges had agreed to spare Fouquet.

Cyrien Besnard de Rézé, one of the judges drawn from the ranks of the *maîtres des requêtes*, took the floor and spoke at some length. He agreed that Fouquet's administration of state finances had been deplorable.[126] He then reviewed many of the financial charges brought against Fouquet, finding the evidence either not convincing or ambiguous. In the case of the pension on the gabelle, for example, the royal prosecutor could have cleared up the doubt by producing the accounts submitted to Mazarin in 1656. The failure (or refusal) to do so was "troubling" (*donne de la peine*), and, he reminded his listeners, it was for the accuser to provide proof of the crime.[127]

After hurling this thunderbolt, Besnard charged into the 6 million livres transaction. He agreed that its complicated circumstances and the testimony of Jeannin de Castille and Tabouret gave rise to "legitimate suspicions" against Fouquet. But what about proofs?[128] As he continued, an impatient Séguier interrupted him several times—a discourtesy not visited on the other judges—but was unable to shake him.[129] Nor could the chancellor deflect his conclusion that the charge could not be proved.[130] As for the "crime of state," a thought, as the prosecutors well knew, was not in itself a crime.[131] Finally, Besnard agreed with Ormesson's conclusions and recommendations.[132]

A furious Voysin rose to insist that Fouquet was guilty of all the crimes imputed to him. He had used his office to divert royal revenues for his own purposes and had plotted against the crown. Implicitly criticizing his fellow magistrates inclined to clemency, he denounced the seeking of "popular approval" in rendering a verdict as "shameful" and contrary to his sense of "honor" and "duty."[133] For his part, he voted for conviction on all charges. Fouquet was too dangerous a man to let loose: banishment would punish France more than Fouquet. He agreed with Sainte-Hélène: death and confiscation of all assets.[134]

Pontchartrain, president of the Paris-based Chambre des comptes, offered his evaluation. Stressing the lack of proofs to tie Fouquet to many of the charges, he sided with Ormesson.[135]

A crestfallen Séguier then rose to give his opinion. He began with a kind of *mea culpa*: he had worked alongside Fouquet for many years but had never suspected any misconduct. He was now convinced. The charges were all proven. Fouquet had abused his office and violated the king's trust, had embezzled the king's money, and had plotted against the state. He agreed with Sainte-Hélène's findings and his recommendations.[136] This was the conclusion of his formal remarks, "for the record." But he continued to speak to his colleagues, almost defiantly. Even if he stood alone in his opinion, he said, he would not change it. He had judged in accordance with his conscience, the demands of justice, and his duty to his king.[137]

The final vote was nine for death: Ferriol, Gisaucourt, Hérault, Noguès, Poncet, Pussort, Sainte-Hélène, Séguier, and Voysin. Thirteen voted for banishment: Besnard, Brillac, Catinat, La Baume, La Toison, Le Féron, Massenau, Moussy, Ormesson, Pontchartrain, Renard, Rocquesante, and du Verdier.

After the judges conferred briefly to conform their sentencing recommendations, the court ruled that Fouquet had been duly convicted of "abuse [of office], and malfeasance [*malversations*]" in the direction of the state's finances and the exercise of his office of superintendant. He was declared banished for life from the kingdom and his assets confiscated to the state, with a small sum allocated to charitable purposes.[138]

Of those voting for death, three had been aligned with Colbert and the prosecution from the beginning: Colbert's uncle Pussort, the prosecutor Talon's brother-in-law Voysin, and Séguier. Poncet, as noted earlier, had some unstated grievance toward Fouquet, despite their ties of blood. Ferriol of Metz and Gisaucourt, from the Grand Conseil, both replacement judges, had consistently voted against Fouquet's requests and motions throughout the trial, as had Noguès of Pau. Hérault had been pressured by Le Tellier into changing his position. Sainte-Hélène, who had rarely strayed from the prosecutor's point of view throughout the process, was said to have ties to Berryer and to harbor ambitions for advancement in his home parlement of Rouen and looked to Colbert for help with this.[139]

Of those voting for banishment, Ormesson and Besnard, both maîtres des requêtes, and Brillac, Renard, and Catinat, all from the Grand'chambre of the Parlement of Paris, were aligned with Lamoignon early in the trial and tended to adopt the same position on issues throughout the process. Pontchartrain had also associated himself with this bloc of votes.[140]

Counting Séguier, 13 of the judges had been drawn from Paris-based institutions. Eight of these (62%) had voted to spare Fouquet, and five had voted for death. With the exception of Pussort, who belonged to both the Grand Conseil and the Chambre des comptes, all the judges who belonged to the courts dealing with crown finances, the Chambre des comptes and the Cour des aides, presumably the ones most familiar with the state's financing arrangements, sided with Ormesson. Of the nine magistrates drawn from the provincial parlements, five (56%) had accepted Ormesson's findings, and four had rallied to Sainte-Hélène. Given that most of the judges who had left the chamber for one reason or another were believed sympathetic to Fouquet, the vote in his favor might have been even more lopsided had they remained on the bench.

"God be praised," wrote Madame de Sévigné. "Our poor friend is saved."[141] If Ormesson is to be believed, the rejoicing was general throughout Paris, even by "the little shopkeepers who showered a thousand benedictions on me without knowing me." He added that at the beginning, those same people would gladly have seen Fouquet put to death, but by the end of the trial they had come to have compassion for him as a victim.[142] He conceded that such feelings were also driven by the general dislike for the current government, meaning Colbert. For the moment, however, Ormesson could bask in the afterglow of his triumph. People drank to his health in taverns, his Jesuit friends rejoiced, and Father Joly told him that the queen mother was pleased with the results.[143] Turenne conveyed his satisfaction, and even d'Artagnan took a moment to whisper in Ormesson's ear that he was an "illustrious man."[144]

Fouquet, too, found a way to convey his thanks. While Ormesson was at the Bastille to complete a few formalities two days after the verdict, Fouquet, standing in a window of d'Artagnan's room, managed to catch the magistrate's eye. He gave him a courtier's bow and shouted he was "his servant." Ormesson, perhaps more moved than he cared to record, returned the bow, but did not speak.[145]

But the ending of the story was not to be as the majority of the judges had determined. Some days earlier, after it seemed likely that enough judges would vote to spare Fouquet, his faithful friend Madame de Sévigné was still worried. She warned her correspondent, "Colbert is so furious that we expect something atrocious and unjust that will send us back into despair."[146]

The marquise guessed right. Colbert did not have to do much to convince Louis XIV to intervene. The king, who had remarked that if the chamber had condemned Fouquet, he would have let Fouquet die, was not prepared to see a man go free who had evaded royal justice by slandering his late prime minister and exposing the organized looting of the state's resources. Shortly before the end of the trial, Louis forbade the queen mother to ask him for clemency in the event of a death sentence. He also warned Turenne forcefully not to interest himself any further in the case. On the day of the chamber's verdict, the king remarked to Louise de la Vallière, that if Fouquet had received a death sentence, he would have let it stand.[147]

Now, for the first and apparently only time in the judicial history of the monarchy, the king exercised his authority not to mitigate a sentence but to aggravate it. Not even the king, however, dared outrage public opinion by imposing a death sentence at this stage. As he complained some days earlier to Colbert, if Ormesson was not willing to hang Fouquet, he could not be expected to do so.[148] Instead, an order in council explained that the king had determined it would be too dangerous to allow Fouquet to leave the kingdom, given his "special knowledge" of the "most important affairs of state." Instead of banishment, the king condemned the former superintendant to life in prison.[149]

"And now this great trial is finished," wrote Ormesson, "which has been the talk of all of France from the day it began to the day it ended . . . I can say that the important errors in the inventories, the acts of hatred and of authority throughout the trial, the forgeries of Berryer and the damage to everyone's private finances, even those of the judges, have been good reasons to spare Fouquet the death penalty."[150]

CHAPTER 9

Aftermath

The Price of Honor and Conscience

If Louis XIV was not willing to brave public opinion and send Fouquet to the death he had been spared by his judges, he was prepared to consign Fouquet to a rigorous, almost nightmarish, captivity. Within hours of the reading of the amended sentence, Fouquet, with d'Artagnan by his side, was hustled into a carriage escorted by 100 musketeers, en route to an undisclosed destination. As the cortège passed through the gates of the Bastille, Fouquet could hear the cheers of passers-by, a last tribute from a Paris largely won over to his cause.[1] D'Artagnan took his prisoner via Grenoble across the Alps, braving the winter's snows and arriving after several weeks at the royal fortress of Pignerol (Pinerolo in Italian), a French outpost on the Italian side of the mountains. Once there, d'Artagnan bid the former superintendant farewell and relinquished custody to its governor, Bénigne de Saint-Mars, a protégé of Le Tellier.

Fouquet was assigned a suite of three rooms in the second story of Pignerol's grim donjon, with two valets as his only companions. On the instructions of Le Tellier, presumably with the king's knowledge, the prisoner was denied all communication with the outside world. He was refused pen and paper, and his reading was limited to religious subjects. He was not permitted to leave his cell except to attend Mass in an improvised chapel across the corridor. Cut off from virtually all human contact except for occasional, formal visits from the governor to determine his physical and mental health, Fouquet was now immersed in a kind of living death.[2]

Le Tellier and his son, and successor after 1666, the marquis de Louvois, oversaw this regime with a pedantic severity—the correspondence with the royal governor survives—that can scarcely be exaggerated.[3] The tedium was relieved in the summer of 1665, when an explosion badly damaged the donjon, and Fouquet had to be moved to a nearby fortress, Pérosse, while the building was repaired.[4] He was returned to Pignerol in August 1666, where the monotony was broken again four years later. This time, several of Fouquet's old servants tried to arrange his escape by bribing members of the garrison. The plot was uncovered, and retribution was swift. One of the plotters and four soldiers were hanged in the courtyard of the fortress. To discourage any more escapes, the windows of Fouquet's cell were reinforced with additional sets of bars and shutters, effectively blocking out the daylight.[5]

The first amelioration of Fouquet's captivity occurred in the fall of 1672, when he and his wife were allowed briefly to correspond about family matters.[6] At about the same time he was allowed pen and ink, which he used to write theological tracts and poetry for his own amusement.[7] A correspondence initiated by Louvois on financial matters in early 1673 was aborted after several exchanges; the minister apparently decided that Fouquet had no useful ideas to offer him.[8] Finally, in April 1674, nearly ten years after his conviction and thirteen years after his arrest, he received permission to exchange two letters a year with his wife.[9]

Fouquet may have owed some of these new liberties to the presence of another prisoner of state at Pignerol, the comte de Lauzun, who had arrived in December 1671. A courtier who had fallen afoul of Louis XIV and a former fiancé of the king's cousin, the duchess de Montpensier, Lauzun was confined under conditions similar to those of Fouquet, who was not informed initially about Lauzun's incarceration. Lauzun, however, proved to be a far more intractable prisoner than the former superintendant and still had powerful friends at court. When Lauzun's sister and a few other relatives were allowed to visit him in 1677, the stories they brought back about his treatment created an uproar in elite circles.[10] For her part, Mademoiselle de Montpensier somewhat naïvely refused to believe the king capable of such severity and blamed Louvois for this harshness.[11]

In the wake of these outcries, Louvois authorized measures in November 1677 that were to apply to both prisoners, including the right to walk on the ramparts, even together, as long as their conversations were monitored. In January 1679 their privileges were expanded to include the right to visit together, to dine with the governor and his officers, to correspond freely with family, and to have greater access to books and gazettes, even the right to receive news (i.e., political news) from the outside world.[12] These concessions were probably tied to the complicated negotiations undertaken by Montpensier to win Lauzun's freedom, in exchange for which she was willing to bestow much of her fortune on the king's son by Madame de Montespan. Fouquet seemingly benefited from the spillover effect. It should be noted, however, that Fouquet's wife and mother were on good terms with Montespan, who may thus have had an incentive to intercede on his behalf as well.[13]

Prior to 1677, Fouquet's jailers believed he was unaware of Lauzun's presence. Unknown to them, however, sometime in 1676 Lauzun had established contact. Anticipating Dumas's Edmond Dantès by a century and a half, he had chiseled an opening connecting his cell to Fouquet's, which was on the level below. The two had thus been visiting clandestinely for some time before Fouquet was officially advised of Lauzun's proximity.[14]

In May 1679, Fouquet finally obtained permission to receive visits from his wife and other family members. A joyous reunion followed of husband, wife, and several grown children, including the eldest, Louis Nicolas, now a young army officer, and the youngest, Louis, who, born in 1661, the year of Fouquet's arrest, could not have had any recollection of his father. Fouquet's aged mother was not capable of making the trip, but she sent a benediction through her daughter-in-law.[15]

In succeeding months, the tone of Louvois's correspondence with Fouquet and with Madame Fouquet shifted markedly, and became almost cordial. As in the case of Lauzun, it was widely rumored that Fouquet was soon to be released, perhaps even pardoned.[16]

But there was to be no happy ending for Fouquet. His health had been failing for some years, and he died suddenly of a stroke in mid-March 1680. His son Louis Nicolas, known as the comte de Vaux, was with him at the time.[17] Two of Fouquet's brothers had predeceased him during his years of captivity: François, archbishop of Narbonne, in 1673, and Basile in 1679. Their mother, the courageous Marie de Maupeou, survived into the following year, 1681.[18]

In the long years of his captivity, the entire Fouquet family had suffered from the king's displeasure. Fouquet's mother, wife (with the children), and his brothers, including the two bishops, had been exiled to remote locations across France, as were many of his friends and confidants.[19] In addition to political disgrace, the family had to contend with financial ruin. At about the same time Fouquet arrived at Pignerol, officials armed with orders from the chamber of justice seized many of his possessions. Any known liquid assets were impounded, as were all of the art treasures, silver and gold plate, and other valuable furnishings found in Fouquet's residences, including the famous library at Saint-Mandé. Some of these items were transferred to the king's palaces while others found their way to the auction block. The crown also offset or canceled Fouquet's many shares in royal borrowings or tax farms and confiscated his remaining offices and the emoluments attached to them. Surprisingly, the crown made few attempts to seize Fouquet's landed properties, perhaps due to the complex terms of land tenure attached to some of them, or to prior mortgage claims, or for other unstated reasons. Neither Vaux-le-Vicomte nor Belle-Isle was confiscated, although the copper and lead piping feeding the waterworks at Vaux were carried off for the crown's benefit and a royal garrison continued to occupy Belle-Isle. In all, more than 10 million livres worth of Fouquet's assets passed to the crown.[20]

This left the family, and Madame Fouquet in particular, with the task of salvaging the family fortune in the face of Fouquet's many creditors, who now surfaced with claims on what remained. Once more, Marie-Madeleine de Castille proved equal to the task. Under the customary law of Paris, she was entitled to recover most of her dower property from her husband's estate, with a status that was privileged or senior to that of other creditors. Shortly after her husband's arrest in 1661 she had taken the initial steps to assert her claims, which eventually totaled nearly 1.4 million livres. Soon she found herself drawn into lawsuits with creditors, who formed a syndicate or consortium to litigate with the Fouquets, and with the crown, to keep the latter from confiscating Fouquet's remaining assets. After a decade of legal battles, Madame Fouquet reached an accommodation with the creditors. In return for a settlement paid to them in installments, she would receive title to some of the Fouquet family estates, including Vaux and Belle-Isle. These last two properties, which had brought such grief to the superintendant, eventually fell into other hands. Vaux was sold in 1705 to maréchal de Villars, while legal ownership of Belle-Isle passed to the crown by virtue of an exchange for the duchy of Gisors in 1718.[21]

If Madame Fouquet's lengthy and heroic struggles stabilized the family's finances, it took much longer for the family to achieve a return to grace in royal eyes. Sons Louis Nicolas and Louis attempted to redeem the family name through military service but were unable to make headway against lingering royal resentment. Discouraged by a lack of normal advancement, both retired to private life.[22]

The last years of the reign of Louis XIV saw the beginning of the family's rehabilitation. In 1711, Armand, duc de Charost, Fouquet's grandson by Marie Fouquet, was named a captain of the royal bodyguard, a prestigious post that required him to spend three months a year in constant attendance on the king. One wonders if either king or captain, during those many days spent in one another's company, ever recalled Nicolas Fouquet's vain appeals a half century earlier for an hour's audience with his royal master. The duke's younger cousins, the sons of Louis Fouquet, Louis-Charles-Auguste (1684–1761) and Louis-Charles-Armand (1693–1747) began their own military careers during the War of the Spanish Succession (1701–1714), serving with distinction at a time when the aged monarch had need of such services. In the same year as Charost's appointment, Louis-Charles-Auguste made a brilliant marriage with a daughter of the aristocratic Durfort family, which was kin to any number of ducal houses, including Turenne's. The king and the rest of the royal family deigned to sign the wedding contract, and Marie-Madeleine de Castille, who lived until 1716, had the joy of greeting wedding guests drawn from the political and social elites of the day.[23]

The groom did more than live up to expectations. In succeeding decades, he became in turn a general officer, minister of state and secretary of war, maréchal of France, duke and peer of the realm, knight of the royal Order of the Holy Spirit, and knight of the Order of the Golden Fleece. With an irony known only to Clio, the muse of history, he is remembered under the name maréchal de Belle-Isle. His younger brother, known as the chevalier de Belle-Isle, also served with great distinction in the wars of mid-century, achieving the rank of lieutenant-general before an untimely death on the battlefield in 1747.

Fouquet's remaining close circle, including the unsinkable Gourville, went their separate ways. Madame du Plessis-Bellière faded into oblivion, living under the protection of her son-in-law's family, the Créqui, on one of her remote country estates. She died in 1675.[24] Paul Pellisson, who had somehow mounted from his own cell in the Bastille a daring and clandestine defense of Fouquet, was released in 1666. With the help of powerful friends, he found redemption in Louis XIV's eyes and was part of a team charged in the later 1660s with editing the *Mémoires*, and recording the life and deeds, of the lord of Versailles. After converting to Catholicism, he received an official appointment as a royal historiographer, an honor he shared with Jean Racine, among others. He died in 1693. La Fontaine returned to Paris in 1664 from exile but never really regained royal favor. In 1684, a reluctant Louis XIV confirmed his election to the Académie française after, said Louis, the poet "promised to behave himself."[25]

Despite Talon's public vow in 1661 of implacable severity against those who had despoiled the state, the many financiers detained by the chamber fared much better than Fouquet. Given the outcome of Fouquet's trial, this was not surprising. The prosecution had put Fouquet at the center of all the financial disorders of the 1650s, but the majority of the court had found the evidence ambiguous or not convincing for most of the charges leveled against him. How effective would that same evidence be against the financiers who had been Fouquet's associates in those transactions? In the end, Colbert's great effort followed the precedents set by earlier chambers of justice. With several exceptions, a conditional general amnesty was issued in 1665. It absolved the financiers and royal financial officials under investigation from all criminal charges on payment of individual indemnities set by the royal council, meaning, in effect, Colbert. These originally totaled 156 million livres, although they were eventually reduced to 110 million livres. A study by Daniel Dessert of these fines and the negotiations for reductions led him to conclude that Colbert used the adjustments to reward those financiers he saw as allies and to penalize those he considered closely aligned with Fouquet.[26]

Prior to the amnesty, three or four very junior officials or minor functionaries had been executed for various forms of embezzlement.[27] None of the major figures, however, suffered any such fate, although several died of natural causes while imprisoned. Two or three others still caught in the web, including Jeannin de Castille, eventually reached accommodations with the crown. The royal amnesty did not extend to Gourville or to Fouquet's clerk Bruant, both of whom had fled the country. The wily Gourville, who had lived briefly under the protection of La Rochefoucauld and the prince of Condé before slipping across the border, benefited from a pardon in 1671 and became the chief financial officer of the Condé family until his death in 1703. Bruant, while living in the Low Countries, received clemency around 1672, served as a diplomatic agent of Louis XIV, returned to France in 1675, and sued Colbert's heirs unsuccessfully in 1684 for the return of some of his property. He died an honored servant of state in 1689.[28]

There were to be consequences for the members of the chamber of justice as well. The refusal of the majority of judges to convict Fouquet on any of the specific instances of financial misconduct with which he had been charged was a check to the ambition of Colbert and the vanity of a young king. Fouquet, who had participated in much of the skirmishing between the Parlement of Paris and the cardinal in the 1650s, understood the lingering hostility of the high court judges toward Mazarin. He had used this resentment to fashion a defense that put Mazarin at the center of the financial mismanagement and corruption of the 1650s. The strategy had evidently worked. Many of the judges had stressed the "conditions" of the time, implying strongly that Mazarin was also at fault, even if, as Ormesson put it, "innocently." By acquitting Fouquet of most of the charges, the judges were restating in less overtly confrontational terms the criticisms and accusations leveled against the cardinal during the Fronde, in effect reaffirming those charges against Mazarin by the same courts from which many of these magistrates had been seconded.

In this context, it is not surprising that many of the judges paid dearly for what the crown may have deemed a continuation of the Fronde by other means. In the months following the trial, the depth of royal displeasure became evident. Raffélis de Rocquesante, whose support of Ormesson may have emboldened his colleagues to follow suit, was exiled to Quimper-Corentin on the pretext of corrupt dealings with, of all people, Berryer.[29] Pontchartrain was denied permission to resign his position in the Chambre des comptes in favor of his son; with his career in ruins, he retired in 1671.[30] Du Verdier and La Baume were excused from further duties in the chamber and sent back to their respective parlements of Bordeaux and Grenoble. Moussy, Brillac, and Massenau were also removed from the panel in evident disgrace.[31]

Nobody was to feel the wrath of Louis XIV more acutely than Olivier d'Ormesson. In the years after the trial of Fouquet, Louis XIV made him a living example of the consequences of integrity. By early 1665, André d'Ormesson was clearly in failing health. In the normal course of events, Olivier could expect to be nominated to his father's seat as a councilor of state. But this required royal approval, and Olivier undertook the traditional lobbying effort to gain the king's consent. His friend Turenne and even the queen mother Anne of Austria raised the matter with Louis as a prelude to a more direct approach by Olivier, who waited on the king in late February. When Louis asked after the senior Ormesson's health, Oliver used his response to introduce the issue of succession. To Olivier's conventional plea to continue in the king's "good graces," Louis replied coldly, "When you have earned them, I will gladly give them to you."[32]

In the months following André d'Ormesson's death in early March 1665, Olivier made repeated appearances at court. Although his friends, including Condé, lobbied on his behalf and made sure he was in the monarch's line of sight, Louis exercised the royal prerogative of overlooking his presence. In December 1665 a replacement for André was announced: Henri Pussort. The rebuke and public disgrace could not have been clearer, doubly so because in the same month Olivier was "excused" from all further duties in the chamber of justice, a royal command conveyed to him by Séguier.[33] In the following year, 1666, Saint-Hélène, who had demanded Fouquet's head, was appointed a councilor of state, as was Voysin in 1667.

Ormesson, however, persisted in his efforts, convinced that sooner or later Louis would relent. He appeared twice at court in 1666, eight times in 1667, ten times in 1668, and once again in late 1669.[34] On all of these occasions, Louis simply ignored him. In June 1670, at the suggestion of Le Tellier, who advised Ormesson that he needed to "break the ice," Ormesson asked for an audience with the king.[35] After listening to Ormesson plead his cause and the "obligation of a judge" to do justice, Louis responded with a noncommittal promise to "consider the things you have said."[36] After three more years of vain solicitations, the last in April 1672, Ormesson, who had already sold his office of *maître des requêtes* in 1667, finally gave up hope.[37]

Thereafter he lived in graceful retirement, busying himself with his friends and his books and enjoying the esteem of many of the grandees of the time. Le Tellier, the eternal rival of Colbert, always treated him cordially, and the prince of Condé even received Olivier and his wife as honored guests at Chantilly.[38] Charles Le Brun, whose works adorned both Vaux-le-Vicomte and Versailles, painted Ormesson's portrait in 1666.[39]

Olivier died in 1686, having lived long enough to see his sons' careers launched but also to lose his promising eldest son, André, two years before his own death. As in the case of Fouquet's offspring, Louis XIV made the point of accepting the services of a younger generation: André was appointed to serve on the *chambre ardente* that investigated the *affaire des poisons* in 1679. Olivier's more remote descendants were to play prominent political roles in the eighteenth century, and his lineage has produced distinguished soldiers, diplomats, and writers down into the twenty-first century. But for Olivier, the only reward for integrity was to be the honor in which his memory is held and which still adorns the name of Ormesson.[40]

Several of the judges who voted for Fouquet's execution later had doubts. In late 1667, Ferriol told Madame Besnard over dinner that he had since changed his mind and wished he could retract his vote for death. Ferriol also said that Sainte-Hélène had confided to him that when he finished his opinion at the end of the trial, he was struck to the heart, lost all appetite, and never got it back.[41] Sainte-Hélène had died some months before this conversation, in April 1667, stricken suddenly in his carriage while passing by the Bastille.[42]

Those who had fought so hard to send Fouquet to the block were well rewarded for their efforts. Despite his failure to deliver the death sentence that Colbert and the king had expected, Pierre Séguier continued to bask in royal favor, although he never became a member of the Conseil d'en haut, the nexus of power under Louis XIV. Confined largely to judicial and administrative functions, he was the nominal head of the various commissions appointed to reform the judicial codes in 1667 and 1670. In 1668, he had the joy of seeing his daughter Charlotte, widow of the duc de Sully, remarry to no less a person than the king's uncle, Henri de Bourbon, duc de Verneuil, a natural son of Henri IV. As father of the bride, the descendant of an apothecary in the Bourbonnais signed his name to the marriage contact alongside the descendants of the House of Bourbon: Louis XIV, Queen Maria Theresa, Philippe d'Orléans, and his spouse, Henrietta Anne of England.[43] Séguier died in 1672, leaving behind a fortune of nearly 4 million livres. Rather than achieving his lifelong ambition of attaining the rank of duke and peer of France, he agreed to the elevation of a grandson to that rank.[44]

Colbert continued his brilliant career, serving as one of Louis XIV's most powerful and trusted ministers until his death in 1683. His achievements are too well known to require any elaboration here. Many of the financial reforms he initiated to great applause in the early 1660s fell apart in the last years of that decade as Colbert, like his predecessors, was faced with the need to fund lengthy and costly wars with an inadequate revenue stream. Historians have long since recognized that financing these conflicts forced him to rely on many of the same financial practices and mechanisms that had cost Fouquet so dearly.[45]

Colbert amassed an enormous personal fortune, estimated at 12 million livres, comparable to that left by Louvois.[46] He married his three daughters to the ducs de Chevreuse, de Beauvillier, and Mortemart. His son, the marquis de Seignelay, later the minister of the navy, was married to a Matignon with lines of descent from the Bourbon and Longueville families. A second son became bishop of Rouen. Three others died on active military service. Colbert's brothers and nephews also enjoyed distinguished careers as high servants of state.

Colbert lived in a style befitting his rank and wealth. His Paris residence was decorated with magnificent tapestries, paintings, and other works of art. His library eventually passed into the hands of the crown and thence into the collections of the Bibliothèque nationale de France.

In 1670 Colbert bought an estate known as Sceaux, not far from Versailles. With the help of Charles Perrault, Le Brun, and Le Nôtre, he created a magnificent residence, surrounded with 700 acres of garden. He received the king and members of the royal family there on several occasions over the years and, in 1677, entertained Louis and the court with a magnificent festival, which included poetry readings, a performance of Racine's *Phèdre,* and a grand display of fireworks.[47]

Colbert's uncle, Henri Pussort, who was only his nephew's senior by four years, continued on as his close collaborator. In 1665 he headed the commission—under Séguier's nominal presidency—charged with compiling a list of all royal ordinances, both civil and criminal, for use by the courts. Just as importantly, the commission was authorized to set out uniform rules of procedure for the royal courts throughout the kingdom. A brainchild of Colbert's, the project was intended not only to improve the quality of royal justice but also to serve as a control device, allowing the crown to rein in what Colbert saw as a judicial system not responsive to the royal will. The civil code resulting from this effort appeared in 1667, and the criminal code in 1670; three ancillary codes followed in later years. Known collectively as the Code Louis by legal historians, they remained the cornerstone of the French judicial system down to the Revolution.

In the commission's work, the echoes of the Fouquet trial were evident. It was Colbert's intention initially to avoid any formal input by the existing royal courts, and the individuals appointed to work with Pussort were all drawn from the Conseil d'État. In addition to Pussort, Séguier, and Colbert, the commission members included Poncet (who was soon excused), Voysin, Boucherat, and Hotman (who had prosecuted the other cases before the chamber of justice), with Oudart Gomont and Nicolas-Joseph Foucault, son of the recorder at Fouquet's trial, as advocates and draftsmen. Initially, none of those magistrates voting in Fouquet's favor were selected, although Catinat, Brillac, and Fayet joined the commission for revision of the criminal law in 1670.[48]

Colbert's attempt to bypass the high courts was thwarted by Lamoignon, who convinced Louis XIV to expand the commission to include representatives from the bench to comment on the proposed codes. This set the stage for exchanges between Lamoignon and Pussort about the rights and safeguards to be accorded to defendants, the autonomy and discretionary powers of judges, penalties to be incurred by judges who failed to adhere to the procedural constraints imposed by the code, and so forth. Some of the debates were memorable. Lamoignon opposed many of the proposed restrictions on traditional safeguards afforded to defendants, including some that Fouquet had made use of, such as the refusal to take an oath or the right to counsel. On the right to counsel, for example, he argued strenuously that such deprivation, rather than trapping the guilty, might cause "innocent people to perish for want of advice."[49] In both the civil and criminal codes, he saved his strongest objections for the code's limitations on judicial discretion and the sanctions threatened against magistrates who departed from the strictest adherence to its provisions. For Lamoignon, centuries of experience had proved that "honor and conscience," rather than fear of punishment, impelled magistrates to do their duty.[50] To this, Pussort found a ready response. "The truth was that the least well enforced ordinances were those that relied on their honor and conscience." The most dramatic clashes between the two occurred during the civil code conferences in February–March 1667, but similar ones erupted over the criminal code during the conferences of June and July 1670.[51]

In the end, virtually all of Pussort's recommendations for restraints and restrictions were adopted, often after the king's intervention to break deadlocks in the commission. Defendants were required to take an oath before interrogation: failure or refusal to do so meant treatment as a "voluntary mute." Counsel was denied in the earlier stages of proceedings (interrogations, confrontations with witnesses, and so forth) and completely for charges of treason or lèse majesté.[52] Much of this seemed to reflect the frustration of Pussort and his partisans at Fouquet's ability to exploit "loopholes" and appeal during his trial to the judicial sense of equity to secure important rulings in his favor. The regime was determined to tolerate no more "trials of Fouquet." The duty of overseeing the adherence of the courts to the new procedures fell to the royal privy council (*conseil privé*). In practice, however, this choice allowed for more nuance in decision making than either Colbert or Pussort would have liked.[53] Many of these provisions came under attack during the Enlightenment by important thinkers, including Montesquieu, who sometimes cited the exchanges between Lamoignon and Pussort, which had been published in the early part of the eighteenth century.

Pussort continued to soldier on, obtaining royal appointments and surviving his illustrious nephew by fourteen years. He became a member of the council of finance in 1672 but was passed over for the post of controller-general at Colbert's death in 1683. Two years later, when Le Tellier died, he failed to win the chancellorship. Ironically, the successful candidate was Louis Boucherat, who had been forced off the chamber of justice by Colbert. At his death in 1697, Pussort left behind a comfortable fortune. Berryer, whose disgrace proved ephemeral, continued to serve under Colbert for another twenty years. At his death in 1686 he, too, left his heirs well provided for.[54]

Over the centuries, Fouquet's reputation did not fare well at the hands of historians. With the notable exception of Jules Lair, until the late twentieth century most historians in France and abroad accepted the official version of events provided by Colbert and his admirers. The great nineteenth-century historian Adolphe Chéruel, for example, who edited Ormesson's journal for publication, passed over Ormesson's findings of falsified evidence and questionable testimony in silence. He felt obliged, however, to include in his introduction to that journal Pussort's rebuttal of Ormesson's presentation to the chamber.[55] Chéruel's two-volume study of Fouquet, which made ample use of archival material, expressed no reservations about the superintendant's culpability or the methods used to prosecute his case.

At the same time, Fouquet has never been entirely without defenders, mostly in the world of letters. Pellisson had used his literary talents to present the first published defense of Fouquet's actions, and La Fontaine used his to appeal for royal clemency. Madame de Sévigné's correspondence provided posterity with a dramatic and sympathetic account of Fouquet's appearances before the chamber, a vision of "innocence persecuted." Her friend Madame de La Fayette, whose comments on Louis XIV's astonishment at Vaux find their way into virtually every account of Fouquet's downfall, also accepted Fouquet's assertion that Louis

XIV had pardoned him for any offenses committed during Mazarin's tenure. But Louis, stampeded by Colbert and Le Tellier, broke his word and plotted with them to arrest Fouquet.[56] The duc de Saint-Simon, in discussing the character of Louis XIV, accused him of opening his personal reign by acting as Colbert's dupe in pursuing Fouquet. Somewhat later, he characterized Fouquet as paying the price for "the millions cardinal Mazarin took, the jealousy of Le Tellier and Colbert, and a little too much gallantry and splendor."[57] Voltaire, in his *History of Louis XIV*, portrayed Mazarin in entirely negative terms but saw in Fouquet a certain "greatness of soul," while accusing Colbert of vindictiveness in the pursuit of his rival. He recognized in the prosecution what Fouquet made obvious, that to try the superintendant was "to disparage the memory of Cardinal Mazarin."[58] The popular novelist Alexandre Dumas also depicted Fouquet sympathetically in his *Vicomte de Bragelonne* and *Louis XIV et son siècle*.[59] Marc Fumaroli's provocative *Le poète et le roi* has updated and restated this literary tradition. For Fumaroli, Fouquet's policies offered "reconciliation, synthesis, and compromise" between the "restored authority of the state" and those forces that had opposed the "excesses of absolutism" since Richelieu's time. Domestic tranquility would be coupled with "diplomacy and peace" abroad.[60] Fouquet's "charm and misfortune," he insists, "would cast a permanent shadow over the early reign of Louis XIV," and even today "they overshadow the radiance of the Great King, just as the prophetic fury of Saint-Simon's *Mémoires* overshadows the closing years of his reign."[61]

In the last decades of the twentieth century, the historical and literary traditions began to converge. The works of Daniel Dessert, Françoise Bayard, Julian Dent, Richard Bonney, and others provided many new insights into the complicated and shadowy world of royal finances in seventeenth-century France. A deeper understanding of that milieu has permitted a reappraisal not just of Fouquet but also of Colbert, and of their predecessors, including Mazarin and Richelieu. A colloquium in Paris in 1983 to commemorate the 300th anniversary of Colbert's death provided a forum for lively exchanges about the Colbert-Fouquet rivalry.[62] It ended with a ringing pronouncement by the distinguished Roland Mousnier that the trial of Fouquet was a "political trial in all its horror . . . Fouquet was not guilty according to the spirit and practices [*habitudes*] of the times. His trial was unjust, tainted with irregularities and manipulations."[63]

Among a wider public, the story of Fouquet is still mesmerizing, perhaps stimulated in part by the remarkable restoration of Vaux-le-Vicomte in the last half century, and its prominence as a major tourist attraction. In March 2011 a made-for-television movie, *Le roi, l'écureuil, et la couleuvre,* with Lorant Deutsch as Fouquet and Carole Richert as Madame de Sévigné, filmed in part at Vaux, aired on France 3.

This change in scholarly and popular opinion has not swayed everyone. Emmanuel Le Roy Ladurie, in his pugnacious survey of ancien régime France, conceded that the superintendant was the scapegoat of a royal coup d'état in 1661 and that Fouquet's heavy debt load suggested that "at least from 1650 onward, he had been relatively honest." He refused, however, to accept Daniel Dessert's portrayal of Fouquet as "a Dreyfus-like figure" and Colbert as "a less than attractive stooge." For Le Roy Ladurie, Dessert's attempt to present Fouquet "as a national hero is tantamount to turning a *baudruche* into a *montgolfière*" (a toy balloon into a blimp or hot air balloon).[64] Perhaps falling prey to the syndrome he decried, Le Roy Ladurie also suggested that Fouquet's "Breton conspiracy" had "something of the Fronde about it."[65] Similar assertions framed his account of Colbert's many achievements, as he politely but firmly dismissed the implications of the works of Dessert, Bayard, Bonney, Bergin, and other scholars.[66]

In a remarkable display of institutional solidarity across the centuries, in 2011, the French Ministry of Justice, on an official website, stipulated that Fouquet was able to exploit brilliantly the faults and irregularities in the prosecution's case. It also accepted that Fouquet was primarily the victim of Louis XIV's wrath. Nevertheless, it upheld the result of the trial, arguing that Fouquet was indeed guilty of "frauds and swindles" (*tromperies et escroqueries*), which could not have been ignored much longer. The judges had succumbed to popular opinion in pronouncing a sentence of banishment instead of the usual punishment of death for peculation. The king refused to accept this defiance and commuted the sentence to perpetual imprisonment. In short, however flawed the means, the end was justifiable.[67]

But academics can also demonstrate intellectual if not institutional continuity. In May 2000, literary scholars and historians gathered for "The Fouquet Years," a two-day conference at Versailles. There, in the palace of the Sun King, a prominent French historian and biographer of Colbert, Jean Meyer, who had participated in the 1983 colloquium, pronounced Fouquet's trial "one of those sad, ambiguous, sordid stories, at times simultaneously grotesque and pathetic, so abundant in our political history."[68]

One can only hope that the shades of Louis XIV and Fouquet were listening.

Appendix

Ministerial Fortunes in Seventeenth-Century France

In the absence of any sense of conflict of interest, and knowing that their offices were revocable at the king's pleasure, many ministers and high-ranking officials made full use of their positions to enrich themselves and their families. At his death, Richelieu left a fortune estimated at 20 million livres, including cash reserves slightly in excess of 4 million livres, while his extended family had also been provided with offices and emoluments to secure comfortable family fortunes.[1] Claude de Bullion, the superintendant of finance 1632–1640, amassed an estate approaching 8 million livres.[2]

The champion exploiter of all was Mazarin. In the decade before the Fronde, the newly minted chief minister managed to build a large income from his various offices and appointments, both lay and ecclesiastical. Contemporaries in the Parlement of Paris estimated his revenues in those years at about 1 million livres. Mazarin's parlementary critics, however, were not in a position to track the cardinal's hidden revenues, derived from his participation in the syndicates lending money to the crown or in the wholesale trafficking in munitions, foodstuffs, and furnishings to the troops in the field. Such activities were usually concealed by the use of "front men," valets or clerks of the cardinal's household who were the parties of record for these transactions. Mazarin also used trusted bankers to provide the same kind of cover, for example, Thomas Contarini, a Venetian, and Barthélemy Hervart, a German Protestant from Augsburg. Taking these investments into account, a modern scholar, Claude Dulong, believes contemporary estimates of Mazarin's income to be off by one-third or more and puts his income at about 1.5 million livres.[3] At least some of Mazarin's wealth was sent out of the country. Dulong has noted that Mazarin had extensive dealings with bankers in Italy, the Rhineland states, Amsterdam, and Antwerp, using them to move some of his assets outside France.[4] In 1641, he was able to purchase the magnificent Palazzo Bentivoglio in Rome, today the Palazzo Rospigliosi-Pallavicini.[5] Even before the Fronde, Mazarin's collections of tapestries, paintings, books, silver, and gems were a source of wonder. The famous 18 diamonds known as the "Mazarins," which the cardinal later bequeathed to the crown of France, were among his holdings. Two of them, the "Sancy" and the "Mirror of Portugal" had been bought through surrogates at bargain prices from Henrietta Maria, the widow of Charles I.[6] Contarini's account books, confiscated and examined by parlementary commissioners during the Fronde, showed that by 1648 the Venetian had already received 8 million livres in deposits from Mazarin.[7] One wonders how much of this was somehow derived from the 31 million livres in royal funds that passed through Contarini's hands in the years 1643–1648.[8] Although a great deal of this early accumulation was dispersed during the Fronde, Mazarin later exaggerated the extent of his losses; much had been secretly recovered by his agents or was out of reach of the Parlement of Paris, thanks in part to the efforts of Colbert and the Fouquet brothers.[9]

On his return to France in February 1653, the cardinal made strenuous efforts to compensate for lost time. His "aboveground" revenues grew to slightly more than 2 million livres per annum in the 1650's, derived from royal pensions and *gages* of office, church benefices, and the income from the vast estates he acquired in the 1650s, which included the duchies of Nevers and Mayenne and lands in Alsace. In June 1658, Colbert estimated the total value of Mazarin's holdings at slightly more than 8 million livres, a fortune that would have made him wealthier than most of the princes or peers of France.[10] By the time of Mazarin's death, scarcely three years after Colbert's estimate, Mazarin's fortune had grown to more than 35 million livres, the largest private fortune ever amassed under the ancien régime, and one that included 8.7 million livres in specie, more than twice the amount of cash left by Richelieu, and four times that left by Henri de Condé, the first prince of the blood, at his death in 1646.[11] Daniel Dessert asks the very sensible question, how was it possible in so short a time, on stated revenues of 2 million livres a year, to grow a fortune this rapidly? In another of his works, Dessert suggests the answer, noting that none of the financial transactions offered in evidence against Fouquet postdated Mazarin's death and also that Mazarin's account books, entrusted to Colbert, were destroyed with the king's consent shortly after Fouquet's trial.[12]

Although details were not known to Mazarin's contemporaries, enough was known about his activities to raise the question during the Fronde and after the cardinal's death. Claude Dulong comments that under the circumstances, it is not surprising that Louis allowed Mazarin's accounting records to be destroyed, preferring not to "lift the veil" on the secret of Mazarin's wealth.[13] Fouquet, however, was to do so, asserting that in the late 1650s more than 22 million livres of state money per annum passed through Mazarin's hands.[14]

Fouquet's colleague Abel Servien was to leave behind the relatively modest fortune of about 3 million livres. Later generations of royal ministers were just as industrious in reaping the rewards of office. Colbert's fortune at his death was estimated to be about 12 million livres; that of Louvois, between 9 and 12 million livres.[15] Both ministers also made sure that their immediate and extended family members were showered with royal appointments and revenues as a foundation for their separate fortunes.

With the exception of the wealth enjoyed by collateral branches of the royal family (Condé, Orléans, etc.), such ministerial fortunes vastly outstripped those of the highest ranks of the old territorial aristocracy (the *noblesse d'épée*) and dwarfed the ones accumulated by the administrative and judicial elites (the *noblesse de robe*) below ministerial status.

Perhaps the most perceptive comment about this phenomenon comes from Claude Dulong, who observed that "the ideal of a poor minister is late in coming [*tardif*] and republican."[16]

Notes

ABBREVIATIONS USED IN THE NOTES

AnF	Archives nationales (France)
BA	Bibliothèque de l'Arsenal
Bastille	*Archives de la Bastille,* ed. François Ravaisson-Mollien, vols. 1–3 (Paris, 1866–1868)
BI	Bibliothèque de l'Institut de France
BM	Bibliothèque Mazarine
BnF	Bibliothèque nationale de France
CC Colbert	Collection Cinq Cents de Colbert
Défenses	*Défenses de M. Fouquet,* 13 vols. (Paris, 1665–1668)
Ms.	Manuscrit
Ms. Fr.	Manuscrit français

INTRODUCTION

1. Dessert, "Chambre de justice," 857.

PRELUDE

1. On Fouquet's arrest, see BnF, CC Colbert 235, fols. iii–xiii; Choisy, *Mémoires,* 98–100; Brienne, *Mémoires,* 3:72–75; the various documents and accounts in *Bastille,* 1:347–64; Foucault, "Récit officiel," 447–53; Colbert, *Lettres,* vol. 2, pt. 1: "Arrestation de Fouquet, Mésures Préparatoires," clxxxix–cxcix; and Lair, *Foucquet,* 2:58–63. Fouquet's account is found in *Défenses,* 13:279–303, "Memoirs and Comments . . . September 5, 1661 to December 9, 1662."

CHAPTER 1: The Long Reach

1. Richet, *Réforme,* 145. On Lamoignon, see Chaussinand-Nogaret, *Élites,* 160.
2. Dessert, *Fouquet,* 18–23.
3. Richet, *Réforme,* 146–48. On Colbert, see Petitfils, *Fouquet,* 20.
4. Dessert, *Fouquet,* 23.
5. On the early Fouquets, see Dessert, *Fouquet,* 23–26, and Petitfils, *Fouquet,* 21–23. On the persistence of these bonds in later generations, see Uzman, "Kinship," 39–43.
6. Lair, *Foucquet,* 1:9–10.
7. Barbiche, *Institutions,* 121–23; Etchechoury, *Maîtres des requêtes,* 19–23, 89–131; Dessert, *Fouquet,* 36–37; Lair, *Foucquet,* 1:15, 1:71–72.

8. Dessert, *Fouquet*, 39–40; Uzman, "Kinship," 33–39. On the *dévots*, see Ranum, *Paris*, 167–94.

9. On the Fouquets and overseas commerce, see Lair, *Foucquet*, 1:48–51, 57–60; Dessert, *Fouquet*, 32–41; Petitfils, *Fouquet*, 29–30; and Uzman, "Kinship," 44–48. See also Boucher, *French Colonial Empire*.

10. Lair, *Foucquet*, 1:20, 39–47 passim.

11. Dessert, *Fouquet*, 43–44.

12. Petitfils, *Fouquet*, 38; Lair, *Foucquet*, 1:61; Saunders, "Library," 2.

13. Lair, *Foucquet*, 1:63–65.

14. Dessert, *Fouquet*, 52–53.

15. Dessert, *Fouquet*, 55; Petitfils, *Fouquet*, 39.

16. Lair, *Foucquet*, 1:66.

17. Petitfils, *Fouquet*, 40.

18. Lair, *Foucquet*, 1:68, 71.

19. Lair, *Foucquet*, 1:74.

20. Lair, *Foucquet*, 1:75–77.

21. Dessert, *Fouquet*, 56–63; Petitfils, *Fouquet*, 42–48 passim.

22. Petitfils, *Fouquet*, 52 and 52 n3.

23. Ormesson, *Journal*, 1:200–201, July 1644; Petitfils, *Fouquet*, 56–59; Dessert, *Fouquet*, 64–66.

24. Lair, *Foucquet*, 1:86–93; Petitfils, *Fouquet*, 59–64; Dessert, *Fouquet*, 65–70.

25. Mazarin, *Lettres*, 2:898, Mazarin to abbé de La Rivière, May 20, 1647.

26. Mazarin, *Lettres*, 2:955, Mazarin to Fouquet, Sept. 30, 1647; Lair, *Foucquet*, 1:93–96.

27. Ranum, *Fronde*, 70.

28. Ranum, *Fronde*, 60–61, 70–71, 86–87, 104–5. See also Moote, *Revolt*, 17–18, 51, 52–63, 77–87.

29. Ranum, *Fronde*, 11, 30–41 passim. For the general narrative of the Fronde, see Ranum, *Fronde*; Lorris, *Fronde*; Moote, *Revolt*; Chéruel, *Minorité de Louis XIV*. On urban unrest, see Beik, *Urban Protest*.

30. Moote, *Revolt*, 28; Ranum, *Fronde*, 8, 11, 36–37.

31. Chauleur, "Traitants," 25–26; Ranum, *Fronde*, 134–35; Moote, *Revolt*, 30–31, 44–47; Hamscher, *Parlement*, xviii–xxi.

32. Ranum, *Fronde*, 91–100 passim.

33. Ranum, *Fronde*, 122; Moote, *Revolt*, 126–27. On the bankruptcy of 1648, see Bonney, *Debts*, 203–10 passim and 320, table IX B.

34. Ranum, *Fronde*, 159–60; Moote, *Revolt*, 151–52.

35. Ranum, *Fronde*, 169–71; Moote, *Revolt*, 158–60.

36. Lair, *Foucquet*, 1:109–13 passim.

37. Lair, *Foucquet*, 1:124, 132–33.

38. Ranum, *Fronde*, 209–11 passim; Moote, *Revolt*, 210–14

39. Lair, *Foucquet*, 1:137–39.

40. On the role of the parquet, see Carbasse, "Introduction," in *Histoire du parquet*, 12–21; Dauchy, "Droits du roi," 55–75; Crépin, "Rôle pénal," 79–103; and David, "Participation," 105–37. See also Barbiche, *Institutions*, 337–38; Chéruel, *Fouquet*, 1:7–8; Lair, *Foucquet*, 1:141–42; and Petitfils, *Fouquet*, 75–77.

41. Lair, *Foucquet*, 1:150–51; Chéruel, *Fouquet*, 1:355–56.

42. Lair, *Foucquet*, 1:150; Dessert, *Fouquet*, 60. For Marie-Madeleine's fortune, see Petitfils, *Fouquet*, 74–77; for ducal and other aristocratic fortunes of the period, see Labatut, *Ducs et pairs*, 144–48, 248–50.

43. Lair, *Foucquet*, 1:164.

44. See, for example, Mazarin, *Lettres*, 4:186, Mazarin to Abbé Fouquet, May 16, 1651; and Lair, *Foucquet*, 1:161–62. According to Moote, *Revolt*, 287, Fouquet was ineffective as procureur général in 1650–1651, due to inexperience, but thereafter played the part Mazarin expected.

45. Lair, *Foucquet*, 1:160–61, 166–67; Moote, *Revolt*, 320. See also Chéruel, "Introduction," in Ormesson, *Journal*, 2:vii–xi. On Basile Fouquet, see Uzman, "Kinship," 120–28.

46. Ranum, *Fronde*, 96; Moote, *Revolt*, 71–73, 316.

47. Chéruel, *Fouquet*, 1:24–27; Lair, *Foucquet*, 1:173; Petitfils, *Fouquet*, 83; Uzman, "Kinship," 129–33.

48. Chéruel, *Fouquet*, 1:27; Lair, *Foucquet*, 1:185; Dulong, *Mazarin et l'argent*, 55–57.

49. Mazarin, *Lettres*, 5:103, Mazarin to Abbé Fouquet, May 4, 1652; Petitfils, *Fouquet*, 84–85.

50. Chéruel, *Fouquet*, 1:114; Lair, *Foucquet*, 1:114; Petitfils, *Fouquet*, 85.

51. Pitts, *Mademoiselle*, 77–81.

52. Chéruel, *Fouquet*, 1:128–29, 144–48; Lair, *Foucquet*, 1:203–8 passim.

53. Chéruel, *Fouquet*, 1:149–50.

54. Chéruel, *Fouquet*, 1:149–50.

55. Chéruel, *Fouquet*, 1:151–71 passim; Petitfils, *Fouquet*, 89–90.

56. Quoted in Chéruel, *Fouquet*, 1:225. See also Bonney, *Debts*, 244–45.

57. BnF, CC Colbert 235: fols. xxii verso–xxiii verso, Joint Commission, January 8, 1653; Chéruel, *Fouquet*, 1:235–38; Lair, *Foucquet*, 1:266–70. On Servien's career, see Duccini, *Guerre et paix*.

CHAPTER 2: The Superintendant at Work

1. For a summary of these disputes, see Hamscher, *Parlement*, 82–118, and Moote, *Revolt*, 355–63.

2. For an overview of the French taxation system in this period, see Collins, *Fiscal Limits*, esp. 108–65; see also Dent, *Crisis in Finance*, 27–43; Bayard, *Monde des financiers*, 22–44; Dessert, *Argent*, 15–26, 42–65; Bonney, *Debts*, 13–17; and Charmeil, *Trésoriers*, 157–74 (tax structure), 359–74 (provincial Estates).

3. Bonney, "Failure," 12; Chéruel, *Fouquet*, 1:332 n1.

4. Bayard, *Monde des financiers*, 45–74; Collins, *Fiscal Limits*, 109–35. On *rentes*, see Béguin, *Financer la guerre*, 23–34. On the sale of offices, see Mousnier, *Vénalité*, and Doyle, *Venality*, 1–25.

5. Bosher, "*Chambres*," 25.

6. Bosher, "*Chambres*," 25; Bonney, *Debts*, 6–7; Dent, "Financial Administration," 249–56; Dent, "Clientèles," 56–58. Charmeil, *Trésoriers*, 410, notes that by the seventeenth century, the terms *partisan* and *traitant* were "virtually synonymous."

7. Bonney, *Debts*, 176–77. See also Chauleur, "Traitants," 18–25, which examines the use of *prête-noms*, 24.

8. Bonney, "Failure," 13–17.

9. Bonney, "Failure," 13–17; on the mechanism of tax leases, see 15–17.

10. Bonney, "Secret Expenses," 830–31; Weiss, *Acquits*, 53–54, 74–76.

11. Bonney, "Secret Expenses," 827; Dent, *Crisis in Finance*, 84–85; Weiss, *Acquits*, 74–76.

12. Bonney, *Debts*, 304 table 1.

13. Bonney, *Debts*, 175, 313 table Vb.

14. Bonney, *Debts*, 228 and 228 n4.

15. Bonney, *Debts*, 225–26.

16. Bonney, *Debts*, 247–48.

17. Dent, *Crisis in Finance*, 78–83.

18. BnF, CC Colbert 235: fols. xxiii verso–xxv, December 24, 1654; Lair, *Foucquet*, 1:342–43, 347; Dent, "Financial Administration," 253–54. On Hervart, see Dulong, *Hervart*; for an overview of Mazarin's business practices, see Dulong, *Mazarin et l'argent*; Dulong, *Fortune*; and Dessert, "Fortune du Cardinal Mazarin."

19. Lair, *Foucquet*, 1:351–52; Bonney, *Debts*, 250–51. Dent, *Crisis in Finance*, 67–68, argues Fouquet was appointed because of his skills at persuasion and because of his status as one of Mazarin's clients, not because of any technical financial skills. See also Dent, "Financial Administration," 246.

20. Bonney, *Debts*, 250–51.

21. Dent, *Crisis in Finance*, 65–66.

22. Dent, *Crisis in Finance*, 69; Dent, "Clientèles," 53–56, 58. Dulong, *Mazarin et l'argent*, 172, notes that initially Fouquet did not object to Hervart's appointment.

23. Dent, *Crisis in Finance*, 73–76; Dent, "Clientèles," 50, 56; Uzman, "Kinship," 26–30, 263–67; Piccioni, "Bruant des Carrières," 424–25.

24. Dent, "Clientèles," 57.

25. For the calculation, see Dessert, *Argent*, 162, who notes that the calculations must be used as approximations, given the difficulties with underlying data. Dessert's figures are gross, before deductions and discounts. Bonney, *King's Debts*, 315–17, provides an estimate that advances from *traités* totaled 240 million livres gross but only about 173 million net of deductions in those same years. Other figures he provides are incomplete and cannot be compared with Dessert's estimates. On the identity of the financiers, see Dessert, "Chambre de justice," 864–65, and Dent, "Clientèles," 56–57.

26. Lair, *Foucquet*, 1:440. See also Dent, *Crisis in Finance*, 68.

27. Dent, *Crisis in Finance*, 69–70. Dent adjusted calculations made by Ormesson to arrive at this figure, 68–69. See also BnF, Ms. Fr. 16533: fols. 15–17, List of Fouquet's Creditors; and BA, Ms. Fr. 7167: fols. 163–77, Assets and Liabilities, 1653, 1661, 1663. *Défenses*, 13:32–38, Interrogation, March 9, 1662.

28. Lair, *Foucquet*, 1:355–56.

29. Lair, *Foucquet*, 1:360–61; Dessert, *Argent du sel*, 171–80. See also *Défenses*, 2:206–19, 4:156–57, and 5:1–13. Dulong, *Mazarin et l'argent*, 62, notes that Fouquet's explanations shifted over time.

30. Lair, *Foucquet*, 1:362–72 passim.

31. Lair, *Foucquet*, 1:365–70; Bluche, *Louis XIV*, 70.

32. Lair, *Foucquet*, 1:379–82; Pujo, *Condé*, 238–39.

33. Mazarin to Colbert, June 12, 1657, in Lair, *Foucquet*, 1:408. See also Bonney, *Debts*, 252–54.

34. Lair, *Foucquet*, 1:407–8.

35. Fouquet to Mazarin, June 26, 1657, in Colbert, *Lettres*, 1:501–3, quote 502.

36. Bonney, *Debts*, 254. Lair, *Foucquet*, 1:427, gives a net figure of 10.5 million livres, as does Dulong, *Mazarin et l'argent*, 157–58.

37. Lair, *Foucquet*, 1:403–5; Petitfils, *Fouquet*, 136–37.

38. *Défenses*, 2:245–62 passim. See also *Bastille*, 2:352–57, December 2, 1664. Lair, *Foucquet*, 1:458–60. In his various pleadings, and interrogations, Fouquet often repeated arguments and explanations. Citations from the *Défenses* in these notes are therefore intended to be representative rather than comprehensive.

39. Lair, *Foucquet*, 1:475–79, quote 478. BnF, CC Colbert 235: fols. xxv–xxvi, Commission, January 28, 1659.

40. Lair, *Foucquet*, 1:479.

41. Dessert, *Fouquet*, 135. For background on commercial activities and partnerships, and privateering, see Dessert, *Fouquet*, 130–44; Petitfils, *Fouquet*, 189–200, 216–26; and Uzman, "Kinship," 44–48, 74–78.

42. Lair, *Foucquet*, 1:453–55; Petitfils, *Fouquet*, 224–25.

43. Dessert, *Fouquet*, 162; Petitfils, *Fouquet*, 225.

44. Petitfils, *Fouquet*, 216–22; Dessert, *Fouquet*, 136–39.

45. Dessert, *Fouquet*, 161–62. For the income of Henri II de Condé in 1651, about 425,000 livres, see Labatut, *Ducs et pairs*, 258.

46. Lair, *Foucquet*, 1:534.

47. *Bastille*, 2:370–73, December 3, 1664. See also *Défenses*, 10:152–53.

48. Pitts, *Mademoiselle*, 18–20. On Richelieu's fortune, see Bergin, *Richelieu*, 293–311.

49. On Fouquet as patron of the arts, see Lair, *Foucquet*, 1:535–39; Fumaroli, *Poète*, 185–91; Petitfils, *Fouquet*, 258–74; Duchêne, "La Fontaine et Fouquet"; McGowan; "La Fontaine"; Châtelain, *Fouquet*; and Bury, "La culture Fouquet."

50. Fumaroli, *Poète*, 181.

51. Fumaroli, *Poète*, 144. On Pellisson's early career, see 138–50, 159–76 passim. See also Ranum, *Artisans*, 236–46.

52. Fumaroli, *Poète*, 167.

53. Lair, *Foucquet*, 1:481.

54. Fumaroli, *Poète*, 181–85.

55. Sévigné, *Lettres*, 1:108–9, Sévigné to Bussy-Rabutin, July 19, 1655.

56. Lair, *Foucquet*, 1:519.

57. Lair, *Foucquet*, 1:420, 540; Dessert, *Fouquet*, 155; Saunders, "Library." A detailed inventory was prepared by royal commissioners after Fouquet's disgrace: BnF, Ms. Fr. 9438: fols. 1–175v., "Inventory of books found at St-Mandé," July 31, 1665.

58. Lair, *Foucquet*, 1:420.

59. Petitfils, *Fouquet*, 171–73.

60. Blunt, *Art and Architecture*, 233. On Le Brun's ceilings, see Mérot, "Vaux-le-Vicomte."

61. Dessert, *Fouquet*, 156.

62. Lair, *Foucquet*, 1:531; Petitfils, *Fouquet*, 179. For details, see Lair, *Foucquet*, 521–31; Dessert, *Fouquet*, 155–57; and Petitfils, *Fouquet*, 173–88.

63. Blunt, *Art and Architecture*, 233; for an overall assessment, see 229–34.

64. Scudéry, "Valterre" in *Clélie*, vol. X, quoted in Lair, *Foucquet*, 1:525.

65. Lair, *Foucquet*, 1:483.

66. Montpensier, *Mémoires*, 3:489.

67. Petitfils, *Fouquet*, 354.

CHAPTER 3: Fall of a Titan

1. Dessert, *Fouquet*, 201; Meyer, *Colbert*, 40. For the family background, see Meyer, *Colbert*, 22–34, 38–45, and Villain, *Fortune de Colbert*, 3–18. See also Bourgeon, *Les Colbert avant Colbert*.

2. Murat, *Colbert*, 1–9; Richardt, *Colbert*, 17–26; Meyer, *Colbert*, 21; Dessert, *Royaume de Colbert*, 83–92; Dessert, *Fouquet*, 200–203; Villain, *Fortune de Colbert*, 27–28.

3. Murat, *Colbert*, 13–15, including Colbert's ingratiating himself with patrons; Lair, *Foucquet*, 1:143–45 passim.

4. Murat, *Colbert*, 16.

5. Murat, *Colbert*, 16.

6. Murat, *Colbert*, 18.

7. Murat, *Colbert*, 21; Dulong, *Mazarin et l'argent*, 51–55, 228.

8. Murat, *Colbert*, 22–30; Dulong, *Fortune*, 133–148.

9. Dent, *Crisis in Finance*, 79. Dulong, *Fortune*, 44–64 passim, details similar practices but mostly for the pre-Fronde period.

10. Murat, *Colbert*, 21–30 passim; Meyer, *Colbert*, 142–47, 150, 153–57. See also Dulong, *Mazarin et l'argent*, 195, 236, and Villain, *Fortune de Colbert*, 47–53.

11. Colbert, *Lettres*, 1:520–30, "Estat des biens, revenus et effects appartenant à Monseigneur," June 1658. Dessert, *Royaume de Colbert*, 58, estimates Mazarin's fortune at 40 million livres in 1661 and at 38–39 million in his earlier *Fouquet*, 205–6, 237. Dulong, *Mazarin et l'argent*, argues for a figure of 30 million livres, 230–32. For further discussion of the cardinal's fortune, see appendix, "Ministerial Fortunes in Seventeenth-Century France."

12. Murat, *Colbert*, 9, 30–31; Meyer, *Colbert*, 147; Villain, *Fortune de Colbert*, 53–54.

13. Dent, *Clientèles*, 47, 50; Murat, *Colbert*, 30–33 passim; Meyer, *Colbert*, 109–10, 147–48, 317–24. Meyer, 321, argues that the "essentials" of Colbert's fortune were acquired "between 1648 and 1661," implying that much of it had to be connected to participations in Mazarin's activities. See also Villain, *Fortune de Colbert*, 65–72.

14. Lair, *Foucquet*, 1:267–70; Chéruel, *Fouquet*, 1:251–53.

15. Colbert, *Lettres*, 1:198–00, Colbert to Mazarin, January 4, 1653, quote 200; Murat, *Colbert*, 19; Chéruel, *Fouquet*, 1:250–51.

16. Murat, *Colbert*, 40, Colbert to Mazarin, June 19, 1654.

17. Murat, *Colbert*, 45–46, Colbert to Mazarin, July 5, 1657.

18. Murat, *Colbert*, 44. On the evolution of the Colbert-Fouquet relationship, see Uzman, "Kinship," 193–208. Fouquet later accused Colbert and Hervart of conspiring against him, *Défenses*, 2:79–87.

19. Murat, *Colbert*, 43–44; Hamscher, *Parlement*, 10.

20. Murat, *Colbert*, 44–45.

21. Dessert, *Royaume de Colbert*, 96–128 passim; Murat, *Colbert*, 45.

22. Lair, *Foucquet*, 1:482–85.

23. Bonney, *Debts*, 256. On Mazarin balancing between rival subordinates, see Uzman, "Kinship," 210–15.

24. Colbert, *Lettres*, 7:164–83, Colbert to Mazarin, "Mémoire," October 1, 1659; 1:380–83, Colbert to Mazarin, October 1, 1659 (letter accompanying "Mémoire" of same date). See also 1:360–62, Colbert to Mazarin, August 31, 1659.

25. Gourville, *Mémoires*, 113–14; Lair, *Foucquet*, 1:491.

26. Dulong, *Mazarin et l'argent*, 180. For Mazarin's later defenses of Fouquet's stewardship against criticisms by Colbert, Servien, et al., see Uzman, "Kinship," 215–35, who notes that overall the relationship was "contradictory," 232.

27. For the entire exchange, see Lair, *Foucquet*, 1:487–96 passim, and Dulong, *Mazarin et l'argent*, 180–85.

28. Bonney, *Debts*, 258; Bonney, "Secret Expenses," 833; Lair, *Foucquet*, 1:506.

29. Bonney, *Debts*, 259.

30. Petitfils, *Fouquet*, 204.

31. Chéruel, *Fouquet*, 1:488–97, "Texte trouvé à St-Mandé" [part 1, 1657], quote 492. On Madame du Plessis-Bellière, see Uzman, "Kinship," 70–71, 78–85, 102–7.

32. Chéruel, *Fouquet*, 1:497–501, "Texte trouvé à St-Mandé" [part 2, 1658–1659]. The text is also reproduced in Dessert, *Fouquet*, 354–62. See also Lair, *Foucquet*, 1:411–16, 471–74; Petitfils, *Fouquet*, 202–6, 233–237; Dessert, *Fouquet*, 254–57; and Murat, *Colbert*, 46–55. On the break with Basile Fouquet, see Uzman, "Kinship," 268–78.

33. Gourville, *Mémoires*, 125–26.

34. On this controversial point, Murat, *Colbert*, 46–55, takes it very seriously, as does Petitfils, *Fouquet*, 204. Dessert, *Fouquet*, 254–57, is dismissive, arguing that not a word in the text was directed against the king or state and that Fouquet did not dominate Brittany, effectively governed by La Meilleraye. Lair, *Foucquet*, 1:416, is also dismissive, while Chéruel, *Fouquet*, 1:379, saw this planning as "authentic" and continuing after Mazarin's death. Le Roy Ladurie, *Ancien Régime*, 136, sees an incipient Fronde in the plan, an opinion shared by Meyer, *Colbert*, 174–77.

35. Treasure, *Mazarin*, 301–2; Petitfils, *Fouquet*, 317.

36. Dessert, *Royaume de Colbert*, 58–68. Choisy, *Mémoires*, 57.

37. Choisy, *Mémoires*, 77. Petitfils, *Fouquet*, 321–22, believes some of this happened but expresses reservations about the details.

38. Dessert, *Royaume de Colbert*, 68; Lair, *Foucquet*, 1:568; Choisy, *Mémoires*, 58. On Ondedei, see Treasure, *Mazarin*, 328.

39. Bonney, *Debts*, 261–62.

40. Pitts, *Mademoiselle*, 136–40 passim.

41. Brienne, *Mémoires*, 3:36–38, quote 36.

42. Bluche, *Louis XIV*, 98–99; Petitfils, *Fouquet*, 327; Choisy, *Mémoires*, 73; Lair, *Foucquet*, 2:6.

43. Louis XIV, *Mémoires*, 35.

44. Petitfils, *Fouquet*, 328.

45. Lair, *Foucquet*, 2:2–6; Choisy, *Mémoires*, 87.

46. Choisy, *Mémoires*, 68–69, 82. On the complex set of considerations leading to Louis's actions, see Meyer, *Colbert*, 172–81.

47. Louis, XIV, *Mémoires*, 34. On the drafting of this section, see Sonnino's comments, 4–7.

48. Bonney, *Debts*, 265.

49. *Défenses*, 13:156, Interrogation, March 16, 1662; Petitfils, *Fouquet*, 324; Choisy, *Mémoires*, 98.

50. Louis XIV, *Mémoires*, 62.

51. Choisy, *Mémoires*, 82.

52. Louis XIV, *Mémoires*, 62. See also *Bastille*, 1:351–55, Coislin to Séguier, September 5, 1661.

53. Louis XIV, *Mémoires*, 62. Some of these accusations, written in the late 1670s, are clearly post-trial in origin. See Dessert, *Royaume de Colbert*, 98–128 passim.

54. On these reports, see Murat, *Colbert*, 61–63. See also Petitfils, *Fouquet*, 310–16; Dessert, *Fouquet*, 141–44; and Lair, *Foucquet*, 1:531–32.

55. Murat, *Colbert*, 63, Colbert du Terron to Colbert, July 24, 1661.

56. Bonney, *Debts*, 270–71; Petitfils, *Fouquet*, 335–37.

57. Gaillard, *Lamoignon*, 169.

58. Louis XIV, *Mémoires*, 62; *Bastille*, 1:351–55, Coislin to Séguier, September 5, 1661; *Bastille*, 1:362–64, Louis XIV to archbishop of Embrun, September 16, 1661.

59. On the temporary alliance between Colbert and Le Tellier, see Uzman, "Kinship," 306–7. *Bastille*, 1:347–51, contains various orders and instructions to d'Artagnan, September 4, 1661; Murat, *Colbert*, 65–70 passim.

60. Brienne, *Mémoires*, 3:49.

61. Choisy, *Mémoires*, 65–66, 91–93; Brienne, *Mémoires*, 3:49–50; Petitfils, *Fouquet*, 344–45, 354.

62. Lair, *Foucquet*, 1:527–29; Petitfils, *Fouquet*, 173–88.

63. Lair, *Foucquet*, 2:46–51; Petitfils, *Fouquet*, 354–58.

64. Choisy, *Mémoires*, 93–94; Brienne, *Mémoires*, 3:48–49; Voltaire, *Louis XIV*, 263.

65. Lafayette, *Princesse d'Angleterre*, 41.

66. Choisy, *Mémoires*, 91; Voltaire, *Louis XIV*, 263. Madame du Plessis-Bellière's supposed letter is preserved in BA, Collection Conrart, Ms. 5420. Uzman, "Kinship," 92–98, 315, puts this approach to La Vallière in the context of Fouquet's network of female informants at court. Lair, *Foucquet*, 2:40–43, sees this misstep as an important part of Fouquet's fall from grace; Chéruel, *Fouquet*, 2:173–74, believes the story true even if the letter is suspect. See also Petitfils, *Fouquet*, 350–52.

67. Choisy, *Mémoires*, 94; Gourville, *Mémoires*,130–33 passim; Petitfils, *Fouquet*, 347–48. On Fouquet's enormous network of informers at court, many of them women, see Uzman, "Kinship," 87–98.

68. Brienne, *Mémoires*, 3:56.

69. Lair, *Foucquet*, 2:56.

70. Brienne, *Mémoires*, 3:57–58.

71. Brienne, *Mémoires*, 3:67–68.

72. Brienne, *Mémoires*, 3:62–63.

73. Hall and Sanders, *D'Artagnan*, 66; Petitfils, *D'Artagnan*, 79.

74. Foucault, "Récit officiel," 448; Lair, *Foucquet*, 2:58.

75. Foucault, "Récit officiel," 448; Lair, *Foucquet*, 2:59; *Bastille*, 1:348, Louis XIV to d'Artagnan, September 4, 1661; 1:347–50, "Mémoire pour M. d'Artagnan," September 4, 1661.

76. Choisy, *Mémoires*, 100–101.

77. Lair, *Foucquet*, 2:68–69; *Bastille*, 1:353, Coislin to Séguier, September 5, 1661.

78. Gourville, *Mémoires*, 134–35.

79. Lair, *Foucquet*, 2:69.

80. For a summary of these measures, see Lair, *Foucquet*, 2: 64–73; Petitfils, *Fouquet*, 364–75; Uzman, "Kinship," 321–28 passim.

81. Gourville, *Mémoires*, 137–38.

82. Choisy, *Mémoires*, 99–100, quote 100; *Bastille*, 1:351–55, Coislin to Séguier, September 5, 1661; Lair, *Foucquet*, 2:61 n3. Uzman, "Kinship," 320–22, argues that Louis's decision to arrest Fouquet at Nantes was intended in part to neutralize the superintendant's network in Brittany and preclude any possibility of armed rebellion by virtue of the king's physical presence there.

CHAPTER 4: Setting the Stage and Writing the Script

1. Bosher, "*Chambres*," 31; Chéruel, *Fouquet*, 2:334–35.

2. Dessert, "Chambre de justice," 857.

3. Bosher, "*Chambres*," 31; Chéruel, *Fouquet*, 2:334–37.

4. Bosher, "*Chambres*," 19–24. Carbasse, *Justice criminelle*, 146–47.

5. Bosher, "*Chambres*," 31.

6. Bosher, "*Chambres*," 27–31; Dent, *Crisis in Finance*, 103–4; Chauleur, "Traitants," 38–44; Lebigre, *Justice*, 103–7.

7. Bosher, "*Chambres*," 24–37.

8. Dent, *Crisis in Finance*, 104.

9. Lair, *Foucquet*, 1:322.

10. Treasure, *Mazarin*, 190; Bonney, *Debts*, 231–33.

11. Lair, *Foucquet*, 1:319–23. On La Vieuville's fall, see Bergin, *Rise of Richelieu*, 246–59.

12. Colbert, *Lettres*, 7:213–18, "Plan de la Chambre de Justice" (1662); see also 7:173–74, October 1, 1659.

13. Ormesson, *Journal*, 2:lxxvii, "Commission," November 15, 1661.

14. Ormesson, *Journal*, 2:lxxvi, "Commission," November 15, 1661; 2:lxxxi n1.

15. Hamscher, *Parlement*, 17–18, 95, 97–98, 101–5 passim; Dulong, *Mazarin et l'argent*, 184–85; Uzman, "Kinship," 201.

16. Colbert, *Lettres*, 7:174, October 1, 1659; Lair, *Foucquet*: 1:508–9. On Talon's ties to Colbert, see Uzman, "Kinship," 204.

17. Ormesson, *Journal*, 2:lxxvi–lxxvii, "Commission," November 15, 1661. For the entire text see 2:lxxvi–lxxx. On jurisdiction to 1635, see 2:lxxxii. For Colbert's evaluation of the court's members, see Colbert, *Lettres*, 7:213–18, "Chambre de Justice." (1662). On Gomont, see Villain, *Fortune de Colbert*, 70–71, 79. On Berryer, see Dornic, *Berryer*, 23–32, for early career; 32–48, on duchy of Mayenne; and 49–82, on forestry transactions, characterized by the author as "gangsterism," 75.

18. Richet, *Réforme*, 158–64.

19. Richet, *Réforme*, 180–84, 196–97; Kerviler, *Séguier*, 4–7
20. Richet, *Réforme*, 192, 216; Kerviler, *Séguier*, 8–9.
21. Richet, *Réforme*, 265–66; Kerviler, *Séguier*, 18–23.
22. Richet, *Réforme*, 266; Kerviler, *Séguier*, 24–25.
23. Richet, *Réforme*, 307–9; Kerviler, *Séguier*, 56–57, 93–94.
24. Richet, *Réforme*, 309.
25. Richet, *Réforme*, 307; Kerviler, *Séguier*, 58–59.
26. Ranum, *Fronde*, 159–60; Kerviler, *Séguier*, 246–54.
27. Richet, *Réforme*, 309–10; Kerviler, *Séguier*, 270–306 passim.
28. Richet, *Réforme*, 312. Kerviler, *Séguier*, 158–166.
29. Richet, *Réforme*, 262–63, 294 table VII; Kerviler, *Séguier*, 18.
30. Sévigné, *Lettres*, 1:131, Sévigné to Pomponne, December 1, 1664.
31. Tallemant des Réaux, *Historiettes*, 1:611–16, "Le chancelier Séguier."
32. Uzman "Kinship," 310, 317. Uzman also outlines the rivalry between Fouquet and Séguier in the last years of Mazarin's ministry, 188–90.
33. Lair, *Foucquet*, 1:456–58. Hamscher, *Parlement*, 105, maintains that both Le Tellier and Fouquet supported Lamoignon's candidacy. On Fouquet's complicated ties to Lamoignon, see Uzman, "Kinship," 229–30, 246–47, 259–60, 279, 281. In his own account, written in April 1662, Lamoignon stressed his strong ties to Le Tellier and asserted that Fouquet approached him with offers of support and friendship. "Relation de la nomination," in Lemoine, *Grande robe*, 265–66. He also insisted that even without Fouquet's help, he would still have been appointed first president, 271, and that Mazarin insisted that the final decision was his and the king's, no one else's, 277 and 279. For background on Lamoignon, see Lemoine, *Grande robe*, 181–230 passim.
34. Lair, *Foucquet*, 1:506–508; Gaillard, *Lamoignon*, 168–69.
35. Chéruel, *Fouquet*, 1:306–7.
36. Gaillard, *Lamoignon*, 172, 179; Lamoignon, "Journal," AnF, 399 AP3 (folios not numbered); Uzman, "Kinship," 347–348; Hamscher, *Parlement*, 125–26. For Colbert's reservations about Lamoignon, see Colbert, *Lettres*, 7:214, "Chambre de Justice" (1662). See above n33 for Lamoignon's efforts to distance himself from any obligation to Fouquet. The date of the "Relation," April 1662, while the trial was under way, is significant here.
37. Uzman, "Kinship," 351–52.
38. Uzman, "Kinship," 355. Colbert counted nine: Colbert, *Lettres*, 7:214, "Chambre de Justice" (1662). See also Colbert, "Notes secrètes," in Depping and Depping, *Correspondance administrative*, 2:33–34.
39. Uzman, "Kinship," 347.
40. Ormesson, *Journal*, 2:10–11; Uzman, "Kinship," 346; Petitfils, *Fouquet*, 386 n7; Cornette, *Mélancolie*, 64. Voysin, too, had crossed swords with Fouquet in the past over patronage: see Uzman, "Kinship," 204–5. On Pontchartrain, see Chapman, *Private Ambition*, 19–21.
41. Chéruel, *Fouquet*, 2:338–40.
42. Lair, *Foucquet*, 2:97.
43. Lair, *Foucquet*, 2:76–90.
44. Lair, *Foucquet*, 2:83, 2:93.
45. *Bastille*, 1:344–46; Petitfils, *Fouquet*, 387.

46. Ormesson, *Journal*, 2:98–99, February 18, 1664.

47. *Bastille*, 1:407–8, Le Tellier to Talhouet, December 14, 1661.

48. Lair, *Foucquet*, 2:105.

49. Chéruel, *Fouquet*, 2:263–70, Fouquet to Le Tellier, September 1661.

50. Lair, Foucquet, 2:108; *Bastille*, 1:369–70, Le Tellier to d'Artagnan, September 27, 1661.

51. Ormesson, *Journal*, 2:10–11, March 3, 1662; Dessert, *Royaume de Colbert*, 123.

52. Ormesson, *Journal*, 2:11, March 4, 1662 [misprinted as March 2 in text].

53. *Défenses*, 13:1–16, Interrogations, March 4 and March 6, 1662; *Bastille*, 2:18, Rouillé to Pomponne, March 18, 1662.

54. *Défenses*, 13:18, Interrogation, March 7, 1662.

55. All of the interrogations can be found in *Défenses*, 13:1–258. On judicial philosophies and norms of the period, see Krynen, *Idéologie*, 79–103, 139–90; Lebigre, *Justice*, 100–103, 214–32; Astaing, *Droits*, 189–213; and Carbasse, *Justice criminelle*, 297–300. On procedure, see Esmein, *Criminal Procedure*, 145–61; Carbasse, *Justice criminelle*, 177–79; and Langbein, *Crime*, 223–43.

56. *Défenses*, 13:44–50, Interrogation, March 9, 1662.

57. *Défenses*, 13:67, Interrogation, March 10, 1662.

58. *Défenses*, 13:65, Interrogation, March 10, 1662.

59. *Défenses*, 13:74–76, Interrogation, March 11, 1662.

60. *Défenses*, 13:79, Interrogation, March 11, 1662.

61. *Défenses*, 13:79–87 passim, Interrogation, March 11, 1662.

62. *Défenses*, 13:95–177, Interrogations, March 14–17, 1662. According to Lair, *Foucquet*, 2:127 n3, some of this is misdated March 13.

63. *Défenses*, 13:151–54, Interrogation, March 16, 1662.

64. *Défenses*, 13:156, Interrogation, March 16, 1662.

65. Gourville, *Mémoires*, 125–26.

66. *Défenses*, 13:161–62, Interrogation, March 17, 1662.

67. *Défenses*, 13:44, Interrogation, March 9, 1662; 13:235–37, Interrogation, March 22, 1662.

68. *Défenses*, 13:207–9, 212–17, Interrogation, March 21, 1662, quote 208; see also 13:242, Interrogation, March 22, 1662.

69. *Défenses*, 13:249–50, March 23, 1662.

70. *Bastille*, 2:12–15, Mme Fouquet the Elder to the King, March 5, 1662.

71. *Bastille*, 2:15–16, Le Tellier to Mme Fouquet the Younger, March 8, 1662.

72. *Bastille*, 2:24–25, Bénigne Bouhier to President Bouhier, March 24, 1662.

73. Mongrédien, *Fouquet*, 122–24.

74. Chapelin to Sévigné, n.d., 1662, quoted in Chéruel, *Fouquet*, 2:321–22.

75. Chéruel, *Fouquet*, 2:322–23.

76. Chéruel, *Fouquet*, 2:506–8, "Confiteor de Fouquet."

77. Pellisson, *Oeuvres*, 1:132. For the entire text, *Discours au Roi*, see 1:130–215.

78. Pellisson, *Oeuvres*, 1:137–45 passim.

79. Pellisson, *Oeuvres*, 1:165–75 passim.

80. Pellisson, *Oeuvres*, 1:175.

81. Pellisson, *Oeuvres*, 1:153–54, 155.

82. Pellisson, *Oeuvres*, 1:183.

83. Pellisson, *Oeuvres*, 1:190–202 passim.

84. Pellisson, *Oeuvres*, 1:147–48, 202–4, 214–15.

85. Ranum, *Artisans*, 246.

86. Pellisson, *Oeuvres*, 2:5–168, "Second Discours au Roi."

87. Pellisson, *Oeuvres*, 2:18–28.

88. Pellisson, *Oeuvres*, 2:92–138.

89. Pellisson, *Oeuvres*, 2:28–45 passim; 2:62–75 passim.

90. Pellisson, *Oeuvres*, 2:86–87.

91. Pellisson, *Oeuvres*, 2:163.

92. Pellisson, *Oeuvres*, 2:169–205, "Considérations Sommaires." For analyses of Pellisson's three essays, see Ranum, *Artisans*, 246–51; Lair, *Foucquet*, 2:137–41, 159–61; and Petitfils, *Fouquet*, 392–93, 397.

93. Mongrédien, *Fouquet*, 101.

94. Voltaire, *Age of Louis XIV*, 363.

95. Fumaroli, *Poète*, 226–27; Chéruel, *Fouquet*, 2:401. On the function of adjuncts, see Storez-Brancourt, "Substituts," 160–67.

96. Fumaroli, *Poète*, 226.

97. Funaroli, *Poète*, 65–66, 231–32. For the verses, see Mongrédien, *Fouquet*, 109–10.

98. Fumaroli, *Poète*, 65–66.

99. Anonymous, *L'innocence persecutée*. For the connection to Molière, see 8–9. The mention in the play is in act 5, scene 1, 1501–4. Editor Baveral-Croissant concludes, 204, that the likeliest author of the poem was La Fontaine. See also Mongrédien, *Fouquet*, 156–68, and Fumaroli, *Poète*, 79–85.

100. Petitfils, *Fouquet*, 394. See also Mongrédien, *Fouquet*, 124.

101. Petitfils, *Fouquet*, 394–95; Mongrédien, *Fouquet*, 392–400; Fumaroli, *Poète*, 222–27.

CHAPTER 5: The Best-Laid Plans of Men and Ministers

1. Lair, *Foucquet*, 2:145–47.

2. Lair, *Foucquet*, 2:148–49. On this transaction, see also Pellisson, *Oeuvres*, 2:92–138, "Second Discours au Roi."

3. Ormesson, *Journal*, 2:12–13, June 14–17, 1662; *Bastille*, 2:45, Louis XIV to d'Artagnan, June 19, 1662.

4. Ormesson, *Journal*, 2:18–19, June 27–28, 1662; *Bastille*, 2:53 n1. On the legal concept of "voluntary mute," see Astaing, *Droits*, 247, 396–97. On a similar principle in contemporary English law, see Hale, Wilson, and Dogherty, *Pleas*, 2:314–21.

5. Ormesson, *Journal*, 2:20, July 5 and July 7, 1662.

6. *Bastille*, 2:47–48, Louis XIV to d'Artagnan, June 23, 1662; 2:51–52, Louis XIV to d'Artagnan, June 29, 1662; Petitfils, *Fouquet*, 397.

7. *Bastille*, 2:55–57, Register of Parlement, July 19 and July 27, 1662. On the regular courts' dislike of royal evocations, quarrels over jurisdiction, etc., see Parker, "Sovereignty," 57–58; 71; Kitchens, "Judicial *Commissaires*," 327, 329; and Hamscher, *Parlement*, 107–9, 124–25.

8. *Bastille*, 2:59–61, Mme Fouquet the Younger to Louis XIV, July 30, 1662.

9. *Bastille*, 2:62–63, Register of Parlement, August 2, 1662.

10. Lair, *Foucquet*, 2:170–71.

11. *Bastille*, 2:81–84, Chamber of Justice, September 26, 1662.

12. *Bastille*, 2:81–84, Chamber of Justice, September 26, 1662; Gaillard, *Lamoignon*, 170. See also AnF, 399 AP3, Lamoignon, "Journal," September 1662 (folios not numbered).

13. Hamscher, *Parlement*, 125. In his journal, Lamoignon noted that he had been a friend of Fouquet's initially, then an opponent because of his opposition to the crown's financial policies. Either sentiment, he noted, would preclude a magistrate participating in a proceeding: AnF, 399 AP3, September 1662.

14. Gaillard, *Lamoignon*, 170; AnF, 399 AP3, Lamoignon, "Journal," September 1662.

15. BnF, CC Colbert 235: fols. 226–312. See also Lair, *Foucquet*, 2:166–69.

16. *Bastille*, 2:86–87, Chamber of Justice, October 5, 1662; Ormesson, *Journal*, 2:21, October 5, 1662; Chéruel, *Fouquet*, 2:353; Cherchève, "Procès de Fouquet," 110.

17. Ormesson, *Journal*, 2:22, October 10, 1662; Gaillard, *Lamoignon*, 172–73. On traditional grounds for recusal, see Astaing, *Droits*, 135, 213–26.

18. Gaillard, *Lamoignon*, 173.

19. AnF, 399 AP3, Lamoignon, "Journal," October 12, 1662, et seq. The same quote is found in Gaillard, *Lamoignon*, 174. Ormesson, *Journal*, 2:22, October 11, 1662.

20. AnF, 399 AP3, Lamoignon, "Journal," October 12, 1662, et seq.; Gaillard, *Lamoignon*, 174.

21. AnF, 399 AP3, Lamoignon, "Journal," October 12, 1662, et seq.; Gaillard, *Lamoignon*, 175; Ormesson, *Journal*, 2:21–23, October 10–11, October 21, 1662; *Bastille*, 2: 91–92, Chamber of Justice, October 22, 1662; Lair, *Foucquet*, 2:173–77.

22. Solnon, *Ormesson*, 70–77; Ormesson, *Journal*, 1:xxxii–xxxviii. Excerpts of André d'Ormesson's memoirs for 1650–1654 are printed in Ormesson, *Journal*, 2:635–707.

23. Solnon, *Ormesson*, 38–39, 138.

24. Solnon, *Ormesson*, 83. See also Ormesson, *Journal*, 1:64, June 5, 1643. For general background on Olivier, see Solnon, *Ormesson*, 81–87. For his career to 1662, see Ormesson, *Journal*, 1:xxxviii–xliv.

25. Solnon, *Ormesson*,150, 166–67. On Ormesson and Lamoignon, see Gaillard, *Lamoignon*, 175, and Colbert, *Lettres*, 7:216, "Chambre de Justice" (1662).

26. Ormesson, *Journal*, 1:xli.

27. Solnon, *Ormesson*, 97–98.

28. Ormesson, *Journal*, 1:xli–xlii, xliv; Solnon, *Ormesson*, 98–100.

29. Ormesson, *Journal*, 2:21, October 10, 1662; Uzman,"Kinship," 258.

30. Colbert, *Lettres*, 7:216, "Chambre de Justice" (1662).

31. Ormesson, *Journal*, 2:22, October 11, 1662.

32. Ormesson, *Journal*, 2:22–26, October 21–December 9, 1662; Lair, *Foucquet*, 2:187–90. On Talon's behavior, see Hamscher, *Parlement*, 125.

33. Hamscher, *Parlement*, 78–80, 125–26. Lamoignon mentioned the issue of *rentes* as a point of disagreement between himself and Colbert: AnF, 399 AP3, Lamoignon, "Journal," n.d.

34. AnF, 399 AP3, Lamoignon, "Journal," December 10, 1662; Gaillard, *Lamoignon*, 176; *Bastille*, 2:103: Colbert to Séguier, December 12, 1662.

35. AnF, 399 AP3, Lamoignon, "Journal," December 11, 1662; Gaillard, *Lamoignon*, 176–77; Ormesson, *Journal*, 2:27, December 12, 1662.

36. Ormesson, *Journal*, 2:27, December 11, 1662. Lemoine, *Grande robe*, 227, dismisses this account of Lamoignon's departure from the chamber and insists that it had been understood that he would not take part in Fouquet's trial, only in those pertaining to others investigated by the chamber. He offers no evidence for this assertion, which also overlooks the role Lamoignon had played in the debates over Fouquet's requests to the chamber in 1662.

37. Ormesson, *Journal*, 2:29, December 22, 1662; Lair, *Foucquet*, 2:194–96 passim.

38. Gaillard, *Lamoignon*, 177–78. See also AnF, 399 AP3, Lamoignon, "Journal," n.d.

39. Gaillard, *Lamoignon*, 179. In his "Journal," Lamoignon criticizes the interference and distortions of judicial process by Colbert et al. in a number of places, and insisted that his actions as presiding magistrate were often the opposite of the complaisance "always expected by those who wielded the royal authority." AnF, 399 AP3, n.d.

40. Ormesson, *Journal*, 2:79–80, January 26, 1664.

41. *Défenses*, 1:159.

42. *Défenses*, 1:61–259, "Extracts." Lair, *Foucquet*, 2:191–92.

43. *Défenses*, 13:279–303, "Memoirs and Comments."

44. Ormesson, *Journal*, 2:30–32, December 29, 1662–January 22, 1663. Ormesson's date of December 29 is incorrect per Lair, *Foucquet*, 2:202 n1, which provides the correct date as January 19, consistent with the date of the second petition, January 21, as noted in Ormesson. See also *Bastille*, 2:110, Chamber of Justice, January 19, 1663.

45. *Défenses*, 1:32–36, Fouquet to the Chamber of Justice, January 1663; *Défenses*, 3: 396–419, Fouquet to the Chamber of Justice, January 1663 (petition against Talon).

46. Ormesson, *Journal*, 2:32–35, January 30, 1663; Lair, *Foucquet*, 2:204.

47. Ormesson, *Journal*, 2:36–37, January 31, 1663.

48. Ormesson, *Journal*, 2:37–40, February 1 and 3, 1663.

49. On Bordeaux, see Dulong, *Mazarin et l'argent*, 172; Lair, *Foucquet*, 1:67 and 1:342.

50. Ormessson, *Journal* 2:40–41, April 6, 1663.

51. Lair, *Foucquet*, 2:250; Ormessson, *Journal* 2:40–41, April 6, 1663.

52. *Bastille*, 2:102, Bulliaud to Fabricius, December 7, 1662; *Bastille*, 2:126–27, Le Tellier to Royal Procureur, Soissons, April 1663; Lair, *Foucquet*, 2:192.

53. Montgrédien, *Fouquet*, 124–25; Chéruel, *Fouquet*, 2:370; Lair, *Foucquet*, 2:201.

54. *Défenses*, 2:148–61 passim, "Points."

55. *Défenses*, 2:139, "Points." The presentation, subdivided into sections, encompasses the entirety of *Défenses*, vol. 2.

56. *Défenses*, 2:141, "Points."

57. *Défenses*, 2:295, "Points."

58. *Défenses*, 2:25–29, "Points."

59. *Défenses*, 2:77–78, 259–60, 262, "Points."

60. *Défenses*, 2:209–10, "Points."

61. *Défenses*, 2:215, "Points."

62. *Défenses*, 2:231, "Points."

63. *Défenses*, 2:54 (quote), 79, 41 (Talon), "Points."

64. *Défenses*, 2:28–29, "Points."

65. *Défenses*, 2:215, 265, 318, "Points."

66. On these investigations, 1641–1652, see Dulong, *Mazarin et l'argent*, 19–55 passim; on Hervart, ibid., 168. See also Bonney, *Debts*, 234–35, and Bonney, "Remonstrances," 20–22.

67. *Défenses*, 2:333–45 passim, 345 (annual income), "Points."

68. *Défenses*, 2:97, "Points."

69. *Défenses*, 2:350, "Points."

70. *Bastille*, 2:115–16, Mme Fouquet the Younger to Louis XIV, February 2, 1663.

71. Lair, *Foucquet*, 2:209.

72. Ormesson, *Journal*, 2:38, February 3, 1663.

73. *Bastille*, 2:135, Louis XIV to Besmaux, July 31, 1663.

74. *Bastille*, 2:128–29, Mortoge to Colbert, May 20, 1663.

CHAPTER 6: To Do Justice without Consideration of Fortune or Self-Interest

1. Ormesson, *Journal*, 2:39–40, February 3, 1662.

2. Talon's charges and Fouquet's responses are printed in *Défenses*, 3:1–395, with Talon's accusations in italics and Fouquet's responses in roman type; see esp. 3:1–40. For a summary, see Lair, *Foucquet*, 2:236–42.

3. All of the exchanges are printed in *Défenses*, vols. 3–5.

4. See *Défenses*, vol. 4, esp. 4:139–40 (on Mazarin's orders).

5. *Défenses*, 5:10–17.

6. On Jeannin de Castille, Tabouret, and this transaction, see *Défenses*, 9:1–73, esp. 20, also 2:245–62, esp. 253, and 10:231. On the misdated documentary evidence, see *Défenses*, 5:86, 92.

7. *Défenses*, 5:236–64.

8. *Défenses*, 5:279–99, quote 298–99.

9. *Défenses*, 3:40.

10. *Défenses*, 4:391.

11. *Défenses*, 4:392.

12. *Défenses*, 4:392.

13. *Défenses*, 4:61.

14. *Défenses*, 6:72–73.

15. *Défenses*, 8:31–66.

16. *Défenses*, 6:55.

17. *Défenses*, 6:38–39.

18. *Défenses*, 7:136.

19. *Défenses*, 8:4, 6, quote 4.

20. *Défenses*, 7:38, 86.

21. *Défenses*, 7:133–34.

22. *Défenses*, 7:205–6.

23. *Défenses*, 4:319.

24. *Défenses*, 7:41–53.

25. *Défenses*, 7:23.

26. Ormesson, *Journal*, 2:43, August 7, 1663; 2:48–49, October 19, 1663.

27. Ormesson, *Journal*, 2:44, August 7, 1663. According to Lair, the correct date for this exchange is August 13, Lair, *Foucquet*, 2:266.

28. Ormesson, *Journal*, 2:46–48, August 29–31, 1663.

29. Ormesson, *Journal*, 2:45–46, August 22–23, 1663.

30. Ormesson, *Journal*, 2:45–46, August 23, 1663.

31. Ormesson, *Journal*, 2:46, August 27, 1663; *Bastille*, 2:144, Chamber of Justice, August 27, 1663.

32. *Bastille*, 2:144 n1, Colbert to Louis XIV, August 27, 1663; Ormesson, *Journal*, 2:46, August 27, 1663.

33. *Bastille*, 2:145–46, Talon to Colbert, August 1663.

34. *Défenses*, 3: 173–74. Ormesson, *Journal*, 2:42–43, July 11, 1663; Uzman, "Kinship," 345.

35. *Bastille*, 2:134, Louis XIV to Besmaux, June 18, 1663.

36. *Bastille*, 2:147–48, Chamber of Justice, September 26, 1663.

37. Ormesson, *Journal*, 2:61, November 29, 1663.

38. Ormesson, *Journal*, 2:60–61, November 27, 1663. On Chamillart and his ties to both Colbert and Le Tellier, see Pénicaut, *Faveur et pouvoir*, 33–44.

39. *Défenses*, 3:1 verso (pagination irregular); Lair, *Foucquet*, 2:249.

40. Ormesson, *Journal*, 2:49–50, October 19–26, 1663.

41. Ormesson, *Journal*, 2:51, October 29, 1663.

42. Ormesson, *Journal*, 2:53–55, November 14–15, 1663.

43. Ormesson, *Journal*, 2:71, January 6, 1664.

44. BnF, CC Colbert 236: fols. 179–211v. BnF, Ms Fr. 10229: fols. 443–69; Ormesson, *Journal*, 2:72, January 7, 1664; Lair, *Foucquet*, 2: 279–80.

45. Ormesson, *Journal*, 2:74–75, January 17, 1664; BnF, Ms Fr. 10229: fols. 468–69.

46. Ormesson, *Journal*, 2:74, January 16, 1664.

47. Lair, *Foucquet*, 2:281.

48. Ormesson, *Journal*, 2:75–77, January 19, 1664; BnF, CC Colbert 236: fols. 212–18, Chamber of Justice, January 19, 1664.

49. Ormesson, *Journal*, 2:77–78, January 26, 1664; 2:86–87, January 30, 1664.

50. Ormesson, *Journal*, 2:79–81 January 26, 1664, quote 81.

51. Ormesson, *Journal*, 2:83–84, January 29, 1664, quote 84.

52. Ormesson, *Journal*, 2:86, January 30, 1664.

53. Ormesson, *Journal*, 2:82, January 29, 1664; 2:96, February 11, 1664.

54. Ormesson, *Journal*, 2:84–85, January 30, 1664.

55. Ormesson, *Journal*, 2:88, January 31, 1664.

56. Ormesson, *Journal*, 2:91, February 4, 1664.

57. Ormesson, *Journal*, 2:100, February 19, 1664.

58. Ormesson, *Journal*, 2:106, March 5, 1664; 2:109, March 15, 1664; *Défenses*, 12:2, 3, 98–99, 118–49.

59. Ormesson, *Journal*, 2:112–13, March 29, 1664.

60. Ormesson, *Journal*, 2:112–13, March 29, 1664.

61. See above n58.

62. Ormesson, *Journal*, 2:115–16, April 3, 1664; BnF, CC Colbert 236: fols. 237v–240, Chamber of Justice, April 3, 1664.

63. Ormesson, *Journal*, 2:113, March 29, 1664.

64. Ormesson, *Journal*, 2:117–18, April 5, 1664.

65. Ormesson, *Journal*, 2:105, March 4, 1664.

66. Ormesson, *Journal*, 2:118, April 17, 1664.

67. Ormesson, *Journal*, 2:120, April 20, 1664; 2:134, May 2, 1664.

68. Ormesson, *Journal*, 2:124, April 25, 1664.

69. Ormesson, *Journal*, 2:120, April 20, 1664, quote; see also 2:124, April 25, 1664.

70. Ormesson, *Journal*, 2:132–33, May 1, 1664.

71. Ormesson, *Journal*, 2:133–34, May 2, 1664; see also 2:141, May 7, 1664. For the story that Boucherat recused himself on grounds of kinship, see Brienne, *Mémoires*, 3:77.

72. Ormesson, *Journal*, 2:136–38, May 3, 1662.

73. Ormesson, *Journal*, 2:141–42, May 6–7, 1664.

74. Ormesson, *Journal*, 2:138, May 3, 1664.

75. Ormesson, *Journal*, 2:138–39, May 3, 1664.

76. *Bastille*, 2:194–98, Hotman to Colbert, June 16, 1664; Ormesson, *Journal*, 2:159–61, June 16, 1664.

77. *Bastille*, 2:198, Pequot to Colbert, June 16, 1664.

78. Ormesson, *Journal*, 2:142–43, May 13, 1664.

79. Ormesson, *Journal*, 2:151–53, June 10, 1664; Béguin, *Financer la guerre*, 38–40.

80. Ormesson, *Journal*, 2:161, June 17, 1664.

81. Ormesson, *Journal*, 2:151, June 10, 1664; 2:161, June 17, 1664; 2:164, June 25, 1664.

82. Ormesson, *Journal*, 2:148, June 5, 1664, quote; see also 2:164, June 24, 1664.

83. Ormesson, *Journal*, 2:171–75 passim, July 7–8, 1664, quotes 175; *Bastille*, 2:205–8, Chamber of Justice, July 7, 1664.

84. Ormesson, *Journal*, 2:176–77, July 10, 1664; BnF, CC Colbert 236: fols. 250–60, Chamber of Justice, July 10, 1664.

85. Ormesson, *Journal*, 2:185, July 27, 1664.

86. Ormesson, *Journal*, 2:149–50, June 6, 1664.

87. Ormesson, *Journal*, 2:189–93, July 30, 1664, quote 190. See also *Bastille*, 2:209–10, Chamber of Justice, July 30, 1664.

88. Ormesson, *Journal*, 2:193–95, July 31, 1664.

89. BnF, CC Colbert 236: fol. 282–82v. For Fouquet's motions on this matter in July–August 1664, see BnF, Ms. Fr. 10229: fols. 476–99.

90. Ormesson, *Journal*, 2:205–6, August 19, 1664.

91. Ormesson, *Journal*, 2:208–9, August 24, 1664.

92. Ormesson, *Journal*, 2:209–10, August 25–28, 1664. On standards of proof, see Esmein, *Criminal Procedure*, 255–70.

93. Ormesson, *Journal*, 2:210–211, August 28, 1664.

94. BnF, CC Colbert 236: fols. 285v–99v, Chamber of Justice, August 29, 30, 1664; Ormesson, *Journal*, 2:211–12, Aug. 30, 1664; *Bastille*, 2:211–13, Chamber of Justice, August 29, 1664; Lair, *Foucquet*, 2:319–22.

95. Ormesson, *Journal*, 2:212, August 31, 1664.

96. Ormesson, *Journal*, 2:212, August 31, 1664.

97. BnF, CC Colbert 236: fols. 299v–325, Chamber of Justice, September 1 and 5, 1664; Ormesson, *Journal*, 2: 212–13, September 1, 1664; Lair, *Foucquet*, 2:323.

98. Ormesson, *Journal*, 2:213–16 passim, September 1–11, 1664.

99. Ormesson, *Journal*, 2:218, September 14, 1664.

100. BnF, CC Colbert 236: fols. 330v–34v, Chamber of Justice, September 17, 1664; Ormesson, *Journal*, 2:219–20, September 17, 1664; *Bastille*, 2:218–21, Chamber of Justice, September 17, 1664.

101. Ormesson, *Journal*, 2:204, August 14, 1664.

CHAPTER 7: A Performance beyond Comparison

1. Ormesson, *Journal*, 2:234–35, October 23, 1664; BnF, CC Colbert 236: fol. 356, Chamber of Justice, October 23, 1664.
2. Ormesson, *Journal*, 2:213, September 1, 1664.
3. Ormesson, *Journal*, 2:222, September 25, 1664; 2:225, October 4, 1664.
4. Ormesson, *Journal*, 2:227, October 7, 1664.
5. Ormesson, *Journal*, 2:231, October 16, 1664.
6. Ormesson, *Journal*, 2:234–35, October 23, 1664.
7. Ormesson, *Journal*, 2:238–39, November 12–13, 1664. This attack forms the entirety of *Défenses*, vol. 12. See esp. 12:2–54, 98–149, 270.
8. Ormesson, *Journal*, 2:237–38, November 10, 1664; 2:239, November 13, 1664; BM, Ms. 2257, Gomont Papers: fols.156–57v, November 8, 1664.
9. *Bastille*, 2:229, Chamber of Justice, November 14, 1664. As noted in the bibliography, the *Bastille* transcript of these sessions follows BnF, CC Colbert 237: fols. 1–146v. Another copy is found in BnF, Ms. Fr. 7628.
10. *Bastille*, 2:238, Chamber of Justice, November 14, 1664.
11. *Bastille*, 2:240, Chamber of Justice, November 14, 1664.
12. *Bastille*, 2:241, Chamber of Justice, November 14, 1664.
13. *Bastille*, 2:243, Chamber of Justice, November 14, 1664.
14. *Bastille*, 2:244, Chamber of Justice, November 14, 1664.
15. For the entire session, see *Bastille*, 2:225–45, Chamber of Justice, November 14, 1664; Ormesson, *Journal*, 2:239–45, November 14, 1664; BM, Ms. 2257, Gomont Papers: fols. 160v–61v, November 15, 1664.
16. *Bastille*, 2:249, Chamber of Justice, November 17, 1664.
17. *Bastille*, 2:235, Chamber of Justice, November 17, 1664.
18. *Bastille*, 2:258, Chamber of Justice, November 17, 1664.
19. *Bastille*, 2:256, Chamber of Justice, November 17, 1664.
20. For the entire session, see *Bastille*, 2:247–60, Chamber of Justice, November 17, 1664; Ormesson, *Journal*, 2:246–47, November 17, 1664; and Sévigné, *Lettres*, 1:120–21, Sévigné to Pomponne, November 17, 1664.
21. *Bastille*, 2:265, Chamber of Justice, November 18, 1664.
22. *Bastille*, 2:267, Chamber of Justice, November 18, 1664.
23. For the entire session, see *Bastille*, 2: 261–73, Chamber of Justice, November 18, 1664; Ormesson, *Journal*, 2:247–49, November 18, 1664; and Sévigné, *Lettres*, 1:121, Sévigné to Pomponne, November 18, 1664.
24. Ormesson, *Journal*, 2:249, November 18, 1664.
25. On this transaction, see *Bastille*, 2:274, n1, Chamber of Justice, November 20, 1664.
26. *Bastille*, 2:278, Chamber of Justice, November 20, 1664. See also *Défenses*, 11:125–269.
27. *Défenses*, 11:250–52.

28. *Bastille,* 2:282, Chamber of Justice, November 20, 1664.

29. *Bastille,* 2:282, Chamber of Justice, November 20, 1664. For the entire session, see *Bastille,* 2:274–86, Chamber of Justice, November 20, 1664, and Ormesson, *Journal,* 2:250–51, November 20, 1664.

30. Ormesson, *Journal,* 2:250–51, November 20, 1664; Sévigné, *Lettres,* 1:123–24, Sévigné to Pomponne, November 20, 1664.

31. *Bastille,* 2:286, November 20, 1664. For the text, see *Défenses,* 11:12–124, and Lair, *Foucquet,* 2:350.

32. *Bastille,* 2:291, Chamber of Justice, November 21, 1664.

33. *Bastille,* 2:293, Chamber of Justice, November 21, 1664.

34. *Bastille,* 2:295, Chamber of Justice, November 21, 1664.

35. *Bastille,* 2:296–97, Chamber of Justice, November 21, 1664; Ormesson, *Journal,* 2:252, November 21, 1664; Sévigné, *Lettres,* 1:124, Sévigné to Pomponne, November 21, 1664. For the entire session, see *Bastille,* 2:287–97, November 21, 1664.

36. *Bastille,* 2:297–303, Chamber of Justice, November 22, 1664; Ormesson, *Journal,* 2:252, November 22, 1664.

37. *Bastille,* 2:317 and 319, Chamber of Justice, November 27, 1664. For the entire sessions, see *Bastille,* 2:308–14, Chamber of Justice, November 26, 1664, and *Bastille,* 2:315–23, Chamber of Justice, November 27, 1664.

38. Ormesson, *Journal,* 2:253–54, November 26–November 27, 1664; Sévigné, *Lettres,* 1:127, Sévigné to Pomponne, November 26, 1664.

39. Sévigné, *Lettres,* 1:123–24, Sévigné to Pomponne, November 20, 1664.

40. Ormesson, *Journal,* 2:251, November 20, 1664; Sévigné, *Lettres,* 1:126–27, Sévigné to Pomponne, November 24, 1664.

41. *Bastille,* 2:322, Chamber of Justice, November 27, 1664.

42. *Bastille,* 2:308, Chamber of Justice, November 26, 1664.

43. *Bastille,* 2:308–9, Chamber of Justice, November 26, 1664; Ormesson, *Journal,* 2:253, November 26, 1664.

44. Sévigné, *Lettres,* 1:128, Sévigné to Pomponne, November 27, 1664.

45. Ormesson, *Journal,* 2:255, November 28, 1664; *Bastille,* 2:328, Chamber of Justice, November 28, 1664. For the entire session, see *Bastille,* 2:323–31, Chamber of Justice, November 28, 1664.

46. BM, Ms. 2257, Gomont Papers: fols. 161v–62, November 30, 1664.

47. BM, Ms. 2257, Gomont Papers: fol. 162, November 30, 1664; Ormesson, *Journal,* 2:255–56, November 28, 1664.

48. BM, Ms. 2257, Gomont Papers: fol. 162 ("appearances"); 162v ("king's cause"), November 30, 1664.

49. BM, Ms. 2257, Gomont Papers: fol. 163–63v, quote 163 ("own mouth"), November 30, 1664. See also *Bastille,* 2:334–35 Chamber of Justice, December 1, 1664. Lair, *Foucquet,* 2:358.

50. *Bastille,* 2:335, Chamber of Justice, December 1, 1664.

51. *Bastille,* 2:339, Chamber of Justice, December 1, 1664. For the entire session, see *Bastille,* 2:334–43, Chamber of Justice, December 1, 1664.

52. *Bastille,* 2:350–51, Chamber of Justice, December 2, 1664.

53. *Bastille,* 2:356, Chamber of Justice, December 2, 1664.

54. Ormesson, *Journal,* 2:260, December 2, 1664.

55. Sévigné, *Lettres*, 1:132, Sévigné to Pomponne, December 2, 1664.

56. *Bastille*, 2:345, Chamber of Justice, December 2, 1664. For the entire session, see *Bastille*, 2:343–57, Chamber of Justice, December 2, 1664.

57. *Bastille*, 2:365–69 passim, Chamber of Justice, December 3, 1664.

58. *Bastille*, 2:369–70, Chamber of Justice, December 3, 1664.

59. *Bastille*, 2:370–71, quote 371, Chamber of Justice, December 3, 1664.

60. *Bastille*, 2:371, Chamber of Justice, December 3, 1664. For the entire session, see *Bastille*, 2:357–73, Chamber of Justice, December 3, 1664; Ormesson, *Journal*, 2:261, December 3, 1664.

61. *Bastille*, 2:375, Chamber of Justice, December 4, 1664.

62. *Bastille*, 2:376, Chamber of Justice, December 4, 1664.

63. *Bastille*, 2:377, Chamber of Justice, December 4, 1664.

64. *Bastille*, 2:377, Chamber of Justice, December 4, 1664.

65. *Bastille*, 2:377–78, Chamber of Justice, December 4, 1664.

66. Sévigné, *Lettres*, 1:136, Sévigné to Pomponne, December 9, 1664; see also same to same, 1:133–34, December 4, 1664. Ormesson, *Journal*, 2:263, December 4, 1664.

67. *Bastille*, 2:378–79, Chamber of Justice, December 4, 1664.

68. *Bastille*, 2:380–81, quote 381, Chamber of Justice, December 4, 1664.

69. *Bastille*, 2:381, Chamber of Justice, December 4, 1664.

70. *Bastille*, 2:382, Chamber of Justice, December 4, 1664.

71. *Bastille*, 2:383, Chamber of Justice, December 4, 1664.

72. *Bastille*, 2:384, Chamber of Justice, December 4, 1664.

73. *Bastille*, 2:386, Chamber of Justice, December 4, 1664.

74. *Bastille*, 2:386–87, Chamber of Justice, December 4, 1664.

75. *Bastille*, 2:387, Chamber of Justice, December 4, 1664.

76. *Bastille*, 2:388, Chamber of Justice, December 4, 1664.

77. *Bastille*, 2:388–89, Chamber of Justice, December 4, 1664. For the entire session, see *Bastille*, 2:373–89, Chamber of Justice, December 4, 1664. See also Ormesson, *Journal*, 2:264–65, December 4, 1664; Sévigné, *Lettres*, 1:133–34, Sévigné to Pomponne, 1:133–34, December 4, 1664; 1:135–36, same to same, December 9, 1664; BM, Ms. 2257, Gomont Papers: fols. 163v–66, December 4, 1664.

CHAPTER 8: The Honor and Conscience of Judges

1. BM, Ms. 2257, Gomont Papers: fol. 162v, November 30, 1664.

2. Ormesson, *Journal*, 2:264–65, December 4, 1664; Sévigné, *Lettres*, 1:134, Sévigné to Pomponne, December 4, 1664.

3. *Bastille*, 2:322, Chamber of Justice, November 27, 1664; Ormesson, *Journal*, 2:256–57, November 28–30, 1664.

4. Sévigné, *Lettres*, 1:135, Sévigné to Pomponne, December 9, 1664.

5. *Bastille*, 2:389, Chamber of Justice, December 4, 1664.

6. Sévigné, *Lettres*, 1:122, Sévigné to Pomponne, November 18, 1664.

7. Lair, *Foucquet*, 2:337. On Boucherat, see chapter 6 n71. See also Brienne, *Mémoires*, 3:77.

8. Ormesson, *Journal*, 2:260, December 2, 1664.

9. Sévigné, *Lettres*, 1:134, Sévigné to Pomponne, December 5, 1664.

10. Astaing, *Droits*, 412–13.

11. Astaing, *Droits*, 51–53 passim, 65–66.

12. Esmein, *Procedure*, 256–71; Carbasse, *Justice criminelle*, 165–68.

13. Astaing, *Droits*, 73–80, 122–33, 189–98, 295, 301–3; Lebigre, *Justice*, 182–87; Esmein, *Procedure*, 258–66. See also Langbein, *Crime*, 224–29 passim.

14. Astaing, *Droits*, 301; Lebigre, *Justice*, 193–95. Esmein, *Procedure*, 270, attributes this expression to Muyart de Vouglans, *Instituts du droit criminal* (1757), who was enunciating a long-established legal maxim.

15. *Code Louis*, 1:39, "Procès Verbal," February 2, 1667; 1:489, "Procès Verbal," March 17, 1667. The phrase seems to have been a favorite of Lamoignon's. He used it earlier, in his April 1662 "Relation de la nomination," in which he has Mazarin exhorting him to serve as premier president "with honor and conscience": Lemoine, *Grande robe*, 279. On the magistrate's moral obligations, see Krynen, *Idéologie*, 78–103; Thireau, "Le bon juge"; and Renoux-Zagamé, "Conscience du juge."

16. Esmein, *Procedure*, 154–56, 171–72, 229–32; Astaing, *Droits*, 183–84, 197–98, 268–80.

17. AnF, Ormesson Papers, 144 AP71: dossiers 8, 9. For an analysis of Ormesson's calculations, see Dent, *Crisis in Finance*, 68–70.

18. Sévigné, *Lettres*, 1:137, Sévigné to Pomponne, December 10, 1664.

19. On the presentations, see Ormesson, *Journal*, 2: 266–70, December 9–12, 1664, and Sévigné, *Lettres*, 1: 135–38, Sévigné to Pomponne, December. 9–11, 1664.

20. Ormesson, *Journal*, 2:269–70, December 12, 1664.

21. Ormesson, *Journal*, 2:271, December 14, 1664.

22. Ormesson, *Journal*, 2:779, December 13, 1664.

23. Ormesson, *Journal*, 2:779, December 13, 1664.

24. Ormesson, *Journal*, 2:780–83, December 13, 1664.

25. Ormesson, *Journal*, 2:783, December 13, 1664.

26. Ormesson, *Journal*, 2:784, December 13, 1664.

27. Ormesson, *Journal*, 2:784–85, December 13, 1664.

28. Ormesson, *Journal*, 2:785–86, December 13, 1664.

29. Ormesson, *Journal*, 2:786–87, December 13, 1664.

30. Ormesson, *Journal*, 2:788–90, December 13, 1664.

31. Ormesson, *Journal*, 2:792, December 13, 1664.

32. Ormesson, *Journal*, 2:793, December 13, 1664.

33. Ormesson, *Journal*, 2:793, December 13, 1664.

34. Ormesson, *Journal*, 2:795, December 13, 1664; second quote 2:798.

35. Ormesson, *Journal*, 2:796–97, December 13, 1664.

36. Ormesson, *Journal*, 2:797, December 13, 1664.

37. Ormesson, *Journal*, 2:94–95, February 8, 1664.

38. Ormesson, *Journal*, 2:797, December 3, 1664. See also Dulong, *Mazarin et l'argent*, 189.

39. Ormesson, *Journal*, 2:798–99, December 13, 1664.

40. Ormesson, *Journal*, 2:797–98, December 13, 1664; quote 797.

41. Ormesson, *Journal*, 2:799, December 13, 1664; the entire summation is at 2:776–99. See also BnF, CC Colbert 237: fols. 150v–71. The French term *malversation de fonds publics* corresponds to "fraudulent conversion" or "misappropriation of public money," per Pollak, *Lexique juridique*, 24.

42. Ormesson, *Journal*, 2:795–96, December 13, 1664; *Défenses*, 3:81, 420–32.

43. Ormesson, *Journal*, 2:272, December 14, 1664.

44. Ormesson, *Journal*, 2:272–73, December 15–16, 1664.

45. Sévigné, *Lettres*, 1:139, Sévigné to Pomponne, December 17, 1664.

46. BnF, CC Colbert 237: fols. 172v–73, Chamber of Justice, December 15, 1664.

47. BnF, CC Colbert 237: fol. 177v, Chamber of Justice, December 16, 1664.

48. BnF, CC Colbert 237: fol. 174v, Chamber of Justice, December 15, 1664; fol. 177v, Chamber of Justice, December 16, 1664.

49. BnF, CC Colbert 237: fols. 178v–79, Chamber of Justice, December 16, 1664.

50. BnF, CC Colbert 237: fols. 179–81v, Chamber of Justice, December 16, 1664.

51. BnF, CC Colbert 237: fol.181, Chamber of Justice, December 16, 1664. On regicide as the one recognized "crime of thought," see Laingui and Lebigre, *Droit pénal*, 1:51, 71–73. See also Carbasse, *Justice criminelle*, 226–27, 259, 297–300.

52. BnF, CC Colbert 237: fols. 182v–83, Chamber of Justice, December 16, 1664.

53. BnF, CC Colbert 237: fols. 183v–84, Chamber of Justice, December 16, 1664. See also Ormesson, *Journal*, 2:272–74, December 15–16, 1664; Sévigné, *Lettres*, 1:139, Sévigné to Pomponne, December 17, 1664.

54. Sévigné, *Lettres*, 1:141, Sévigné to Pomponne, December 17, 1664.

55. Sévigné, *Lettres*, 1:138, Sévigné to Pomponne, December 11, 1664.

56. Ormesson, *Journal*, 2:290–92 passim, January 1–3, 1665; Uzman, *Kinship*, 348.

57. Ormesson, *Journal*, 2:291–93 passim, January 3–5, 1665; Uzman, *Kinship*, 348, 353–55.

58. Ormesson, *Journal*, 2:265–66, December 6, 1664. This Claude Joly (1610–1678), pastor of Saint-Nicolas-des-Champs, and later bishop of Agen, should not be confused with a namesake, Claude Joly (1607–1700), canon of Notre Dame and a prominent Frondeur and author.

59. Sévigné, *Lettres*, 1:125–26, Sévigné to Pomponne, November 24, 1664.

60. BnF, CC Colbert 237: fols. 187v–88v, Chamber of Justice, December 17, 1664.

61. BnF, CC Colbert 237: fol. 198v, Chamber of Justice, December 17, 1664.

62. BnF, CC Colbert 237: fols. 199–200, Chamber of Justice, December 17, 1664.

63. BnF, CC Colbert 237: fols. 204v–5, Chamber of Justice, December 17, 1664.

64. BnF, CC Colbert 237: fol. 210, Chamber of Justice, December 17, 1664.

65. BnF, CC Colbert 237: fols. 211–21 passim, Chamber of Justice, December 17, 1664.

66. BnF, CC Colbert 237: fols. 221–41v, Chamber of Justice, December 17, 1664.

67. BnF, CC Colbert 237: fols. 246–46v, Chamber of Justice, December 17, 1664.

68. BnF, CC Colbert 237: fols 246, 247, Chamber of Justice, December 17, 1664.

69. BnF, CC Colbert 237: fols. 249–49v, quote 249v, Chamber of Justice, December 17, 1664.

70. Sévigné, *Lettres*, 1:139–40, Sévigné to Pomponne, December 17, 1664. This comment is not found in Ormesson, *Journal*, or in the chamber minutes.

71. Ormesson, *Journal*, 2:275–76, December 17, 1664; Sévigné, *Lettres*, 1:139–40, Sévigné to Pomponne, December 17, 1664; BnF, CC Colbert 237: fols. 249v-50, Chamber of Justice, December 17, 1664.

72. BnF, CC Colbert 237: fols 250–53v, Chamber of Justice, December 18, 1664.

73. BnF, CC Colbert 237: fol. 258v, Chamber of Justice, December 18, 1664.

74. BnF, CC Colbert 237: fols. 267v–71, Chamber of Justice, December 18, 1664.

75. BnF, CC Colbert 237: fol. 271, Chamber of Justice, December 18, 1664.

76. BnF, CC Colbert 237: fol 271v, Chamber of Justice, December 18, 1664.

77. For the entire presentation, see BnF, CC Colbert 237: fols. 253v–74, December 18, 1664.

78. BnF, CC Colbert 237: fol. 275v, Chamber of Justice, December 18, 1664.

79. BnF, CC Colbert 237: fol. 278, Chamber of Justice, December 18, 1664.

80. BnF, CC Colbert 237: fol. 283v, Chamber of Justice, December 18, 1664.

81. BnF, CC Colbert 237: fols. 284v–85, Chamber of Justice, December 18, 1664. For the entire presentation, see BnF, CC Colbert 237: fols. 274–85, December 18, 1664.

82. BnF, CC Colbert 237: fols. 285v–89v, Chamber of Justice, December 18, 1664.

83. BnF CC Colbert 237: fols. 291–93 passim, Chamber of Justice, December 18, 1664.

84. BnF, CC Colbert 237: fol. 293, Chamber of Justice, December 18, 1664.

85. BnF, CC Colbert 237: fols. 293v–94, Chamber of Justice, December 18, 1664.

86. BnF, CC Colbert 237: fols 294–94v, Chamber of Justice, December 18, 1664.

87. BnF, CC Colbert 237: fols. 295v–97, Chamber of Justice, December 18, 1664.

88. For the entire presentation, see BnF, CC Colbert 237: fols. 289v–98, Chamber of Justice, December 18, 1664. See also Ormesson, *Journal*, 2:277, December 18, 1664; Sévigné, *Lettres*, 1:142, Sévigné to Pomponne, December 19, 1664.

89. Ormesson, *Journal*, 2:278, December 18, 1664.

90. Ormesson, *Journal*, 2:278–79, December 19, 1664.

91. BnF, CC Colbert 237: fols. 297v–302, Chamber of Justice, December 19, 1664; Ormesson, *Journal*, 2:279, December 19, 1664.

92. BnF, CC Colbert 237: fols. 302–2v, Chamber of Justice, December 19, 1664; Ormesson, *Journal*, 2:279, December 19, 1664.

93. BnF, CC Colbert 237: fols. 302v–3v, Chamber of Justice, December 19, 1664.

94. BnF, CC Colbert 237: fol. 302v, Chamber of Justice, December 19, 1664.

95. BnF, CC Colbert 237: fol. 303v, Chamber of Justice, December 19, 1664.

96. BnF, CC Colbert 237: fol. 303v, Chamber of Justice, December 19, 1664.

97. BnF, CC Colbert 237: fol. 304, Chamber of Justice, December 19, 1664. The entire presentation is in fols. 302v–4. Ormesson, *Journal*, 2: 279–80, December 19, 1664.

98. BnF, CC Colbert 237: fol. 312, Chamber of Justice, December 19, 1664.

99. BnF, CC Colbert 237: fol. 313, Chamber of Justice, December 19, 1664.

100. BnF, CC Colbert 237: fol. 313v, Chamber of Justice, December 19, 1664. For the opinion, see CC Colbert 237: fols. 304–13v, Chamber of Justice, December 19, 1664. Ormesson, *Journal*, 2:279, December 19, 1664.

101. BnF, CC Colbert 237: fol. 313v, Chamber of Justice, December 19, 1664.

102. BnF, CC Colbert 237: fol. 314, Chamber of Justice, December 19, 1664.

103. BnF, CC Colbert 237: fol. 313, Chamber of Justice, December 19, 1664.

104. For the entire presentation, see BnF, CC Colbert 237: fols. 313v–15v, Chamber of Justice, December 19, 1664. See also Ormesson, *Journal*, 2:280, December 19, 1664.

105. Sévigné, *Lettres*, 1:142, Sévigné to Pomponne, December 19, 1664.

106. BnF, CC Colbert 237: fols. 316–17, Chamber of Justice, December 20, 1664.

107. BnF, CC Colbert 237: fol. 319v, Chamber of Justice, December 20, 1664.

108. BnF, CC Colbert 237: fols. 320v–22, Chamber of Justice, December 20, 1664.

109. BnF, CC Colbert 237: fol. 322, Chamber of Justice, December 20, 1664.

110. Ormesson, *Journal*, 2:281, December 20, 1664. For the entire presentation, see BnF, CC Colbert 237: fols. 316–22, Chamber of Justice, December 20, 1664.

111. BnF, CC Colbert 237: fols. 322–22v, Chamber of Justice, December 20, 1664.

112. BnF, CC Colbert 237: fol. 323v, Chamber of Justice, December 20, 1664.

113. BnF, CC Colbert 237: fol 324, Chamber of Justice, December 20, 1664.

114. BnF CC Colbert 237: fol. 325v, Chamber of Justice December 20, 1664.

115. BnF, CC Colbert 237: fol. 327, Chamber of Justice, December 20, 1664. For the entire presentation, see BnF, CC Colbert 237: fols. 322–27, Chamber of Justice, December 20, 1664. Ormesson, *Journal*, 2:281, December 20, 1664.

116. BnF, CC Colbert 237: fols. 327–27v, Chamber of Justice, December 20, 1664; Ormesson, *Journal*, 2:281, December 20, 1664.

117. BnF, CC Colbert 237: fols. 327v–28, Chamber of Justice, December 20, 1664.

118. BnF, CC Colbert 237: fol. 328, Chamber of Justice, December 20, 1664.

119. BnF, CC Colbert 237: fol. 328v, Chamber of Justice, December 20, 1664.

120. BnF, CC Colbert 237: fol. 328v, Chamber of Justice, December 20, 1664.

121. For the entire presentation see BnF, CC Colbert 237: fols. 327v–29, Chamber of Justice, December 20, 1664. Ormesson, *Journal*, 2:281–82, December 20, 1664.

122. BnF, CC Colbert 237: fols. 329–30, Chamber of Justice, December 20, 1664.

123. BnF, CC Colbert 237: fol. 329v, Chamber of Justice, December 20, 1664.

124. BnF, CC Colbert 237: fols. 329v–30, Chamber of Justice, December 20, 1664. For the earlier session, see BnF, CC Colbert 236: fol. 346, Chamber of Justice, October 14, 1664.

125. BnF, CC Colbert 237: fol. 330v, Chamber of Justice, December 20, 1664. For the entire presentation, see CC Colbert 237: fols. 329–30v, Chamber of Justice, December 20, 1664. Ormesson, *Journal*, 2:282, December 20, 1664.

126. BnF, CC Colbert 237: fols. 331v–32, Chamber of Justice, December 20, 1664.

127. BnF, CC Colbert 237: fol. 353v, Chamber of Justice, December 20, 1664.

128. BnF, CC Colbert 237: fol. 364v, Chamber of Justice, December 20, 1664.

129. For the interruptions, see BnF, CC Colbert 237: fols. 365v, 366, Chamber of Justice, December 20, 1664.

130. BnF, CC Colbert 237: fol. 367v, Chamber of Justice, December 20, 1664.

131. BnF, CC Colbert 237: fol. 367v, Chamber of Justice, December 20, 1664.

132. BnF, CC Colbert 237: fol. 367v, Chamber of Justice, December 20, 1664. For the entire presentation, see BnF, CC Colbert 237: fols. 330–67v, Chamber of Justice, December 20, 1664. Ormesson, *Journal*, 2:282, December 20, 1664.

133. BnF, CC Colbert 237: fol. 368v, Chamber of Justice, December 20, 1664.

134. BnF, CC Colbert 237: fols. 368–68v, Chamber of Justice, December 20, 1664; Ormesson, *Journal*, 2:282, December 20, 1664

135. Ormesson, *Journal*, 2:282, December 20, 1664; BnF, CC Colbert 237: fol. 368v, Chamber of Justice, December 20, 1664. Ormesson states that Pontchartrain reviewed the major charges and agreed with his finding. The official chamber record gives no text and simply records Pontchartrain's concurrence with Ormesson.

136. BnF, CC Colbert 237: fols. 369–69v, Chamber of Justice, December 20, 1664.

137. Ormesson, *Journal*, 2:282, December 20, 1664. These comments are not found in the chamber record.

138. Ormesson, *Journal*, 2:283, and 283 n1 for text. See also BnF, CC Colbert 237: fols. 369v–70, Chamber of Justice, December 20, 1664; 376v–77, December 22, 1664.

139. Petitfils, *Fouquet*, 399–400, 444; Lair, *Foucquet*, 2:174.

140. Chéruel, *Fouquet*, 2:346–50 passim; Uzman, *Kinship*, 355, 366 n140.

141. Sévigné, *Lettres*, 1:142, Sévigné to Pomponne, December 20, 1664.

142. Ormesson, *Journal*, 2:283, December 20, 1664.

143. Ormesson, *Journal*, 2:284, December 20–21, 1664.

144. Ormesson, *Journal*, 2:286, December 22, 1664, for d'Artagnan; 2:287–88, December 22, 1664, for Turenne.

145. Ormesson, *Journal*, 2:287–28, December 22, 1664.

146. Sévigné, *Lettres*, 1:142, Sévigné to Pomponne, December 19, 1664.

147. On Louis and the death sentence, see Racine, "Notes et fragments," 287. See also Condé, *Lettres*, 119, Condé to Marie-Louise de Gonzague, December 26, 1664.

148. Ormesson, *Journal*, 2:278, December 18, 1664.

149. Text in *Défenses*, 13:356; see also BnF, CC Colbert 237: fols. 377–78, December 22, 1664. Lair, *Foucquet*, 2:407.

150. Ormesson, *Journal*, 2:288–89, December 31, 1664.

CHAPTER 9: Aftermath

1. Ormesson, *Journal*, 2:287, December 22, 1664.

2. Lair, *Foucquet*, 2:415–417; Petitfils, *Fouquet*, 462; Dessert, *Fouquet*, 266.

3. Dessert, *Fouquet*, 272–73.

4. Lair, *Foucquet*, 2:428–29; Petitfils, *Fouquet*, 465–68 passim; Dessert, *Fouquet*, 268–69.

5. Lair, *Foucquet*, 2:436–37; Petitfils, *Fouquet*, 470–72; Dessert, *Fouquet*, 272–74.

6. *Bastille*, 3:137, Louvois to Mme Fouquet, October 18, 1672; 3:138, Louvois to Mme Fouquet, November 10, 1672.

7. Petitfils, *Fouquet*, 477; Dessert, *Fouquet*, 274.

8. Lair, *Foucquet*, 2:444–45; Petitfils, *Fouquet*, 477; Dessert, *Fouquet*, 278–79.

9. Petitfils, *Fouquet*, 478; Dessert, *Fouquet*, 279–80.

10. Pitts, *Mademoiselle*, 216–17.

11. Pitts, *Mademoiselle*, 215; Montpensier, *Mémoires*, 4:329.

12. Lair, *Foucquet*, 2:465; Petitfils, *Fouquet*, 486–90 passim; Dessert, *Fouquet*, 281–82.

13. Lair, *Foucquet*, 2:457–58; Petitfils, *Fouquet*, 486–87; Dessert, *Fouquet*, 280–81. On Lauzun's negotiations, see La Force, *Lauzun*, 115–38, and Pitts, *Mademoiselle*, 216–19.

14. Lair, *Foucquet*, 2:455–57; Petitfils, *Fouquet*, 478; Dessert, *Fouquet*, 277–78.

15. Lair, *Foucquet*, 2:468–70; Petitfils, *Fouquet*, 490–91; Dessert, *Fouquet*, 284.

16. Lair, *Foucquet*, 2:461–64 passim; Petitfils, *Fouquet*, 492.

17. Lair, *Foucquet*, 2:473; Dessert, *Fouquet*, 286–87.

18. For general accounts of Fouquet's years at Pignerol, see Lair, *Foucquet*, 2:409–74; Dessert, *Fouquet*, 263–86; and Petitfils, *Fouquet*, 456–495. Correspondence and other material pertaining to his captivity is found in *Bastille*, vols. 2–3.

19. Lair, *Foucquet*, 2:419–20; Dessert, *Fouquet*, 303; *Bastille*, 2:393, Boulliau to Rautenstein, Councilor of the duke of Neuberg, December 1664.

20. Lair, *Foucquet*, 2:423–24, 430, 443; Dessert, *Fouquet*, 304–5.

21. Dessert, *Fouquet*, 327 (Vaux), 332 (Belle-Isle). For an overview of the financial

struggle, see Dessert, *Fouquet*, 305–17; Petitfils, *Fouquet*, 515–16; and Lair, *Foucquet*, 2:423–24, 430, 441–44.

22. Dessert, *Fouquet*, 325–27.

23. Dessert, *Fouquet*, 330–31.

24. Uzman, "Kinship," 325–26.

25. On Pellisson, see Ranum, *Artisans*, 251–77 passim. On La Fontaine, see Fumaroli, *Poète*, 100–105, 274–89, 414–22, quote 421. For an overview of the measures taken against Fouquet's close collaborators, see Uzman, "Kinship," 320–28 passim.

26. Dessert, "Lobby," 1308. For a list of the individual fines and subsequent modifications, see Dessert, "Chambre de justice," 871–81. See also Dent, *Crisis in Finance*, 107–8; Bonney, *Debts*, 266; and Bonney, "Failure," 32. For an overview, see Dessert, *Fouquet*, 269–71, and Petitfils, *Fouquet*, 473–75.

27. Dent, *Crisis in Finance*, 161–62.

28. Dessert, *Fouquet*, 280. Dent, *Crisis in Finance*, 160, states incorrectly that Bruant never returned from exile. On Bruant's later career and rehabilitation, see Piccioni, "Bruant des Carrières," 437–44 passim. On the suit against the Colberts, see Villain, *Fortune de Colbert*, 347–51. On Gourville's later career, see Lebigre, introduction to Gourville, *Mémoires*, 14–20; Freudmann, *Gourville*, 87–158; and Béguin, "Gourville."

29. Lair, *Foucquet*, 2:423; Brienne, *Mémoires*, 3:77; Petitfils, *Fouquet*, 473.

30. Chapman, *Private Ambition*, 11, 17–18; Petitfils, *Fouquet*, 473.

31. Petitfils, *Fouquet*, 473; Lair, *Foucquet*, 2:423.

32. Ormesson, *Journal*, 2:309, February 17, 1665; Solnon, *Ormesson*, 114.

33. Ormesson, *Journal*, 2:432, December 23, 1665; Solnon, *Ormesson*, 113–15.

34. Solnon, *Ormesson*, 116.

35. Ormesson, *Journal*, 2:588, June 10, 1670.

36. Ormesson, *Journal*, 2:591–92, June 16, 1670.

37. Solnon, *Ormesson*, 116–17.

38. Ormesson, *Journal*, 2:572, October 1669; Solnon, *Ormesson*, 118.

39. Solnon, *Ormesson*, 167; Ormesson, *Journal*, 2:412–13, November 30, 1665; 2:438, January 14, 1666.

40. On the later Ormessons, see Solnon, *Ormesson*, 173–505.

41. Ormesson, *Journal*, 2:531–32, December 20, 1667.

42. Ormesson, *Journal*, 2:504, April 22, 1667; Brienne, *Mémoires*, 3:77, 3:77 n1.

43. Richet, "Séguier," 312; Kerviler, *Séguier*, 360.

44. Richet, "Séguier," 315; Kerviler, *Séguier*, 378–97; Labatut, *Ducs et pairs*, 96–97.

45. Dessert, "Lobby," 1328; Bonney, "Secret Expenses," 835; Dent, *Crisis in Finance*, 233; Antonetti, "Colbert," 189–210. Bonney also argues, in "Fouquet-Colbert Rivalry," 112–14, that Colbert's ascendancy in 1661 ended the abuse of the *ordonnances de comptants* to conceal true borrowing costs and curbed the prior autonomy of ministers of finance. In a strong defense of Colbert, Le Roy Ladurie, *Ancien Régime*, 163–64, maintains that even in the most difficult circumstances, the borrowing costs under Colbert were never as high as those during the Fouquet years.

46. Meyer, "Cas Fouquet," 21–22, 22 n13. Corvisier, *Louvois*, 502–3, estimates Louvois's fortune at about 9 million livres.

47. Murat, *Colbert*, 219–29; Villain, *Fortune de Colbert*, 285–302.

48. Full lists of the commission members and representatives of the courts for the civil code are found in *Code Louis*, vol. 1, *Procès-Verbal*, 3, and, for the criminal code participants, in *Code Louis*, vol. 2, *Procès-Verbal*, 2. See also Esmein, *Procedure*, 198–201, 207–8. Esmein, 201, notes the participation of Fouquet's former counselors, Auzanet and Lhoste, among the *avocats* appointed to help draft the *ordonnances*. The identification of the younger Foucault is noted in Chapman, *Private Ambition*, 36. For the earlier meetings of the original commission in 1665, see Colbert *Lettres*, 6:361–401, which includes *procès-verbaux* for the meetings in September and October 1665, as well as a letter from Auzanet, 396–401, dated December 1669, summarizing the effort to date.

49. *Code Louis*, 2:162, *Procès-Verbal*, June 17, 1670.

50. *Code Louis*, 1:39, *Procès Verbal*, February 2, 1667. See also *Code Louis*, 1:181, *Procès-Verbal*, February 16, 1667, and Lamoignon's long speech, *Code Louis*, 1:487–92, *Procès-Verbal*, March 17, 1667.

51. *Code Louis*, 1:237, *Procès-Verbal*, February 24, 1667, quote. For exchanges during the criminal code conferences of June and July 1670, see *Code Louis*, vol. 2, *Procès-Verbal*. See esp. the conferences of June 17, 1670, 2:154–78 passim. For narrative summaries, see Esmein, *Procedure*, 183–210; Hamscher, *Parlement*, 155–95; Lemoine, *Grande robe*, 232–38; and Boulanger, "Justice et absolutisme." See also Gaillard, *Lamoignon*, 183–93, and Krynem, *Idéologie*, 191–212, which concentrates on the Pussort-Lamoignon exchanges.

52. On the criminal code provisions, see Esmein, *Procedure*, 211–50 For an updated perspective, see André Laingui, introduction, *Code Louis*, 2:vii–xxv, and his notes, 2:47–66. See also Boulet-Sautel, "Colbert et la législation," 119–32, and Carbasse, *Justice criminelle*, 177–90.

53. Hamscher, *Conseil Privé*, 35–40, 54–64, 69–79, 147–53.

54. Pillorget, "Pussort," 265–66, on promotions; on Pussort's fortune, estimated at 1,354,000 livres, see 269–74. On Berryer, see Dornic, *Berryer*, 111–17 (later career); 190–200 (fortune and heirs).

55. Ormesson, *Journal*, 2:lxxxix–xcvi.

56. Lafayette, *Princesse*, 39–41.

57. Saint-Simon, *Mémoires*, ed. Truc, 4:942–43, 5:400 (Mazarin et al.).

58. Voltaire, *Louis XIV*, 66–67, 262–26, quotes 264 and 265. See also Meyer, *Colbert*, 172.

59. On Dumas, see Grell, "En guise d'introduction," 3–5.

60. Fumaroli, *Poète*, 203–20, quote 214. Fumaroli's views have not gone unchallenged. See the critical review by Robert A. Schneider, in *H-France* 3 (2003), http:h-france.net/vol3reviews/schneider2.html.

61. Fumaroli, "Favourite Manqué," 240. This article repeats in shorter form much of the argument and language used in Fumaroli, *Poète*, chapter 4, as cited in n60 above.

62. Mousnier and Favrier, *Nouveau Colbert*, 210–15.

63. Mousnier and Favrier, *Nouveau Colbert*, 327.

64. Le Roy Ladurie, *Ancien Régime*, 133–35, quotes 134.

65. Le Roy Ladurie, *Ancien Régime*, 136. As noted in chapter 3, Meyer, *Colbert*, 174–77, although sympathetic to Fouquet's plight, also sees a real conspiracy or incipient uprising in the plan.

66. Le Roy Ladurie, *Ancien Régime*, 136, 136 nn15–17, 137, 163–69.

67. Ministry of Justice, "Procès de Fouquet." The text in its entirety is worth quoting:

> Certains papiers compromettants ayant été, comme nous l'avons vu, falsifiés, le procureur général ne put empêcher l'éclatement au grand jour de plusieurs contradictions dans l'acte d'accusation. Fouquet, avec une extraordinaire précision, récusa une à une les accusations et discuta chaque point : il démontra ainsi sa difficulté à acquérir la charge de surintendant des finances (il s'endetta lourdement pour cela) et surtout son enrichissement relatif selon lui comparé aux grandes fortunes du royaume constituées à cette époque. Plus insidieusement, il n'omettra pas de préciser que les largesses dont il avait pu bénéficier avaient aussi profité à d'autres personnes, tel Colbert par exemple.
>
> Malheureusement pour lui, la réalité des faits le rattrapait de toute façon et, bien qu'il fut finalement plus l'objet du courroux du roi qu'autre chose, ses tromperies et escroqueries ne pouvaient être ignorées plus longtemps.
>
> "L'audience" ne dura pas moins de trois ans et demi et déchaîna les passions pendant tout ce laps de temps. La pression royale sur les juges fut alors proportionnellement équivalente à la popularité inédite de l'accusé, compliquant doublement la tâche de la Chambre de justice. Quant aux avocats de l'ancien surintendant, ceux-ci produisirent plus de 10 volumes de mémoires en défense.
>
> On remarquera que la peine prononcée par les juges ne correspond pas à celle normalement prévue pour punir le péculat : au lieu d'être condamné à mort, on enjoint Nicolas Fouquet de quitter le royaume de France.
>
> Cette clémence, due probablement à la pression populaire ainsi qu'à la durée relativement longue du procès, est considérée comme totalement injustifiée aux yeux du roi et de son entourage.
>
> En réaction à ce qui fut donc perçu comme un premier défi au pouvoir absolu mis en place par le jeune roi, Louis XIV n'hésita pas à modifier lui-même la sentence pour la commuer en peine de prison à vie. Nicolas Fouquet finira alors ses jours enfermé dans la forteresse de Pignerol, sa détention alimentant d'ailleurs les hypothèses les plus folles de certains historiens : Fouquet a-t-il été forcé de revêtir le célèbre "Masque de Fer"?

68. Meyer, "Cas Fouquet," 11. See as well Meyer, *Colbert*, 150, 172.

APPENDIX

1. Bergin, *Richelieu*, 246, 248–49. See also Bergin's caution on valuations, 243–63 passim.

2. Labatut, "Fortune de Bullion," 11.

3. Dulong, *Fortune*, 47–48, 136. See also Bergin, "Mazarin and His Benefices," and Treasure, *Mazarin*, 275–82.

4. Dulong, *Fortune*, 133.

5. Dulong, *Fortune*, 74.

6. Dulong, *Fortune*, 63.

7. Treasure, *Mazarin*, 378 n12. On the parlementary inquiries during the Fronde about Mazarin's dealings with Contarini and other foreign bankers, see Dulong, *Mazarin et l'argent*, 19–29; Bonney, *Debts*, 234–235; and Bonney, "Remonstances."

8. Dulong, *Fortune*, 16.

9. Dulong, *Fortune*, 91, 101.

10. Colbert, *Lettres*, 1:520, "Estat de biens . . . de Monseigneur," June 1658. See also Dessert, *Fouquet*, 237.

11. Dessert, *Fouquet*, 206, 21–217. Dessert compares the lists of assets and revenues of Mazarin and Fouquet in *Fouquet*, 199–229 passim. See also his "Fortune du Cardinal Mazarin," 164, 171, 174. In a later work, *Royaume de Colbert*, Dessert raised his estimate of the cardinal's fortune to 40 million livres. Claude Dulong, who originally used a figure of 38 million livres for Mazarin's estate in *Fortune*, 133, revised her figures downward to about 30 million in *Mazarin et l'argent*, 230–32, taking into account that his heirs did not collect the total of his claims against the royal treasury. It was still, as she reaffirms, 232, a fortune greater than that of the fabulously wealthy Condés at the end of the century. On the Condé fortune, see Roche, "Condé." Béguin, *Princes de Condé*, 53, calculated the Condé fortune at 16.5 million livres in 1651. For an overview of princely and noble fortunes in this period, see Labatut, *Ducs et pairs*, 246–70.

12. Dessert, "Fortune du cardinal Mazarin," 179–80, for the question. See also *Royaume de Colbert*, 52, 144 (on the financial transactions cited against Fouquet); and 69 (on the destruction of Mazarin's account books). Bergin, *Richelieu*, asks the same question about Richelieu, with annual acknowledged revenues of 900,000 to 1 million livres per annum, and he concludes, 256, that the cardinal also "enjoyed substantial concealed revenues" not entered in account books. Bergin also observes, 250, that Richelieu, like Mazarin, and in contrast to Fouquet, "lent as little as possible in the crown's service."

13. Dulong, *Fortune*, 145.

14. Dulong, *Fortune*, 143.

15. Meyer, "Cas Fouquet," 21–22, 22 n13; Meyer, *Colbert*, 109–10, 317–25. Villain, *Fortune de Colbert*, 319–24, using the *inventaire après décès* as his base, arrives at a much lower figure: 4.955 million livres in gross assets, 4.444 million livres net of liabilities. A detailed analysis by Dessert, *Royaume de Colbert*, 243–79, arrives at a figure of 9.3 million livres net of liabilities. Corvisier, *Louvois*, 502–3, estimates Louvois's fortune at about 9 million livres, as does Dessert, *Royaume de Colbert*, 280. On Servien, see Duccini, *Guerre et paix*, 375.

16. Dulong, *Mazarin et l'argent*, 229.

Bibliography

A NOTE ON SOURCES

As a courtesy to the reader, a printed version of a primary source whenever possible is cited in the notes in preference to a manuscript version, even when, as indicated, below, the author has examined both.

The indispensable printed source for Fouquet's trial is his *Défenses*, a compendium of his written responses to the charges against him, together with other motions and demands he filed (recusal of judges, etc.), as well as most of the prosecution's briefs, interrogations, and other important materials. The series was published in the United Provinces 1665–1668 in 13 volumes, probably at the instigation of the Fouquet family, and reprinted in the 1690s in 16 volumes. The series does not contain the transcripts of his appearances before the chamber of justice in November–December 1664, but these were published in Ravaisson-Mollien's *Archives de la Bastille* in the nineteenth century (originals in BnF, Cinq Cents de Colbert 237 and Ms. Fr. 7628), which also contains other useful materials on the trial. Ormesson's enormous *Journal*, edited by Chéruel, provides a running account of the *procès* as it unfolded, including a great deal about the interaction of the judges with one another, with the prosecution, and with the king's ministers, especially Colbert and Le Tellier.

Material on the Fouquet trial and the on tribulations of the many financiers arrested at the same time and examined by the chamber of justice is widely scattered throughout the French archival system. At the Bibliothèque nationale de France, Ms. Fr. 7620 through Ms. Fr. 7628 provide much of the essential documentation of the Fouquet trial. In the Collection Cinq Cents de Colbert, vols. 228–237 contain Foucault's registers of the proceedings of the chamber, in which vols. 235–237 are entirely dedicated to Fouquet's trial. The list of files cited below does not include others that simply contain additional copies of the materials cited herein.

The Archives nationales (France) houses the papers of several important players in Fouquet's trial. The papers of Olivier d'Ormesson include duplicates of documents found elsewhere (interrogations of financiers, etc.), but shed some light on Ormesson's thought process, although his published *Journal* remains key to understanding his role. The Malsherbes family archives contain some of Guillaume de Lamoignon's papers. Lamoignon's account of his appointment as *premier président* of the Parlement of Paris, which has recently been published (see below), suggests his unease about his earlier ties to Fouquet. His Journal of the trial covers the period September 1662–December 1662 and deals with the prosecution's attempts to deprive Fouquet of counsel, the appointment of the *rapporteurs*, and the circumstances surrounding Lamoignon's replacement by Séguier. The balance of the journal provides somewhat disjointed comments and reflections on the chamber, on his complex and troubled relationship with Fouquet, Colbert, Le Tellier et al., and his reservations about the interference by royal officials, chiefly Colbert, in the chamber's deliberations. The papers of Bruant des Carrières offer insights into his role as one of Fouquet's chief subordinates.

The Ms. Gomont at the Bibliothèque Mazarine contains a useful journal of the last weeks of the trial kept by the junior member of the prosecution team. The papers of Jannart conserved at the Bibliothèque de l'Institut de France provide some insights into his efforts on Fouquet's behalf.

UNPUBLISHED SOURCES

BA (Bibliothèque de l'Arsenal)	Ms. Fr. 7167: Papers on Fouquet's Personal Finances.
BI (Bibliothèque de l'Institut de France)	Ms. 1483: Jacques Jannart Papers, Cote 4 CX 333 (VV–EEE) [Printed documents with notations by Jannart].
BnF (Bibliothèque nationale de France)	Cinq Cents de Colbert, vols. 235–37. Ms. Fr. 3168, 7607, 7620–28, 9438, 10228, 10229, 14056, 16533, 23202.
Bibliothèque Mazarine	Ms. 2257: Oudart Gomont Papers and Journal. Ms. 2258: Prosecution Documents.
Archives nationales (France)	144 AP: Ormesson Family Archives, Papers of Olivier d'Ormesson. 399 AP3: Malsherbes Family Archives, Guillaume de Lamoignon Papers: Liasse 1: Account of Lamoignon's nomination as premier président of the Parlement of Paris, April 12, 1662; Liasse 2: Journal of the Chamber of Justice, September–December 1662. 557 AP: Louis Bruant des Carrières Papers.

CONTEMPORARY MEMOIRS, WORKS, AND PRINTED DOCUMENTARY SOURCES

Anonymous. *L'innocence persécutée* [aka *Le livre abominable*]. Ed. Marie-Françoise Baverel-Croissant. Saint-Étienne, 2002.

Brienne, Louis-Henri de Loménie, comte de. *Mémoires*. Ed. Paul Bonnefon. 3 vols., Paris, 1916–1919.

Choisy, François-Timoléon, abbé de. *Mémoires*. Ed. Georges Mongrédien. Paris, 1966.

Code Louis. Ed. Nicola Picardi and Alessandro Giuliani. 2 vols. Milan, 1996.

Colbert, Jean-Baptiste. *Lettres, instructions, et mémoires de Colbert*. Ed. Pierre Clément. 7 vols. Paris, 1861–1873.

———. "Notes secrètes sur le personnel de tous les parlements et cours des comptes du royaume envoyées par les intendants des provinces à Colbert . . . 1663." In Depping, *Correspondance administrative*, 2:33–132.

Condé, Louis, prince de, and Enghien, Henri Jules, duc d'. *Lettres inédites sur la Cour de Louis XIV*. Ed. Emile Magne. Paris, 1920.

Depping, Georges-Bernard, and Guillaume Depping, eds. *Correspondance administrative sous le règne de Louis XIV*. 4 vols. Paris, 1850–1855.

Foucault, Joseph. "Récit officiel de l'arrestation de Fouquet." In *Mémoires du duc de Saint-Simon*, ed. Adolphe Chéruel, vol. 8 (Paris, 1857), 447–53.

Fouquet, Nicolas. *Recueil des défenses de M. Fouquet*. 5 vols. (Series vols. 1–5). N.p., 1665.

———. *Suite du recueil des défenses de M. Fouquet*. 7 vols. (Series vols. 6–12). N.p., 1667.

———. *Conclusion des défenses de M. Fouquet*. 1 vol. (Series vol. 13). N.p., 1668.

Gourville, Jean Hérault, sieur de. *Mémoires*. Ed. Arlette Lebigre. Paris, 2004.

Lafayette [La Fayette], Marie-Madeleine Pioche de la Vergne, comtesse de. *Vie de la princesse d'Angleterre*. Ed. Marie-Thérèse Hipp. Geneva, 1967.

Lamoignon, Guillaume de. "Relation de la nomination . . . à la place du premier président du parlement" (April 14, 1662). In Lemoine, *La grande robe*, 257–85. Also in AN, 399AP 3.

Le Boindre, Jean. *Débats du Parlement de Paris pendant la minorité de Louis XIV*. Vol. 1: 1648–1649. Ed. Robert Descimon, Orest Ranum, and Patricia M. Ranum. Paris, 1997.

———. *Débats du Parlement de Paris pendant la minorité de Louis XIV*. Vol. 2: 1650–1652. Ed. Isabelle Storez-Brancourt. Paris, 2002.

Louis XIV. *Mémoires for the Instruction of the Dauphin*. Ed. and trans. Paul Sonnino. New York, 1970.

Mazarin, Jules. *Lettres du cardinal Mazarin pendant son ministère*. Ed. Adolphe Chéruel and Georges d'Avenal. 9 vols. Paris, 1872–1906.

Montpensier, Anne-Marie-Louise, duchesse de. *Mémoires*. Ed. Adolphe Chéruel. 4 vols. Paris, 1858–1859.

Motteville, Françoise Bertaut, Madame de. *Mémoires*. In *Nouvelle collection des mémoires relatifs à l'histoire de France*, ed. Joseph-François Michaud and Jean-Joseph Poujoulat, vol. 24. Paris, 1857.

Ormesson, Olivier Lefèvre d'. *Journal, et extraits des mémoires d'André Lefèvre d'Ormesson*. Ed. Adolphe Chéruel. 2 vols. Paris, 1860–1861.

Pellisson (-Fontanier), Paul. *Oeuvres choisies de Pellisson, de l'Académie française . . . précédées d'une notice . . . par N.L.M. Desessarts*. 2 vols. Paris, 1805.

Racine, Jean. "Notes et fragments." In *Oeuvres complètes*, ed. Raymond Picard, vol. 2. Paris, 1952.

Ravaisson-Mollien, François. *Archives de la Bastille*. Vols. 1–3. Paris, 1866–1868.

Saint-Simon, Louis de Rouvroy, duc de. *Mémoires*. Ed. Adolphe Chéruel. 13 vols. Paris, 1856–1858.

———. *Mémoires*. Ed. Gonzague Truc. 7 vols. Paris, 1947–1961.

Sévigné, Marie de Rabutin-Chantal, marquise de. *Lettres*. Ed. Emile Gérard-Grailly. 3 vols. Paris, 1953–1957.

Tallemant des Réaux, Gédéon. *Historiettes*. Ed. Antoine Adam. 2 vols. Paris, 1960–1961.

Voltaire [François-Marie Arouet]. *The Age of Louis XIV.* Trans. Martyn P. Pollack. London, 1961.

COLLECTIVE WORKS AND PUBLISHED COLLOQUIA

Bercé, Yves-Marie, ed. *Les procès politiques XIV–XVII siècle*. Rome, 2007.

Bonney, Richard, ed. *Society and Government in France under Richelieu and Mazarin, 1624–1661*. London, 1988.

Bosher, John Francis, ed. *French Government and Society, 1500–1850*. London, 1973.

Cameron, Keith, and Elizabeth Woodrough, eds. *Ethics and Politics in Seventeenth-Century France*. Exeter, UK, 1996.

Carbasse, Jean-Marie, and Laurence Depamdour-Tarride, eds. *La conscience du juge dans la tradition juridique européenne*. Paris, 1999.

Carbasse, Jean-Marie, ed. *Histoire du parquet*. Paris, 2000.

Chaussinand-Nogaret, Guy, ed. *Histoire des élites en France du XVIe au XXe siècle*. Paris, 1991.

Grell, Chantal, Klaus Malettke, and Kornelia Oepen, eds. *Les années Fouquet: politique, société, vie artistique et culturelle dans les années 1650. Colloque, Université de Versaille-Saint-Quentin et al., Versailles, 26–27 mai 2000*. Münster, 2001.

Imbert, Jean, ed. *Quelques procès criminels des XVIIe et XVIIIe siècles*. Paris, 1964.

Mousnier, Roland, ed. *Le conseil du roi de Louis XII à la Révolution*. Paris, 1970.

Mousnier, Roland, and Jean Favier, eds. *Un nouveau Colbert: actes du Colloque pour le tricentenaire de la mort de Colbert* (Paris, October 4–6, 1983). Paris, 1985.

SECONDARY WORKS

Antoine, Michel. *Le coeur de l'État: surintendance, contrôle général, et intendances de finances, 1552–1791*. Paris, 2003.

Antonetti, Guy. "Colbert et le crédit public." In Mousnier and Favier, *Un noveau Colbert*, 189–210.

Astaing, Antoine. *Droits et garanties de l'accusé dans le procès criminel de l'ancien régime*. Aix-en-Provence, 1999.

Barbiche, Bernard. *Les institutions de la monarchie française à l'époque moderne*. Paris, 1999.

Bastid, Paul. *Les grands procès politiques de l'histoire*. Paris, 1962.

Bayard, Françoise. *Le monde des financiers au XVIIe siècle*. Paris, 1988.

Béguin, Katia. "De la finance à l'intendance ou la reconversion réussie de Jean Hérault de Gourville (1625–1703)." *Revue d'histoire moderne et contemporaine* 46 no. 3 (1999): 435–56.

———. *Financer la guerre au XVIIe siècle: la dette publique et les rentiers de l'absolutisme*. Seyssel, 2012.

———. *Les princes de Condé: rebelles, courtisans, et mécènes dans la France du Grand Siècle*. Paris, 1999.

Beik, William. *Urban Protest in Seventeenth-Century France: The Culture of Retribution*. New York, 1997.

Bercé, Yves-Marie. "L'affaire Fouquet dans l'opinion de son temps et sous le regard des historiens." *Le fablier* 5 (1993): 37–42.

Bergin, Joseph. "Cardinal Mazarin and His Benefices." *French History* 1 (1987): 3–26.

———. *Cardinal Richelieu: Power and the Pursuit of Wealth*. New Haven, 1985.

———. *The Rise of Richelieu*. New Haven, 1991.

Bertière, Simone. *Le procès Fouquet*. Paris, 2013.

Bluche, François. *Louis XIV*. Trans. Mark Greengrass. Oxford, 1990.

Blunt, Anthony. *Art and Architecture in France, 1500–1700*. London, 1991.

Bonnefin, Aimé. *La monarchie française (987–1789): constitution et lois fondamentales*. Paris, 1987.

Bonney, Richard. "Cardinal Mazarin and His Critics: The Remonstrances of 1652." *Journal of European Studies* 10 (1980): 15–31

———. "The Failure of the French Revenue Farms, 1600–60." *Economic History Review*, 2nd ser., 32, no. 1 (1979): 11–32.

———. "The Fouquet-Colbert Rivalry and the Revolution of 1661." In Cameron and Woodrough, *Ethics and Politics*, 107–18.

———. *The King's Debts: Finance and Politics in France, 1589–1661*. Oxford, 1981.

———. *Political Change in France under Richelieu and Mazarin, 1624–1661*. Oxford, 1978.

———, ed. *The Rise of the Fiscal State in Europe, c. 1200–1815*. Oxford, 1999.

———. "The Secret Expenses of Richelieu and Mazarin, 1624–1661." *English Historical Review* 91, no. 360 (1976): 825–36.

Bosher, John Francis. "*Chambres de justice* in the French Monarchy." In Bosher, *French Government*, 19–40.

Boucher, Philip. *The Shaping of the French Colonial Empire: A Bio-bibliography of the Careers of Richelieu, Fouquet, and Colbert*. New York, 1985.

Boulanger, Marc. "Justice et absolutisme: la grande ordonnance criminelle d'août 1670." *Revue d'histoire moderne et contemporaine* 47, no. 1 (2000): 7–36.

Boulet-Sautel, Marguerite. "Colbert et la législation." In Mousnier and Favier, *Un Nouvel Colbert*, 119–32.

Bourgeon, Jean-Louis. *Les Colbert avant Colbert*. Paris, 1973.

Burke, Peter. *The Fabrication of Louis XIV*. New Haven, 1994.

Bury, Emmanuel. "La 'culture Fouquet': précieuses et gallants." In Grell, Malettke, and Oepen, *Les années Fouquet*, 101–9.

Carbasse, Jean-Marie. *Histoire du droit*. Paris, 2008.

———. *Histoire du droit pénal et de la justice criminelle*. Paris, 2000.

Chapman, Sara E. *Private Ambition and Political Alliances: The Phélypeaux de Pontchartrain Family and Louis XIV's Government, 1650–1715*. Rochester, NY, 2004.

Charmeil, Jean Paul. *Les trésoriers de France à l'époque de la Fronde*. Paris, 1964.

Châtelain, Urbain Victor. *Le surintendant Nicolas Foucquet, protecteur des letters, des arts, et des sciences*. Paris, 1905.

Chauleur, Andrée. "Le rôle des traitants dans l'administration financière de la France de 1643 à 1653." *XVIIe Siècle* 65 (1964): 16–49.

Cherchève, Frédéric. "Le procès de Nicolas Fouquet." In Imbert, *Quelques procès criminels*, 101–20.

Chéruel, Adolphe. *Histoire de France pendant la minorité de Louis XIV*. 4 vols. Paris, 1878–1880.

———. *Histoire de France sous le ministère de Mazarin*. 3 vols. Paris, 1882.

——. *Mémoires sur la vie publique et privée de Fouquet, surintendant des finances.* 2 vols. Paris, 1862.

Chiffoleau, Jacques. "Le crime de majesté, la politique, et l'extraordinaire." In Bercé, *Les procès politiques*, 577–662.

Collins, James B. *Fiscal Limits of Absolutism: Direct Taxation in Early Seventeenth-Century France.* Berkeley, 1988.

——. *The State in Early Modern France.* Cambridge, UK, 2009.

Cornette, Joël. *La mélancolie du pouvoir: Omer Talon et le procès de la raison d'État.* Paris, 1998.

Corvisier, André. *Louvois.* Paris, 1983.

Crépin, Marie-Yvonne. "Le rôle pénal du ministère public." In Carbasse, *Histoire du parquet*, 79–103.

Dauchy, Serge. "De la défense des droits du roi et du bien commun à l'assistance aux plaideurs: diversité des missions du ministère public." In Carbasse, *Histoire du parquet*, 55–75.

David, Jacqueline. "La participation des gens du roi à la police du royaume pendant l'ancien régime." In Carbasse, *Histoire du parquet*, 105–37.

Delatour, Jérôme. "Les armes en main et les larmes aux yeux: le procès de Cinq-Mars et de Thou." In Bercé, *Les procès politiques*, 351–93.

Dent, Julian. "An Aspect of the Crisis of the Seventeenth Century: The Collapse of the Financial Administration of the French Monarchy (1653–61)." *Economic History Review*, 2nd ser., 20, no. 2 (1967): 241–56.

——. *Crisis in Finance: Crown, Financiers, and Society in Seventeenth-Century France.* Newton Abbot, UK, 1973.

——. "The Role of Clientèles in the Financial Élite of France under Cardinal Mazarin." In Bosher, *French Government*, 41–69.

Depambour-Tarride, Laurence. "Répresenter une conscience: le portrait de Guillaume de Lamoignon par Robert Nanteuil." In Carbasse and Depambour-Tarride, *La conscience du juge*, 195–228.

Dessert, Daniel. "L'affaire Fouquet." *L'histoire* 32 (1981):39–47.

——. *Argent, pouvoir, et société au Grand Siècle.* Paris, 1984.

——. *L'argent du sel, le sel de l'argent.* Paris, 2012.

——. "Finances et société au XVIIe siècle: à propos de la Chambre de Justice de 1661." *Annales: économies sociétés civilisations* 29, no. 4 (1974): 847–81.

——. *Fouquet.* Paris, 1987.

——. "Le 'laquais-financier' au Grand Siècle: mythe ou réalité?" *XVIIe Siècle* 122 (1979): 21–36.

——. "Pouvoir et finance au XVIIe siècle: la fortune du cardinal Mazarin." *Revue d'histoire modern et contemporaine* 23 (1976): 161–81.

——. *Le royaume de Monsieur Colbert, 1661–1683.* Paris, 2007.

Dessert, Daniel, and Jean-Louis Journet. "Le lobby Colbert: un royaume, ou une affaire de famille?" *Annales: économies sociétés civilisations* 30, no. 6 (1975): 1303–36.

Dornic, François. *Louis Berryer, agent de Mazarin et de Colbert.* Caen, 1968.

Doyle, William. *Venality: The Sale of Offices in Eighteenth-Century France.* New York, 1996.

Drazin, Charles. *The Man Who Outshone the Sun King.* Philadelphia, 2008.

Duccini, Hélène. *Guerre et paix dans la France du Grand Siècle: Abel Servien, diplomate et serviteur de l'État (1593–1659)*. Seyssel, 2012.

Duchêne, Roger. "La Fontaine et Fouquet: un pédant parmi les gallants." *Le fablier* 5 (1993): 31–36.

Dulong, Claude (Badalo-). *Banquier du roi: Barthélemy Hervart, 1606–1676*. Paris, 1951.

——. *La fortune de Mazarin*. Paris, 1990.

——. *Mazarin et l'argent: banquiers et prête-noms*. Paris, 2002.

Esmein, Adhémer. *A History of Continental Criminal Procedure, with Special Reference to France*. Trans. John Simpson. Boston, 1913.

Etchechoury, Maïté. *Les maîtres des requêtes de l'hôtel du roi sous les derniers Valois (1553–1589)*. Paris, 1991.

Fernandez-Lacôte, Hélène. *Les procès du cardinal de Richelieu: droit, grâce, et politique sous Louis le Juste*. Seyssel, 2010.

Freudmann, Félix R. *L'étonnant Gourville (1625–1703)*. Geneva, 1960.

Fumaroli, Marc. *Le poète et le roi: Jean de La Fontaine et son siècle*. Paris, 1997.

——. "Nicolas Fouquet, the Favourite Manqué." In *The World of the Favourite*, ed. J. H. Elliott and L. W. B. Brockliss, 239–55. New Haven, 1999.

Gaillard, Gabriel Henri. *Vie ou éloge historique de M. de Malesherbes, suivie de la vie du premier président Lamoignon, son bisaïeul*. Paris, 1805.

Goldner, Erik. "Corruption on Trial: Money, Power, and Punishment in France's *Chambre de Justice* of 1716." *Crime, histoire, et sociétés* 17, no. 1 (2013): 5–28.

Goubert, Pierre. *Mazarin*. Paris, 1990.

Grell, Chantal. "En guise d'introduction: Nicolas Fouquet au tribunal de l'histoire." In Grell, Malettke, and Oepen, *Les années Fouquet*, 1–10.

Guéry, Alain. "Les finances de la monarchie française sous l'Ancien Régime." *Annales: économies sociétés civilisations* 33, no. 2 (1978): 216–39.

Hale, Matthew, George Wilson, and Thomas Dogherty. *The History of the Pleas of the Crown*. 2 vols. London, 1800.

Hall, Geoffrey F., and Joan Sanders. *D'Artagnan: The Ultimate Musketeer*. Boston, 1964.

Hamscher, Albert N. *The Conseil Privé and the Parlements in the Age of Louis XIV: A Study in French Absolutism*. Philadelphia, 1987.

——. *The Parlement of Paris after the Fronde, 1653–1673*. Pittsburgh, 1976.

——. *The Royal Financial Administration and the Prosecution of Crime in France, 1670–1789*. Newark, NJ, 2012.

Hurt, John J. *Louis XIV and the Parlements*. Manchester, UK, 2002.

Imbert, Jean. "Principes généraux de la procédure pénale (XVIIe–XVIIIe siècles)." In Imbert, *Quelques procès criminels*, 101–20. Paris, 1964.

Kerviler, René. *Le chancelier Pierre Séguier*. Paris, 1874.

Kettering, Sharon. *Patrons, Brokers, and Clients in Seventeenth-Century France*. Oxford, 1986.

Kitchens, James H., III. "Judicial *Commissaires* and the Parlement of Paris: The Case of the Chambre de l'Arsenal." *French Historical Studies* 12 (1982): 323–50.

Klaits, Joseph. *Printed Propaganda under Louis XIV: Absolute Monarchy and Public Opinion*. Princeton, 1976.

Kleinman, Ruth. *Anne d'Autriche*. Paris, 1993.

Krynen, Jacques. *L'idéologie de la magistrature ancienne*. Paris, 2009.

Labatut, Jean-Pierre. "Aspects de la fortune de Bullion." *XVIIe Siècle* 60 (1963): 11–37.

——. "Le chancelier Boucherat (1616–1699)." In Mousnier, *Le conseil du roi*, 87–101.

——. *Les ducs et pairs de France au XVIIe siècle*. Paris, 1972.

La Force, Auguste-Armand, duc de. *Lauzun: un courtisan du grand roi*. Paris, 1913.

Laingui, André. "Nouveauté et permanence dans le droit criminel au XVII siècle." In *Destins et enjeux du XVIIe siècle*, ed. Yves-Marie Bercé, 71–84. Paris, 1984.

Laingui, André, and Arlette Lebigre. *Histoire du droit pénal*. 2 vols. Paris, 1979.

Lair, Jules Auguste. *Nicolas Foucquet* [*sic*]. 2 vols. Paris, 1890.

Langbein, John H. *Prosecuting Crime in the Renaissance*. Cambridge, MA, 1974.

Lebigre, Arlette. *La justice du roi*. Paris, 1988.

Leiner, Wolfgang. "Nicolas Fouquet au jeu des miroirs." In *Études sur la littérature française du XVIIe siècle*, ed. Volker Schröder and Rainer Zaiser, 251–73. Paris, 1996.

Lemoine, Yves. *La grande robe, le mariage et l'argent: histoire d'une grande famille parlementaire, 1560–1660*. Paris, 2000.

Le Roy Ladurie, Emmanuel, *The Ancien Régime: A History of France, 1610–1774*. Trans. Mark Greengrass. Oxford, 1996.

Lorris, Pierre-Georges. *La Fronde*. Paris, 1961.

Lossky, Andrew. *Louis XIV and the French Monarchy*. New Brunswick, NJ, 1994.

Mandrou, Robert. *Louis XIV en son temps*. Paris, 1973.

McGowan, Margaret. "L'éloge et la discrétion: l'art de peindre chez La Fontaine." *Le fablier*, 5 (1993): 23–29.

Mérot, Alain. "Temple des Muses, Palais du Soleil: les plafonds peints par Charles Le Brun au château de Vaux-le-Vicomte." In Grell, Malettke, and Oepen, *Les années Fouquet*, 111–23.

Mettam, Roger. *Power and Faction in Louis XIV's France*. Oxford, 1988.

Meyer, Jean. "Le cas Fouquet: faut-il réhabiliter Fouquet?" In Grell, Malettke, and Oepen, *Les années Fouquet*, 11–32.

——. *Colbert*. Paris, 1981.

Ministry of Justice (France). "Le procès de Nicolas Fouquet." August 23, 2011. Available at www.justice.gouv.fr/histoire-et-patrimoine-10050/proces-historiques-10411/le-proces-de-nicolas-fouquet-22693.html (accessed August 11, 2012).

Mongrédien, Georges. *L'affaire Fouquet*. Paris, 1956.

Moote, A. Lloyd. "The French Crown versus Its Judicial and Financial Officials, 1653–83." *Journal of Modern History* 34 (1962): 146–60.

——. *The Revolt of the Judges: the Parlement of Paris and the Fronde 1643–1652*. Princeton, 1971.

Morand, Paul. *Fouquet, ou le soleil offusqué*. Paris, 1961.

Mousnier, Roland. *La vénalité des offices sous Henri IV et Louis XIII*. 2nd ed. Paris, 1971.

Murat, Inès. *Colbert*. Trans. Robert Francis Cook and Jeannie Van Asselt. Charlottesville, VA, 1984.

Parker, David. "Sovereignty, Absolutism, and the Function of the Law in Seventeenth-Century France." *Past and Present* 122 (1989): 36–74.

Pénicaut, Emmanuel. *Faveur et pouvoir au tournant du Grand Siècle: Michel Chamillart*. Paris, 2004.

Petitfils, Jean-Christian. *Fouquet*. Paris, 1998.

——. *Le véritable d'Artagnan*. Paris, 1999.

——. "Louis XIV et Fouquet." In Grell, Malettke, and Oepen, *Les années Fouquet*, 35–47.

Piccioni, Camille. "Bruant des Carrières, premier commis de Fouquet." *Revue d'histoire diplomatique* 43, no. 1 (1929): 422–44.

Pillorget, René. "Henri Pussort, oncle de Colbert (1615–1697)." In Mousnier, *Le conseil du roi*, 255–74.

Pitts, Vincent. *La Grande Mademoiselle at the Court of France, 1627–1693*. Baltimore, 2000.

Pollak, Liliane. *Lexique juridique français-anglais: termes courant du droit public et privé*. Scarborough, ON, 1995.

Pujo, Bernard. *Le grand Condé*. Paris, 1995.

Ranum, Orest. *Artisans of Glory*. Chapel Hill, 1980.

——. *The Fronde: A French Revolution, 1648–1652*. New York, 1993.

——. *Paris in the Age of Absolutism*. University Park, PA, 2002.

Renoux-Zagamé, Marie-France. "Répondre de l'obéissance: La conscience du juge dans la doctrine judiciaire à l'aube des temps modernes." In Carbasse and Depambour-Tarride, *La conscience du juge*, 155–93.

Richardt, Aimé. *Colbert et le colbertisme*. Paris, 1997.

Richet, Denis. *De la Réforme à la Révolution*. Paris, 1991.

Roche, Daniel. "Aperçus sur la fortune et les revenus des princes de Condé à l'aube du 18e siècle." *Revue d'histoire moderne et contemporaine* 14 (1967): 217–43.

Saunders, E. Stewart. "Politics and Scholarship in Seventeenth-Century France: The Library of Nicolas Fouquet and the College Royal." *Journal of Library History* 20 (1985): 1–24.

Shennan, Joseph H. *The Parlement of Paris*. Thrupp, UK, 1998.

Soll, Jacob. *The Information Master: Jean-Baptiste Colbert's Secret State Intelligence System*. Ann Arbor, 2009.

Solnon, Jean-François. *Les Ormesson au plaisir de l'État*. Paris, 1992.

Soman, Alfred. "La justice criminelle aux XVI–XVIIe siècles: le Parlement de Paris et les sièges subalternes." In *Actes du 107e Congrès National des Sociétés Savantes (Brest, 1982), Section de philologie et d'histoire jusqu'à 1610*, 1:15–52. Paris, 1984.

Storez-Brancourt, Isabelle. "Dans l'ombre de Messieurs les gens du roi: le monde des substituts." In Carbasse, *Histoire du parquet*, 157–204.

Thireau, Jean-Louis. "Le bon juge chez les juristes français du XVIe siècle." In Carbasse and Depambour-Tarride, *La conscience du juge*, 131–53.

Touzery, Mireille. "Le gouvernement des finances sous l'ancien régime: organigrammes, listes, et tableaux." *Annuaire-bulletin de la Société de l'histoire de France* (2004): 61–101.

Treasure, Geoffrey. *Mazarin: The Crisis of Absolutism in France*. London, 1997.

Uzman, Betty Tuba. "Kinship, Friendship, and Gratitude: Nicolas Foucquet's Patronage Network 1650–1661." Ph.D. diss., Johns Hopkins University, 1989.

Villain, Jean. *La fortune de Colbert*. Paris, 1994.

Weiss, France. *Acquits et ordonnances de comptant: histoire des fonds secrets sous l'ancien régime*. Paris, 1939.

Wolf, John B. *Louis XIV*. New York, 1968.

Index

The term *gallery* refers to illustrations located after page 78.